1 Fundamentals

1.1. Why Design Programs — isn't Coding and Testing Enough?

The short answer to the above question is — no, coding and testing are not enough. But is it really necessary to design programs? That depends, of course, on what we mean by the word "design". All programmers design their programs in one way or another. The real question is — how?

Before we get on to the benefits of proper program design and the particular merits of JSP, let us consider some of the concepts currently in use in the art of programming. First of all, how is programming traditionally performed? In many cases, the programmer starts coding his program just as soon as he has understood the program specification. Perhaps he will start by drawing a flowchart but usually he doesn't really feel productive until he has committed some elegant statements to paper. He couldn't be more wrong! If the programmer does not complete the design of his program before coding he will be forced to solve each problem as it arises. With each problem, his chances of making a mistake will increase. And his program will suffer.

In fact, the experience and skill of the programmer should be particularly concentrated on the design of his program. After all, coding as such is rarely more than the mechanical application of programming language rules.

The difference between a program developed from a rudimentary design and one based on a carefully accomplished design stage can be depicted as in figure 1.1.

It is not neccessarily true that a program will be finished faster just because a lot of work has been devoted to its design. However, it is almost always true that the program will be correct first time round. Programmers who have applied JSP in practice have found during the test stage that their programs have few if any logical errors. In addition, the programs are easy to maintain. By limiting maintenance costs, the total cost of a program during its useful life will be considerably reduced. If we accept the idea that coding should be postponed until the program design is finished, then we must also recognize that the programmer is particularly productive during the design stage.

Flow-charting · Coding (interleaved design) · Test · Production runs

Design · Coding · Test · Production runs

Fig 1.1

Program design, yes — but how? There are a lot of opinions on how to design a program. Isn't it enough to choose a method at random and apply it? Are there any arguments that particularly support JSP? Yes, there are!

1. A program, designed according to JSP, is based upon data structures. (This implies both the choice of proper program components and the creation of correct relations between them. Structured programming in general leaves the programmer alone with his/her intuition).

2. Following the JSP rules, you design your program step by step, each step being clearly defined. A good method should allow you to concentrate on specific stages. Then the final result will be less dependent on divine inspiration.

3. It follows from the above that different programmers applying JSP, will present similar solutions to the same problem. The train of thought is easier to follow for the maintenance programmer (and for the program designer himself!).

4. JSP has solutions to problems in which the data structures are incompatible (structure clashes and program inversion, chapter 2).

5. Error handling problems are resolutely tackled with JSP (backtracking, chapter 3).

6. The JSP notation can easily be taught to non-EDP people. This facilitates communication between end users and EDP professionals.

£9.95

Leif Ingevaldsson

JSP – A Practical Method of Program Design

Studentlitteratur Chartwell-Bratt Ltd

This book was first published in Swedish in 1977.
The title of the original edition:
JSP – en praktisk metod för programkonstruktion
Studentlitteratur Lund 1977

Second edition

Printed in Sweden
Studentlitteratur, Lund
ISBN/Studentlitteratur 91-44-15752-5
ISBN/Chartwell-Bratt 0-86238-107-X

Printing: 9 10 11 12 13 | 1996 95 94 93 92

Contents

Preface

This book is intended for both students and experienced programmers. Its subject is Jackson Structured Programming, a method of program *design* applicable to all programming languages. Most of the solutions given in this book are COBOL solutions since COBOL is easy to understand even for those of you who don't actually use it in your programming work. However, some Fortran and Algol solutions are also included.

If you flip quickly through this book, you will see that I have used the tape symbol quite a few times. Don't let this mislead you into believing that the problems are purely tape oriented. Many of the exercises deal with sequential data (see overleaf) but the method itself is by no means restricted to just sequential data.

The reference book is, of course, M. A. Jackson's "Principles of Program Design" published by the Academic Press, London, in 1975.

It is impossible for me to give the names of all the people who have helped me with their encouragement and advice during my work on this book. To them, my gratitude and thanks. I am particularly indebted to Michael Jackson himself for illuminating the very nature of common and important programming problems (most of the problem types in this book emanate from him), to my colleague Dick Nelson at Michael Jackson Systems International, to my friends at Saab Univac for their invaluable advice on the contents of this book and their presentation, to Robert Kellagher for his conscientious scrutiny of my English and, last but not least, to my dear wife Ella-Britt who has struggled with my manuscript at the typewriter.

There are no summarizing quotations at the beginning of each chapter, the quotations file having been exhausted by other authors. The only quotation used in this book is one that you have never seen before. You will find it at the bottom of this page.

Leif Ingevaldsson

"The only quotation used in this book is one that you have never seen before."
(From JSP — A Practical Method of Program Design)

Foreword to the second edition

It has been felt that a minor facelift of this book would be of benefit. We have introduced a rather different and more modern format for the schematic logic in JSP. The chapter on backtracking has been extended somewhat. One hopefully clearer backtracking exercise has replaced another. Finally, I have added three appendices. Appendix 1: coding rules for COBOL, Ada and Pascal, appendix 2:a survey of program design tools and appendix 3:a reading list. Please feel free to go out and buy an older edition of the book from some antiquarian bookseller and check whether I have forgotten something!

Your ever-devoted author.

An Introductory Exercise:

The tape symbol

Is this a tape?

Fig 0.1

No, it's all members processed in a data base set.

Is this a tape?

Fig 0.2

No, it's all DB records with a common property in a relational data base.

Is this a tape?

Fig 0.3

No, it's a file of input messages from a terminal.

Is this a tape?

Fig 0.4

No, it's a file of output messages to a terminal.

Is this a tape?

Fig 0.5

No, it's a yo-yo.

Is this a tape?

Fig 0.6

No, it's a sequentially processed direct access file.

Is this a tape?

Fig 0.7

Yes, it is!

Arguments against JSP? Yes:

1. It is difficult to create data structure diagrams and combine them. Comment: this activity is really a test of creativity and experience. A JSP programmer is unlikely to get bored!

2. Structure diagrams and other design documentation will be rather extensive. Comment: drawings of advanced technical products covering all levels from survey to individual components will always be extensive, and a program is an advanced technical product.

Isn't modular programming just as good as JSP? Let's consider this for a moment. When dividing a program into modules, the division is based upon functions. This sounds attractive enough, but there are risks: the total program structure could very well deviate in places from the structures of the data to be processed. The program will then be unnecessarily complicated and may "blow up" when the program is exposed to an unexpected (but according to the specification valid) combination of input data.

Another proposed remedy for entangled program design is, for instance, GO TO-less programming. Undisciplined use of GO TO gives rise to the so called "spaghetti syndrome". As soon as you want to modify a program somewhere, the program will be affected in several more or less expected places. Of course, this could be remedied by not using GO TO at all. However, then you must use PERFORM and FOR statements. These functions are not implemented in all languages and are unusable in special cases (jumps out of and returns to a subroutine). JSP uses GO TO but in a few well defined ways. We will return to these GO TO's later on.

The so called system matrix is primarily an elegant and very compressed documentation method. There are, however, no specific rules yet on how to create the matrix step by step.

Another method, based upon data structures, has been developed in France: LCP (Lois de Construction des Programmes). The basic LCP principles are similar to basic JSP principles. LCP does not, however, include any methods for handling incompatible data structures or error handling problems.

There are other concepts within programming, such as top-down design, HIPO, chief programmer team and structured walk-through. JSP is applicable in connection with these concepts.

The expression "structured programming" is used for varying concepts. What they all have in common is the exclusive use of three component types: sequence, iteration and selection. Often, when people say structured programming they really mean structured *coding* only.

The three component types are used in JSP too, but in addition, *the program structure and the data structures are matched.* This is necessary to achieve a correct *program design.* Consequently, JSP deals with *design* of structured programs.

Why is it so important to have the data structures controlling the program structure? Well, when designing an EDP system you have to start from the end user's real world. The information within the system is a model of the real world and is expressed by data. Hence, data is a model of the real world. A customer file includes data concerning customers, a trivial statement maybe, but the customers exist (hopefully) in the real world. A stock file reflects the situation in a stock department. A file comprising technical measuring records tells us something about the behaviour of the system measured. If the program structure is based upon the data structures, then the program is firmly established in the real world. And here is the point: When the end user wants additional information on customers, it's easy for the programmer to modify the program because there is one and only one component in the program which processes customers. The entity "customer" does not occur in different program components which process the customer file using different conditions based upon programming technique. Programming technique is alien to the end user. The end user's demands start from the end user's real world. The program structure must reflect this real world.

Program design according to JSP is divided into well defined stages:

1. Draw the data structures (including any internal data structures).
2. Combine these data structures into one basic program structure.
3. List the operations and allocate them.
4. Write the schematic logic (a pseudocode).

Stages 1 and 2 demand the major part of the programmer's creativity and experience. Stage 3 is easier. Providing stages 1 and 2 are correctly performed, you will always find obvious places to allocate the operations in the program structure. Stage 4 is a verbal description of the program. Coding, using the schematic logic as a base, is done very easily. The rules for translating the schematic logic into code are simple. The translation can also be done automatically. There are several precompilers for Cobol and Fortran, all of them more or less advanced. The most advanced precompiler known is the one designed by Michael Jackson Systems Limited.

1.2. The Three Component Types and their Graphical Representation

Inasmuch as this book deals with structured program design it is impossible to avoid mentioning two names: Böhm and Jacopini. These two gentlemen proved in 1966 that all programming problems can be solved by using only three program component types. However, three conditions must exist:

1. The program shall have one starting point and one exit point, no more, no less.
2. There must exist one path through every node (= junction in a flowchart:  ).
3. There must not be any "loose ends".

These conditions are easy to satisfy.

Dijkstra has pointed out that data also can be described by using the same types of component.

The three component types were mentioned in the preceding section: sequence, iteration and selection.

Sequence — first, then
Iteration — over and over again
Selection — either or

Iteration needs a comment. Two alternatives are shown in figure 1.2.

The left alternative is based upon the *iterating condition* V_{iter}, i.e. the iteration *is going on* as long as the condition V_{iter} is true. The right alternative is based upon the *terminating condition* V_{term}, i.e. the iteration *terminates* as soon as the condition V_{term} is true. Consequently the following is valid:

$$V_{term} = \overline{V_{iter}}$$

Both alternatives are equivalent. Note that an iterated component (C in figure 1.2) may be performed *zero* times, that is if the condition causes the iterated part not to be performed the first time the iteration is performed! (This probably sounds a little confusing, but you must bear in mind that the iteration *includes* the condition, the iterated part does not. Look once again at figure 1.2!) Consequently, DO-statements in Fortran are not usable. Here, the condition test is performed at the end, so all statements referred to are always executed at least once. Such a component is sometimes called repetition and is not in accordance with the definition of iteration.

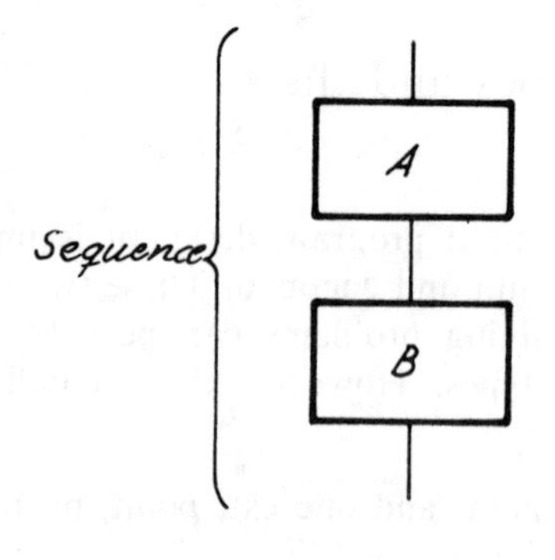

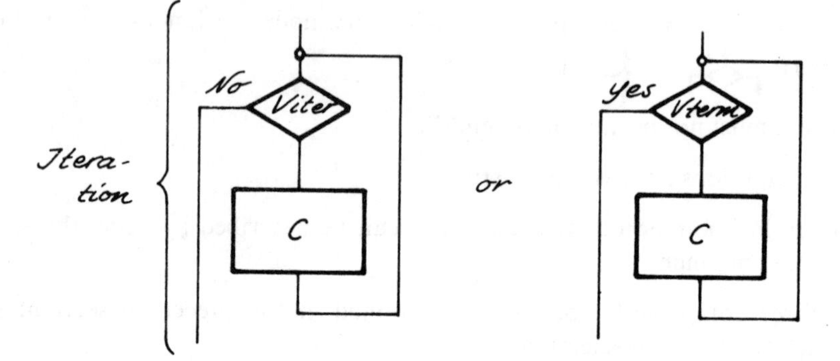

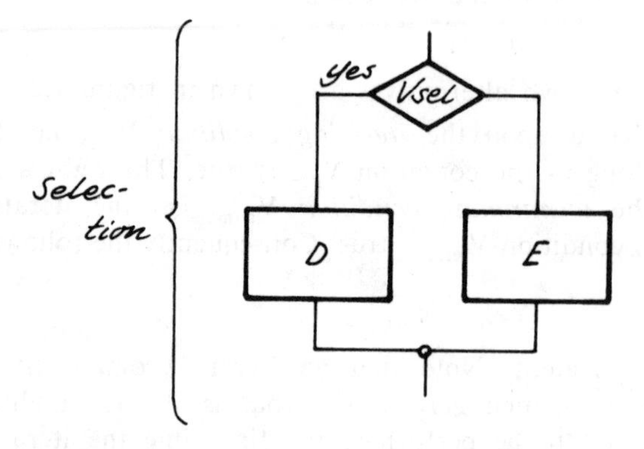

Fig 1.2

Figure 1.2 shows the three component types, expressed by flowchart symbols. These symbols can be used — but we prefer not to! The reason why will be discussed later on.

Let's now look at the graphical representation we shall use for the *sequence* component, figure 1.3.

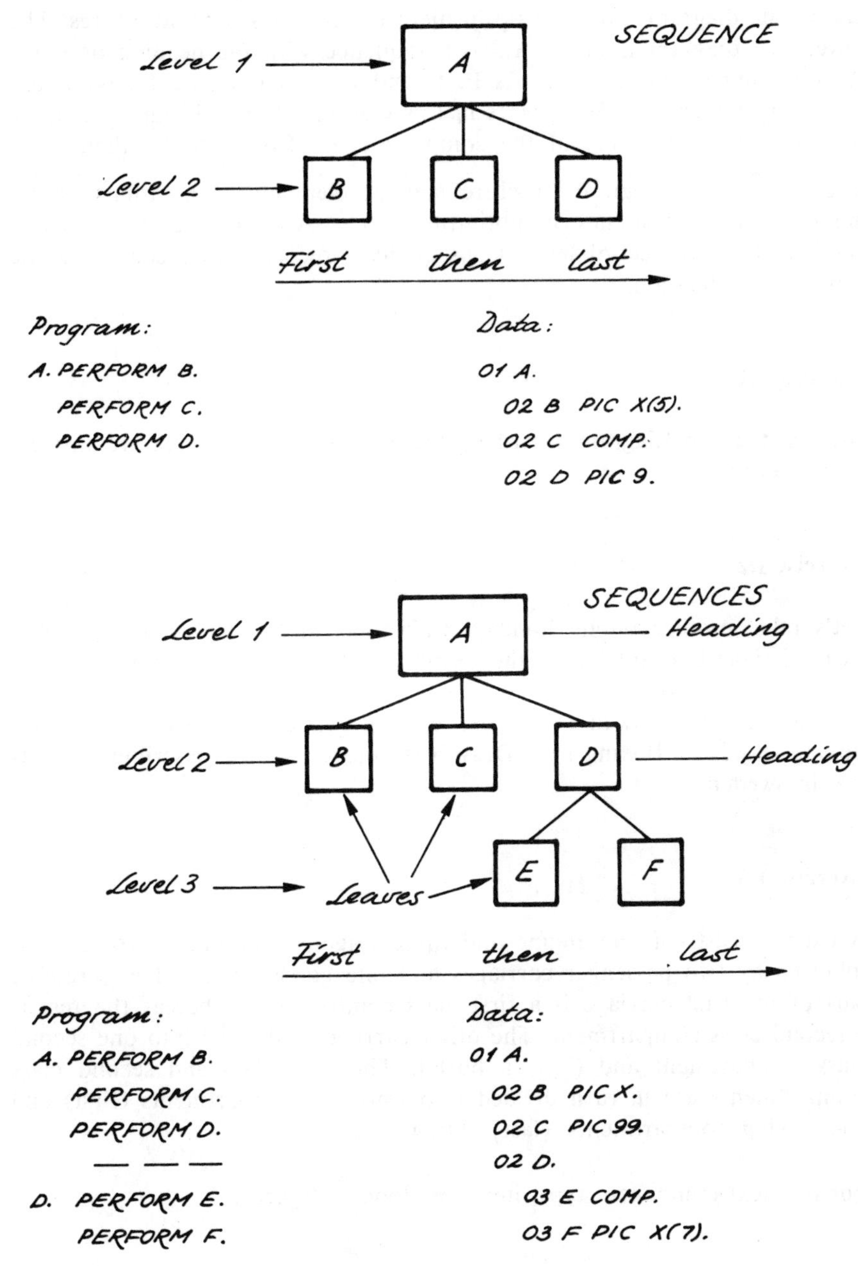

Fig 1.3

If you are used to flowcharts you must exert yourself a little to think along other lines. Note that the *chronological* order is *horizontal* in a JSP diagram. The diagrams are built up in hierarchical levels, tree structures. The lowermost diagram in figure 1.3 is a sequence with the heading or name A consisting of the components B, C and D in that order. B and C are leaves or elementary components in this diagram. D is a heading or name of a sequence consisting of the components E (first) and F (then).

The leaves in a program structure may be elementary operations (statements), paragraph names or subroutine names. A data structure is usually detailed down to record level. Consequently, records often constitute the leaves of the diagram.

Exercise 1.1

Draw a structure diagram describing the days of Easter. (There are answers in chapter 5).

Exercise 1.2

Let's take another public holiday: Christmas in Sweden. The highlights on Christmas Eve are lunch, the exchange of Christmas presents and the consumption of rice pudding in that order. Christmas Day starts with a church service followed a number of hours later by Christmas dinner. Boxing Day is . . . Boxing Day. Draw a structure diagram describing Christmas in Sweden.

Exercise 1.3

A train consists of one engine and three wagons. The engine comes first followed by two passenger carriages and one goods wagon. The foremost part of the first carriage is a first class compartment whereas the rest is a second class compartment. The other carriage is divided into one second class compartment and (last) a buffet. The first class and second class compartments are in turn divided into smoking compartments (first) and no-smoking compartments (last). Draw etc.

For the next component type, iteration, look at figure 1.4.

ITERATIONS

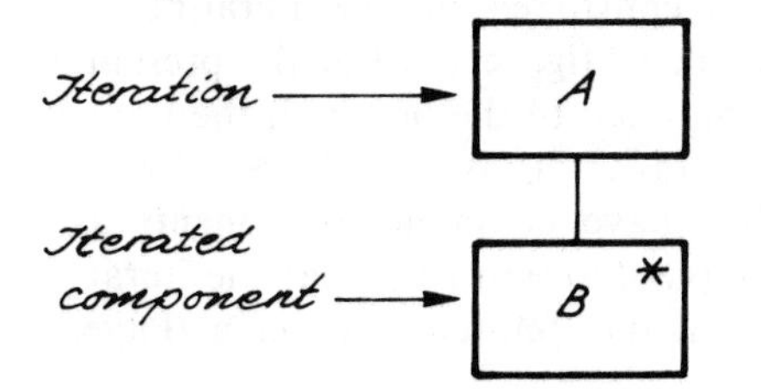

Program:
A. PERFORM B N TIMES.

Data:
01 A.
02 B PIC X(5)
OCCURS N TIMES.

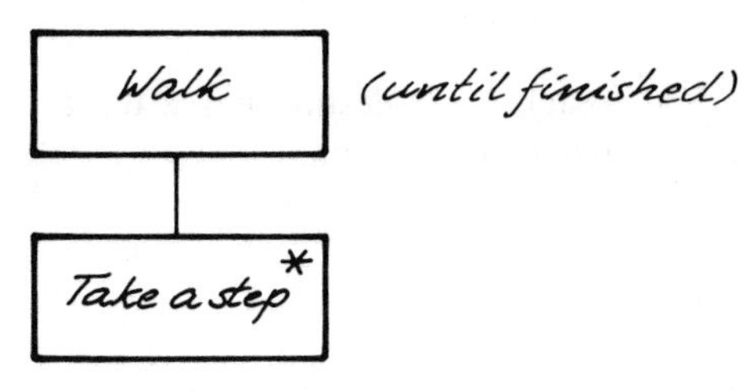

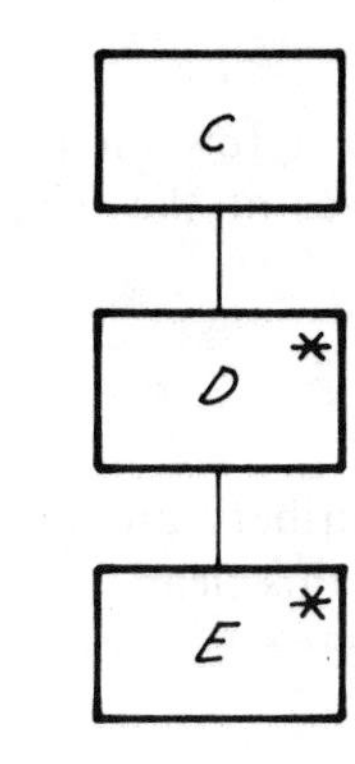

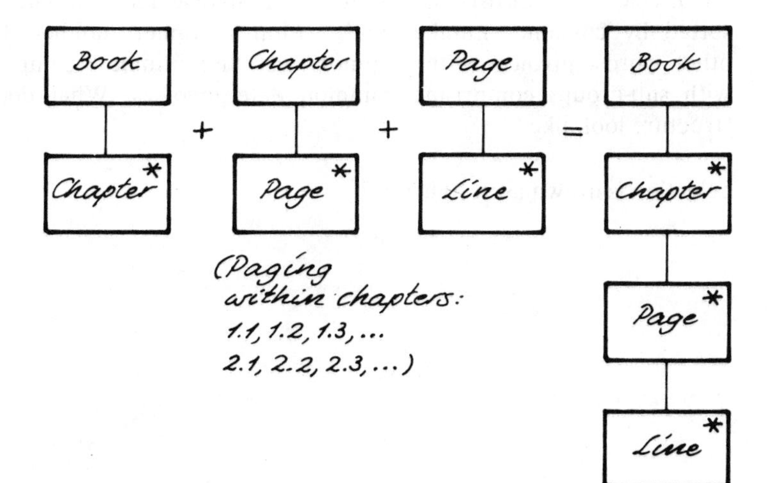

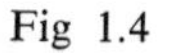
Fig 1.4

In general, the iterated component (the box with an asterisk) may occur zero or more times. *How* many times is controlled by the iterating or terminating condition as in the walk example in figure 1.4. For the present, we may put this condition into the diagram, close to the box with the iteration name. An iteration of an iteration of an . . . etc is feasible. See figure 1.4. You may combine structures, if they have common components as in the book example in figure 1.4. The simple iteration Book has the iterated component Chapter. Chapter has in turn the iterated component Page, and so on.

Exercise 1.4

You are out for a row on the river. You reach your destination after a number of strokes of the oars. Draw the structure diagram.

Exercise 1.5

Telephone subscribers are grouped by code numbers. Draw a structure diagram making this clear.

Exercise 1.6

An invoice file consists of a number of invoice records. The records are sorted by customer number and, within customer number, by date. In other words, invoices with common customer numbers comprise a group with sub-groups comprising common date invoices. What does the data structure look like?

Selection is drawn as in figure 1.5.

SELECTIONS

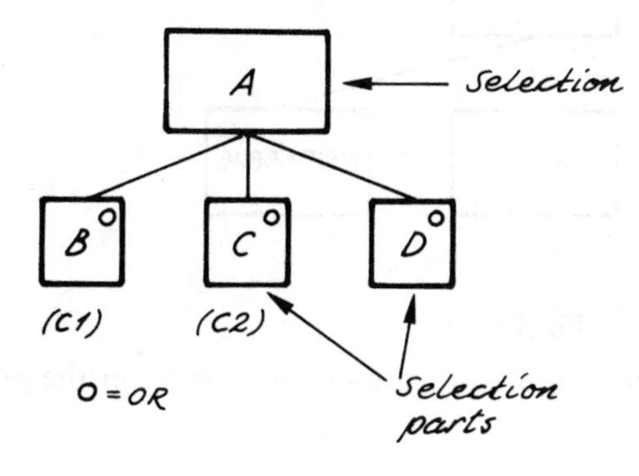

Program:

```
A. IF COND = C1
        PERFORM B
   ELSE IF COND = C2
        PERFORM C
   ELSE
        PERFORM D.
```

Data:

```
01 A.
  02 B PIC 999.
  02 C REDEFINES B.
  02 D REDEFINES B.
```

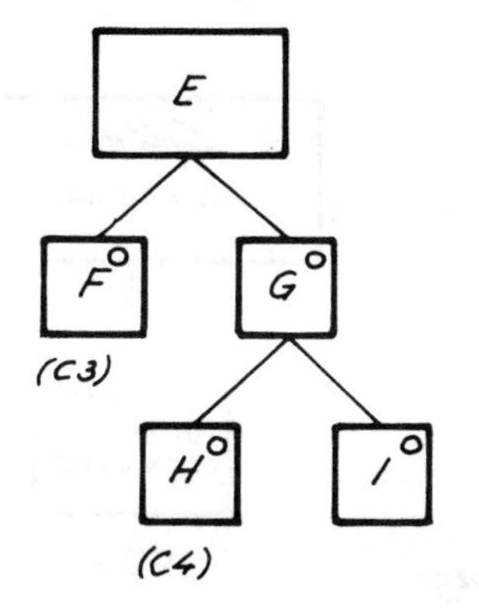

Fig 1.5

The last selection part shall *always be condition-less.* This forces you to check the completeness of the program specification. If, for instance, there is a file with two record types, T1 and T2, somewhere in the program structure there will be two selection parts, each processing one record type: IF RECTYPE = 1 THEN PERFORM PT1 ELSE PERFORM PT2. Now, if the record is not a type 1 record then it must *necessarily* be a type 2 record. But what if there is a record which is neither of type 1 nor type 2? That's it! You had better ask the originator of the program specification if a third alternative should not be included. The answer could very well be: Yes please, and print out RECORD TYPE ERROR as well (figure 1.6).

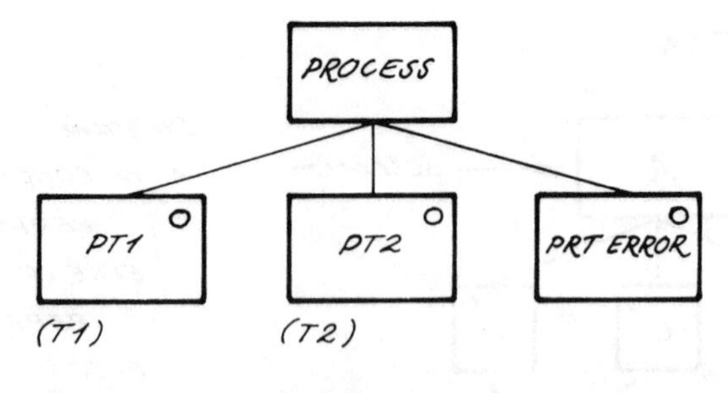

Fig 1.6

In practice problems of this kind are of course more complex, but the principle is the same.

Selection with only one selection part exists too. In this case it can be depicted as in figure 1.7. Figure 1.7a is preferable because it shows explicitly the empty selection part: either you are lucky and your number is found in the lottery prize list or it doesn't exist at all in the prize list.

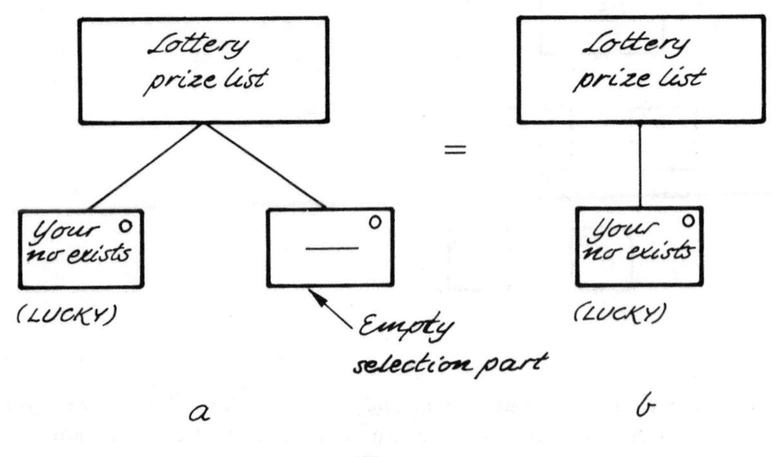

Fig 1.7

Exercise 1.7

As a motorist, you drive on the lefthand side or the righthand side of the road, depending on which country you are in. If you drive right down the middle of the road, you violate the traffic laws. Describe this with a JSP diagram.

Exercise 1.8

If you phone me, my telephone number could be engaged or not. If it's not engaged, either my wife or I answer, or there is nobody at home. Describe etc.

Up to now we have discussed structures comprised of only one type of component at a time. Of course, the component types may be mixed. You must however make sure that each box belongs to one and only one of the three component types. An example will show you what we mean. In figure 1.8a you will find a file comprising records, where all the records have the same properties.

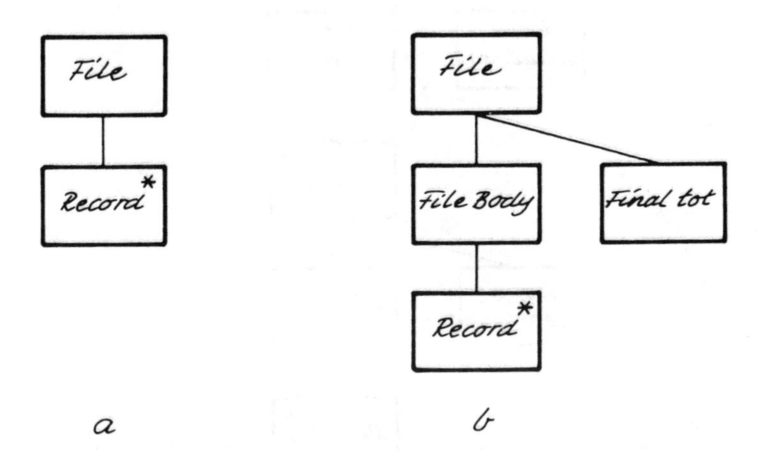

Fig 1.8

In figure 1.8b the file is supplemented with a special record at the end, a final total. All the other records (preceding the final total) are collected under the heading File Body. File is accordingly a sequence of first File Body and last Final Total. File Body is an iteration of Record. If you had added the final total immediately after the iterated component Record in figure 1.8a, File would have been both an iteration and a sequence. A component like this must not be included in the component type set.

Before you start drawing structures with mixed component types, we would like to give you a small demonstration. A report file is divided into groups. Each group begins with a heading. The lines, not being headings, can be of two types: type 1 or type 2. The report file begins with a main heading. (Here the problem description is finished). To be able to draw a correct structure diagram you must distinguish the entities in different levels. You should ask the following question: are there any entities which can be placed immediately under the heading Report File? Yes, the main heading comes first in the report file. Accordingly, the Report File is a sequence of Main Heading and the rest, figure 1.9. The rest could be named Report Body. What does this consist of? A lot of groups (at least some). Report Body is consequently an iteration of Group. Group must in turn be a sequence of first Group Heading, followed by the rest, a Group Body. This is an iteration of Report Line, which must be a selection of either Type 1 or Type 2.

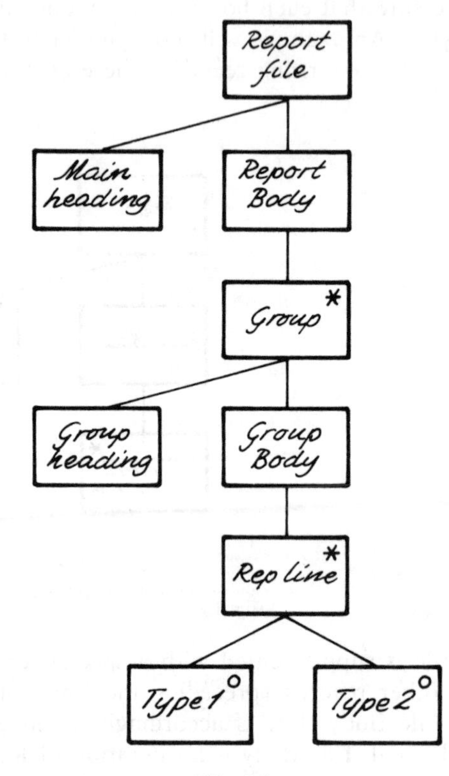

Fig 1.9

Let's remind you:

First — then: sequence
Over and over again: iteration
Either — or: selection

Note that *a box alone* doesn't indicate to which component type it belongs. You must always look at the next level below. Each box in a diagram is a heading only. Consequently, the leaves in a structure diagram can never be considered to be anything other than elementary components, figure 1.10.

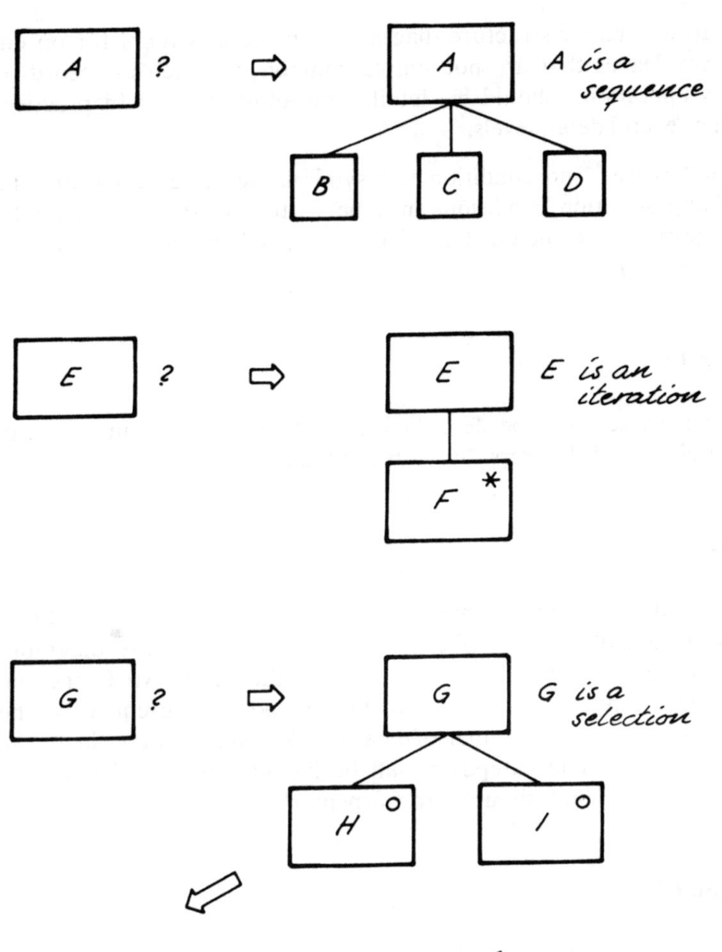
A
?
A
A is a sequence
B
C
D
E
?
E
E is an iteration
F *
G
?
G
G is a selection
H o
I o

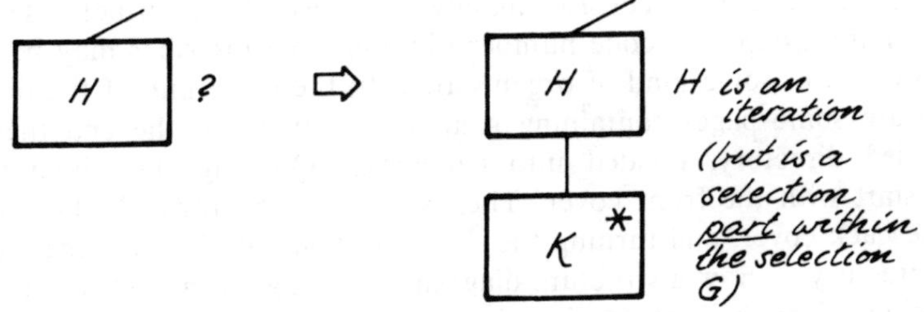
H
?
H
H is an iteration (but is a selection part within the selection G)
K *

Fig 1.10

Never draw a larger structure diagram than there is room for on one A4-page! Any leaves that are not simple components, such as records or elementary operations, should be detailed on another page. In practice there are often several detail levels.

Note that there is no condition test symbol. Iterating or terminating conditions and selection conditions may be written in the structure diagrams. The conditions are included anyway in the schematic logic to which we will return later on.

Exercise 1.9

A pearl necklace may be described as a clasp half, a string of pearls and another clasp half. Express this with a JSP diagram.

Exercise 1.10

Mr Carpenter is going to make a fence around his summer house. But first he would like to describe the fence with a structure diagram. Every second fence board shall be long and every other short. Mr Carpenter would like to have long boards nearest to the gateposts (consequently, the fence will consist of an odd number of boards). The fence is considered to begin with a gatepost. The gateposts shall be included in the diagram. There is only one gate. What should Mr Carpenter's diagram look like?

Exercise 1.11

A telephone directory consists mainly of a list of subscribers. The subscribers are grouped in code number divisions. A subscriber may be a man or a woman or some kind of organisation. In the beginning of the directory there are some pages containing general directions, at the end there is a classified directory, divided into categories. Opening the directory you may start with the front cover. Then you can skim through the directory to the back cover, and turning the directory you will discover the back (of the directory). Draw a structure diagram, covering all the entities in the description. (You had better tick the entities to check your diagram).

1.3. A Simple Programming Problem

In this section we will discuss a simple problem. And, dear reader, don't skip this section just because the problem is simple! You see, we use a simple problem to explain why a flowchart is not a good tool and why you should base the program structure upon the data structure. At the same time we will discuss some important stages of JSP.

Problem

A table is to be created and printed. Each element shall be the quotient of the column number and the line number. Initial values of both Column and Line number = 1 and terminal values = 6. The table shall look like this (Col no and Line no don't belong to the table):

	Col no					
	1	2	3	4	5	6
Line no 1	1.00					
2	0.50	1.00				
3	0.33	0.67	1.00			
4	0.25	0.50	0.75	1.00		
5	0.20	0.40	0.60	0.80	1.00	
6	0.17	0.33	0.50	0.67	0.83	1.00

A flowchart solution is shown on page 26.

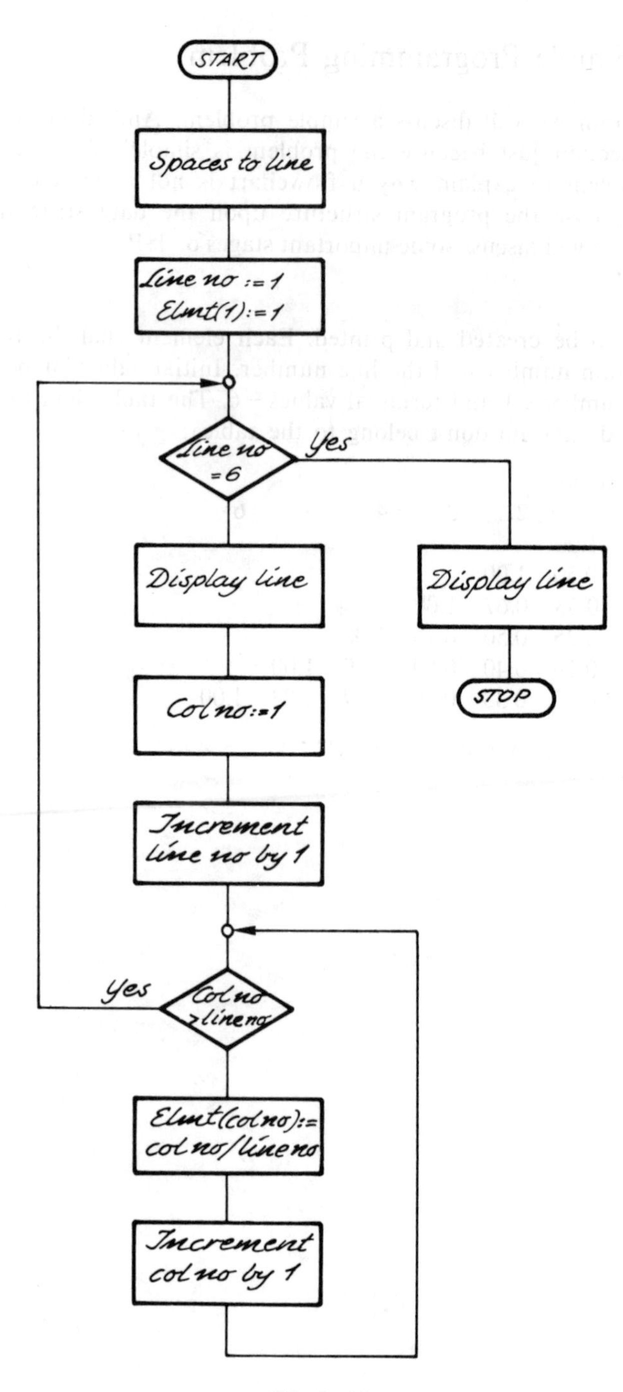
START
Spaces to line
Line no := 1
Elmt(1) := 1
Line no = 6
Yes
Display line
Display line
STOP
Col no := 1
Increment line no by 1
Yes
Col no > line no
Elmt(col no) := col no/line no
Increment col no by 1

Fig 1.11

Cobol code:

———

```
DATA DIVISION.
WORKING-STORAGE SECTION.
       01  LINE.
           02 ELEMENT OCCURS 6 PICTURE ZZZ9.99.
       01  WOR.
           02 LINE-NO PICTURE 99.
           02 COL-NO PICTURE 99.
PROCEDURE DIVISION.
INITIATION.
           MOVE SPACES TO LINE.
           MOVE 1 TO LINE-NO.
           MOVE 1 TO ELEMENT(1).
           PERFORM BUILD-LINE UNTIL LINE-NO = 6.
           DISPLAY LINE.
           STOP RUN.
BUILD-LINE.
           DISPLAY LINE.
           MOVE 1 TO COL-NO.
           ADD 1 TO LINE-NO.
           PERFORM CALC-ELEM UNTIL COL-NO > LINE-NO.
CALC-ELEM.
           DIVIDE COL-NO BY LINE-NO GIVING
           ELEMENT (COL-NO) ROUNDED.
           ADD 1 TO COL-NO.
```

Algol code:

(As the problem is not intended to demonstrate how to put spaces into an array or to print an array, we presume the existence of the following standard procedures: spacearray(A[m:n]) and printarray(A[m:n], fpZq.r))

```
begin  integer colnr, lineno;
       real array element [1:6];
       spacearray(element [1:6]);
       element [1] :=1;
       for lineno :=2 step 1 until 6 do
       begin
             printarray(element [1:6], f3Z1.2);
             for colno :=1 step 1 until lineno do
                   element [colno] :=colno/lineno;
       end
       printarray(element [1:6], f3Z1.2);
end
```

alternatively:

```
begin ———
              spacearray(element [1:6]);
              lineno := element [1] := 1;
       pline: if lineno = 6 then go to concline;
              printarray(element [1:6], f3Z1.2);
              colno := 1;
              lineno := lineno + 1;
       pelem: if colno > lineno then go to pline;
              element [colno] := colno/lineno;
              colno := colno + 1;
              go to pelem;
    concline: printarray(element [1:6], f3Z1.2);
end
```

Fortran code:
(As the problem is not intended to demonstrate array processing, we presume the existence of the following standard subroutines: SPCARR (A,I) and PRTARR (A,I).)

```
      INTEGER COLNO, LINENO
      REAL ELEMENT(6)
      CALL SPCARR(ELEMENT,6)
      LINENO=1
      ELEMENT(1)=1
100   IF(LINENO.EQ.6) GO TO 109
      CALL PRTARR (ELEMENT, LINENO)
      COLNO=1
      LINENO=LINENO+1
200   IF(COLNO.GT.LINENO) GO TO 100
      ELEMENT(COLNO)=FLOAT(COLNO)/FLOAT(LINENO)
      COLNO=COLNO+1
      GO TO 200
109   CONTINUE
      CALL PRTARR(ELEMENT, LINENO)
      STOP
      END
```

The above codes look nice and tidy. The iteration components are correct. If you consider "go to" as a statement to be avoided, the Cobol code and the first Algol code must be satisfying. What more could you want? Well, a simple modification demand should give rise to a simple modification of the program. Let's try.

Modification demand A: the upper right half should be printed instead as:

1.00	2.00	3.00	4.00	5.00	6.00
	1.00	1.50	2.00	2.50	3.00
		1.00	1.33	1.67	2.00
			1.00	1.25	1.50
				1.00	1.20
					1.00

Modification demand B: the lower left half should be printed upside down, i.e.:

0.17	0.33	0.50	0.67	0.83	1.00
0.20	0.40	0.60	0.80	1.00	
0.25	0.50	0.75	1.00		
0.33	0.67	1.00			
0.50	1.00				
1.00					

Modification demand C: a "rectangular" table should be printed involving the column numbers 6 to and including 10 and the line numbers 1 to and including 4, i.e.:

6.00	7.00	8.00	9.00	10.00
3.00	3.50	4.00	4.50	5.00
2.00	2.33	2.67	3.00	3.33
1.50	1.75	2.00	2.25	2.50

The modification demands (they are to be considered one at a time) are modest. It should just be a question of changing the initiation and termination values of the column and line numbers. But is this enough? No, unfortunately not. For instance, the first line is printed in the beginning, containing just one element with the value = 1.00. This will not be changed even if we change the initiation and termination values in appropriate places. And the modification demand B forces us to place the operation "spacing line" elsewhere. The simplest way would perhaps be to rewrite the whole program. However, isn't it an unsatisfactory feeling, being forced to rewrite the program to meet such a tiny demand? As we said before: minor modification demands should give rise to small program modifications. How to design a program to achieve this goal? Well, the program should be a model of the real world. The real world is represented by data. Thus, let's start by studying the data structures and then base the program structure on them.

In this miniature problem we have just one data structure to analyse: that of the table. The data structure of the table and the basic program structure are shown in figure 1.12.

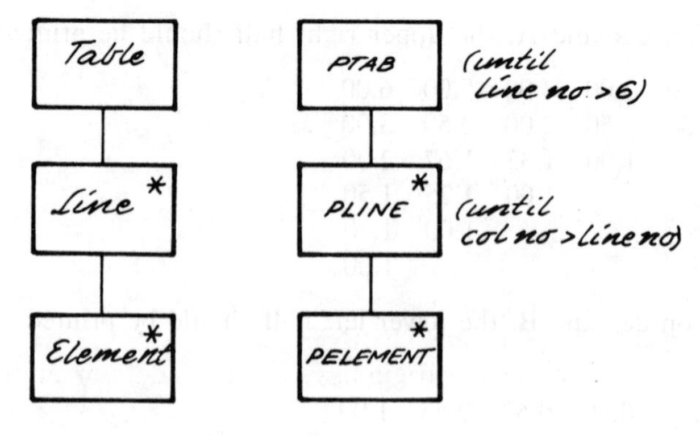

Fig 1.12

The next stage is to make an operations list:

1. Space line
2. Print line
3. Stop
4. Calc. element
5. Initiate line no
6. Increment line no by 1
7. Initiate col no
8. Increment col no by 1

Note that it doesn't matter in what order the operations are listed. We wanted to emphasize this by placing "Stop" somewhere in the middle.

Fig 1.13

Now we draw the boxes of the basic program structure somewhat apart without any relation line, figure 1.13. We draw it like this to be able to insert any necessary bodies (cf. figures 1.8b and 1.9). It is now time to allocate the operations. We are now working with the "atoms" of the problem solution, its simplest components. Thanks to this, we can ask ourselves simple questions, easy to answer correctly, questions about the frequency and order of the operations (check the figure 1.14):

How many times shall we move spaces to line?
Answer: once per process line (PLINE).
Should this be done in the beginning, in the middle or at the end?
Answer: in the beginning.

Operation no 1 is consequently placed under the heading PLINE and in the beginning.

How many times shall we print line?
Answer: once per process line.
Should this be done in the beginning, in the middle or at the end?
Answer: at the end.

Thus, we hang up operation no 2 at the end under PLINE.

How many times shall we stop the program execution?
Answer: once per program execution (PTAB).
In the beginning, in the middle or at the end?
Answer: at the end.
How many times shall we calculate element?
Answer: once per process element (PELMT).
(As this operation in the present stage can't be related to
any beginning or end, we place it somewhere under PELMT).

By asking "how many times" and "in the beginning, in the middle or at the end" about the other operations, we will find obvious allocations as in figure 1.14.

After this we have to insert a body box below PTAB, which no longer can be considered an iteration. PTAB has operation no 3 at the end (first — last: sequence). The same thing can be said about PLINE. In fig 1.14 the boxes of the basic program structure are drawn with heavy lines.

Before coding, a schematic logic should be written, but we have not yet demonstrated how to write the pseudocode and the program is so small that we dare to code straight from figure 1.14.

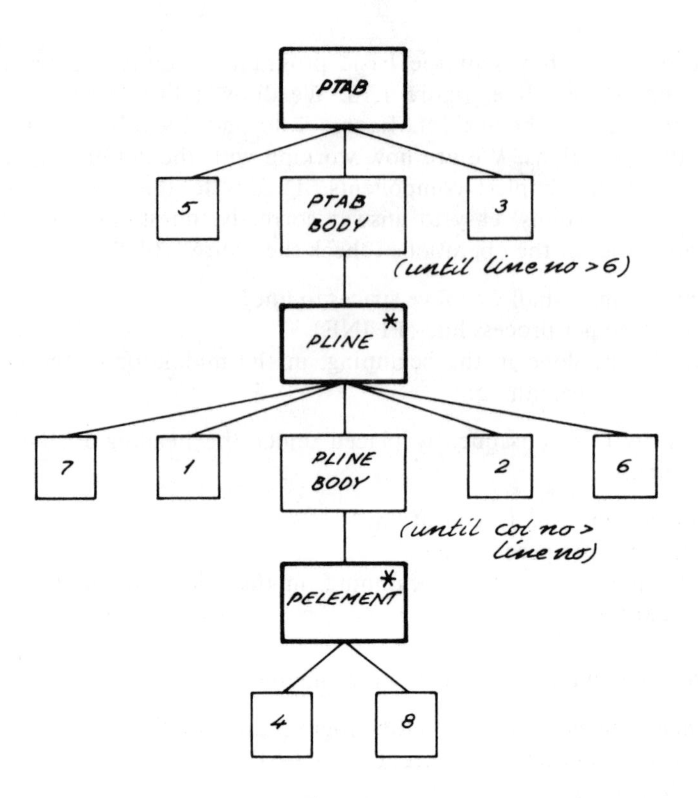

Fig 1.14

Cobol code:

```
PROCEDURE  DIVISION.
PTAB.        MOVE 1 TO LINE-NO.
PTAB-BODY. IF LINE-NO > 6 GO TO PTAB-BODY-END.
PLINE.       MOVE 1 TO COL-NO.
             MOVE SPACES TO LINE.
PLINE-BDY. IF COL-NO > LINE-NO GO TO PLINE-BDY-END.
PELMT.       DIVIDE COL-NO BY LINE-NO GIVING
             ELEMENT (COL-NO).
             ADD 1 TO COL-NO.
PELMT-END. GO TO PLINE-BDY.
PLINE-BDY-END.
             DISPLAY LINE.
             ADD 1 TO LINE-NO.
PLINE-END. GO TO PTAB-BODY.
PTAB-BODY-END.
PTAB-END.  STOP RUN.
```

Algol code:
(In the **for** statement alternative some operations are superfluous, namely those initiating and incrementing column and line numbers i. e. 5, 6, 7 and 8 in figure 1.14. Note that a **for** statement is a composite operation, initiating at one level and incrementing at another).

```
begin
      ———
      for lineno := 1 step 1 until 6 do
                begin
                          spacearray(element[1:6]);
                          for colno := 1 step 1 until lineno do
                               element [colno] := colno/lineno;
                          printarray(element [1:6], f3Z1.2);
                end;
end
```

alternatively

```
begin
      ———
               lineno := 1;
pline:         if lineno>6 then go to plinend;
               colno := 1;
               spacearray(element [1:6]);
pelem:         if colno>lineno then go to pelemend;
               element [colno] := colno/lineno;
               colno := colno + 1;
               go to pelem;
pelemend:
               printarray(element [1:6], f3Z1.2);
               lineno := lineno + 1;
               go to pline;
plinend:
end
```

Fortran code:

```
      DIMENSION ELEMENT(6)
      LINENO=1
100   IF(LINENO.GT.6) GO TO 109
      COLNO=1
      CALL SPCARR(ELEMENT,6)
200   IF(COLNO.GT.LINENO) GO TO 209
      ELEMENT(COLNO)=FLOAT(COLNO)/FLOAT(LINENO)
      COLNO=COLNO+1
      GO TO 200
209   CONTINUE
      CALL PRTARR(ELEMENT, LINENO)
      LINENO=LINENO+1
      GO TO 100
109   CONTINUE
      STOP
      END
```

Let's have a look at how to modify these programs according to the former modification demands A, B and C:

Demand A was about printing the upper right half instead. Consequently the column number must be initiated by the line number and terminated with the value 6. This can easily be done. And "space line" is placed where it should be.

Demand B was the original table, but printed upside down. The line number shall consequently be initiated by 6 and decremented to and including 1. The column number shall start with the value=1 and stop with the value=line number as originally stated.

Finally, demand C can easily be met by changing the initiating and terminating values of the column number and the line number.

"Space line" will of course be done unnecessarily a number of times as long as the original problem is valid. If "space line" is placed in the beginning of the program, it should be considered as an "optimization". The more a program is "optimized", the more hostile it will be to modifications.

Shouldn't it be possible to achieve an easy-to-modify program by using a flowchart? Well, it's not easy to depict for instance the component "process line" in a flowchart. You must use comments. Arriving at a good solution is of course possible by using flowcharts, but in most cases this is true *in spite of* flowcharting, not thanks to it.

What good properties have structure diagrams in contrast to flowcharts? A structure diagram deals with the *static* program structure. This structure is made up as a tree structure. A tree structure can be studied piecemeal. You can focus your attention on one branch at a time without being forced to keep in mind what has been done earlier.

A flowchart describes what will happen when a program is executed. It's too easy to design a hard-to-understand program by flowcharting. The human brain is unable to *simultaneously* grasp more than what corresponds to just a few program statements.

A further drawback concerning flowcharts is the freedom to connect the involved symbols. The risk of creating programs, suffering badly from "spaghetti syndrome", is then impending.

Let's consequently use the JSP diagrams as tools in designing tree structured programs. If we were to use net structures then there will be components occuring in more than one context. This will make the program more difficult to understand. The program structure shall be a synthesis of the data structures, not only input and output data structures but any internal data structures as well.

1.4. Schematic Logic and Coding

The schematic logic is a base, closely connected to the coding. As a matter of fact, the iteration or termination conditions and the selection conditions should be added when you are writing the schematic logic.

The program structure with allocated operations is always the basis of the schematic logic. We have tried to demonstrate in figure 1.15 the connection between program structures and schematic logic. The schematic logic expressions or statements are put into the structure diagrams.

By following the arrows in the picture, you will get the order of the schematic logic expressions.

A structure diagram contains, as you know, a maximum of three component types: sequence, iteration and selection. Moreover, there are elementary components at the lowest level, the leaves of the tree structure. Let's begin by commenting on the leaves.

All leaves in the structure diagram are written in the schematic logic with a concluding semicolon. A leaf is often an elementary operation. This can

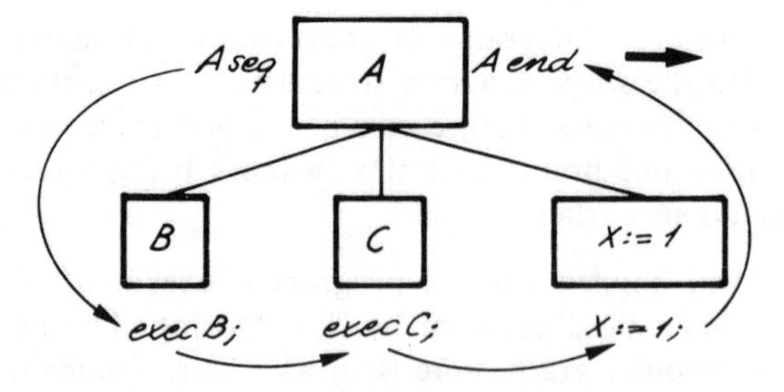


```
A seq
   exec B;
   exec C;
   X:=1;
A end
```

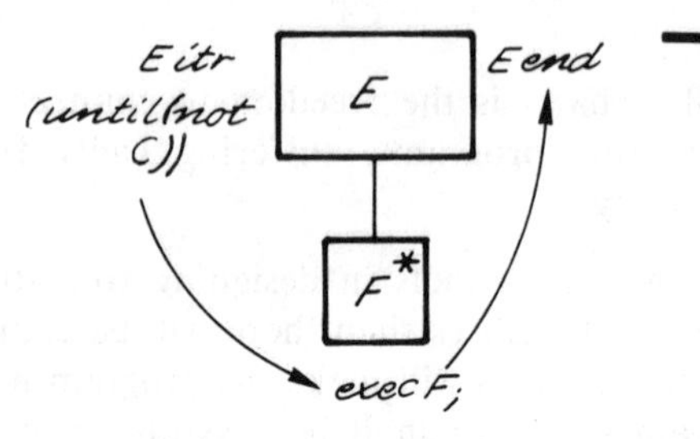


```
E itr until(not C)
   exec F;
E end

E itr while(C)
   exec F;
E end
```

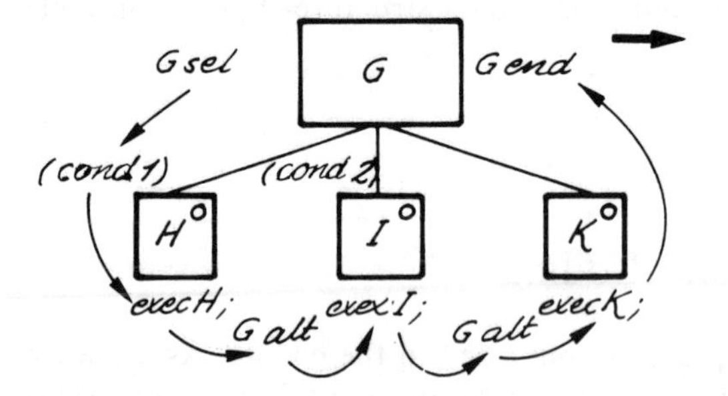


```
G sel (cond 1)
   exec H;
G alt (cond 2)
   exec I;
G alt
   exec K;
G end
```

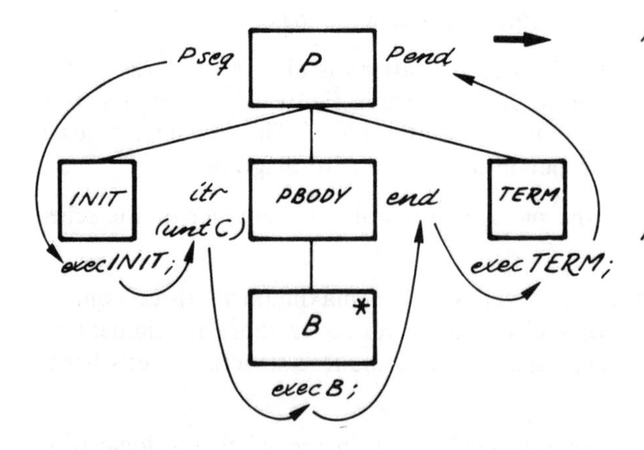


```
P seq
   exec INIT;
   PBODY itr until(C)
      exec B;
   PBODY end
   exec TERM;
P end
```

Fig 1.15

be expressed in plain English (or whatever language you prefer), e.g. "Read customer file;", "ACC := 0;". If you have access to a preprocessor or precompiler, producing code with the schematic logic as input, then the situation is changed. In that case you have to apply the preprocessor manual, of course.

If a leaf consists of many operations (i.e. more than one), you have to put an *exec* before the name of the leaf, e.g. "*exec* B;", "*exec* CALDISCOUNT;". This group of operations is then described by a diagram and a schematic logic on separate pages.

Now we will discuss the components that are not leaves: these begin with the component name followed by component type and end with the component name followed by *end*.

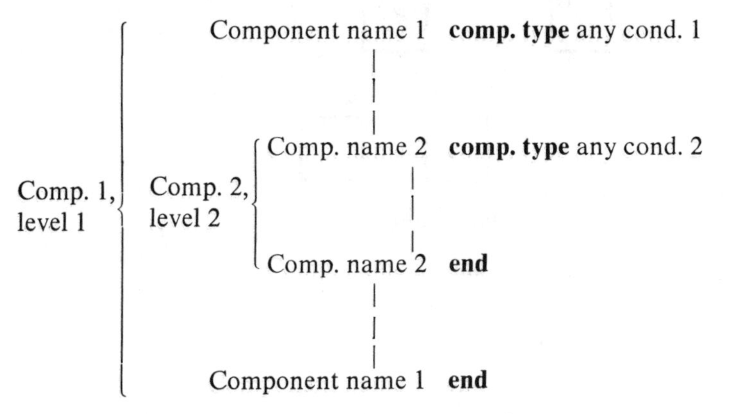

One indent per level transition is required, figure 1.16

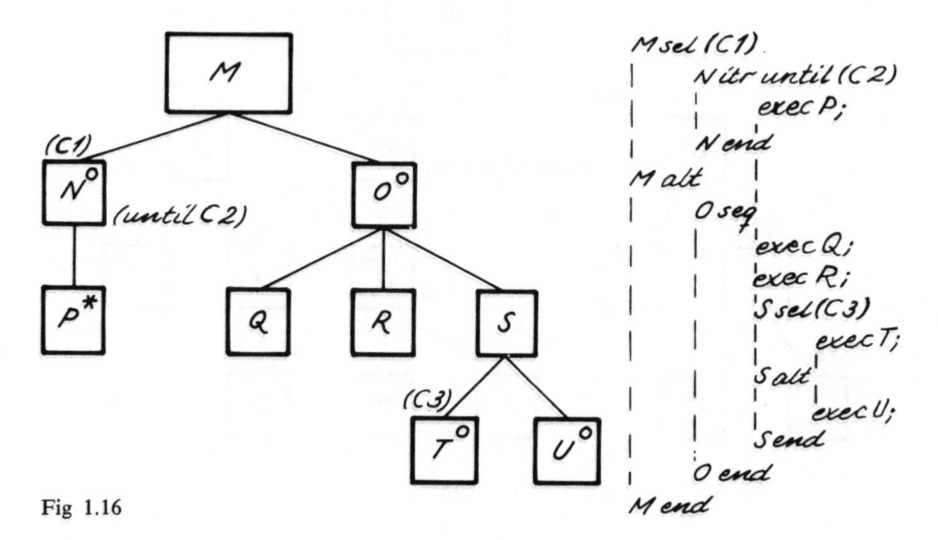

Fig 1.16

Exercise 1.12.

Write the schematic logic according to the structure diagram in figure 1.17.

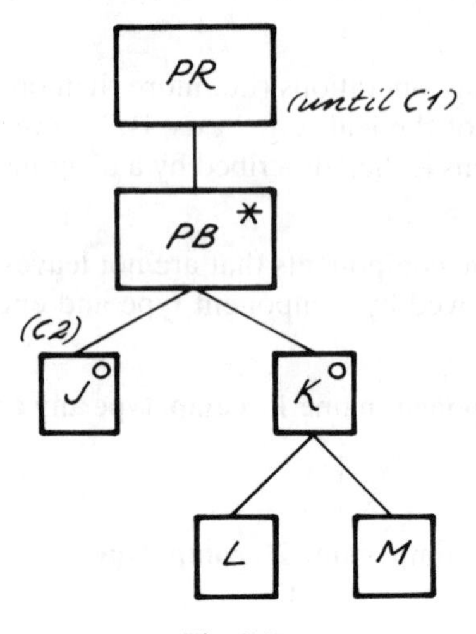

Fig 1.17

Exercise 1.13.

Now do the same exercise on figure 1.18.

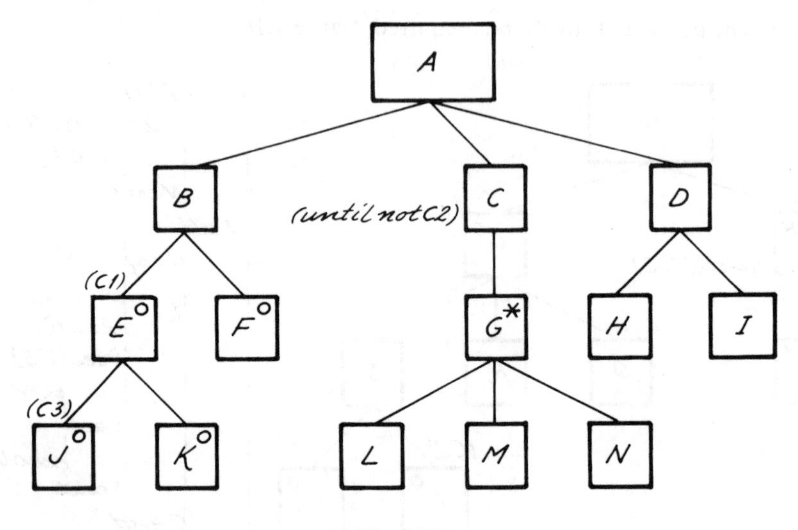

Fig 1.18

Exercise 1.14.

This is a "backwards exercise":

```
P seq
    open;
    read;
    B itr until (EOF)
        C seq
            X := 1;
            S select C-1
                Q itr until (not T1)
                    N seq
                        exec Y;
                        read;
                    N end
                Q end
            S or
                exec Z;
            S end
        C end
    B end
    close;
P end
```

Draw the structure diagram according to the schematic logic above.

Coding from schematic logic is easy. Take a look at Figure 1.19:

The coding in figure 1.19 contains only simple language facilities, facilities you will find in all problem oriented languages. If you are coding in Cobol you may use PERFORM to create an iteration, for instance. But PERFORM within PERFORM... is not applicable in cases in which the so called program inversion is used. We will deal with program inversion in chapter 2.

The suggested paragraph names and labels in fig 1.19 probably don't need any comments. However, when it comes to Fortran, this matter is a little trickier. Every *end* is numbered XX99. XX are two digits denoting the serial number of the component in the order it appears in the schematic logic. Sequences are numbered XX01, iterations XX02 and selections XX03 with XX04, XX05=alt(1), alt(2) etc. If the first component is a *seq,* the second a **select** and the third an *iter,* then we will arrive at the following numbering:

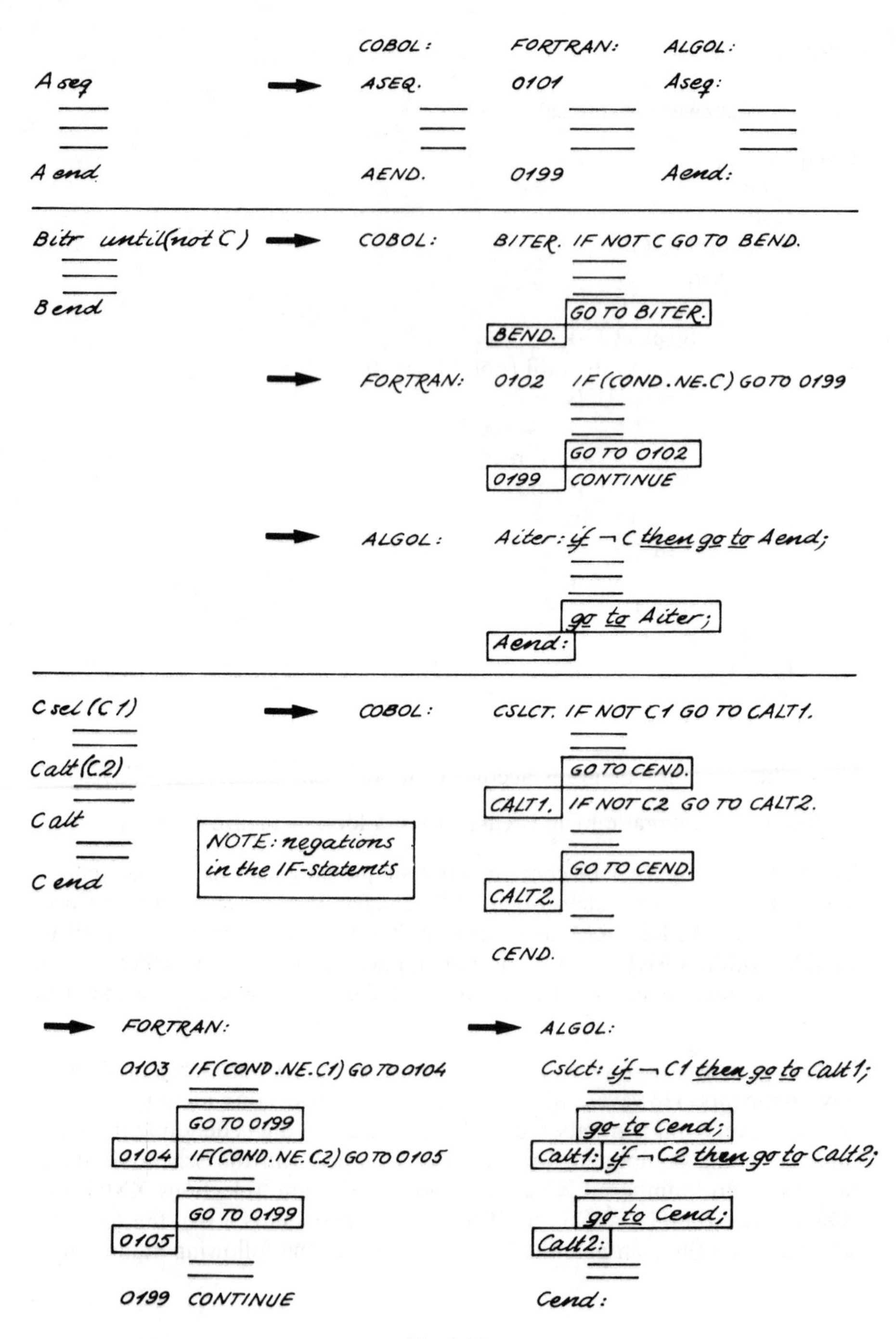
COBOL:
FORTRAN:
ALGOL:
A seq
ASEQ.
0101
Aseq:
A end
AEND.
0199
Aend:
Bitr until(not C)
COBOL:
BITER. IF NOT C GO TO BEND.
Bend
GO TO BITER.
BEND.
FORTRAN:
0102 IF(COND.NE.C) GOTO 0199
GO TO 0102
0199 CONTINUE
ALGOL:
Aiter: if ¬ C then go to Aend;
go to Aiter;
Aend:
C sel (C1)
Calt (C2)
C alt
C end
COBOL:
CSLCT. IF NOT C1 GO TO CALT1.
GO TO CEND.
CALT1. IF NOT C2 GO TO CALT2.
GO TO CEND.
CALT2.
CEND.
NOTE: negations in the IF-statemts
FORTRAN:
0103 IF(COND.NE.C1) GO TO 0104
GO TO 0199
0104 IF(COND.NE.C2) GO TO 0105
GO TO 0199
0105
0199 CONTINUE
ALGOL:
Cslct: if ¬ C1 then go to Calt1;
go to Cend;
Calt1: if ¬ C2 then go to Calt2;
go to Cend;
Calt2:
Cend:

Fig 1.19

```
0101  (seq)                     seq: XX01
      - -                       itr: XX02
      - -                       select: XX03
0203  (select)                  alt(1): XX04
      - -                       alt(2): XX05
      - -                       etc
0204  (alt)
0302  (itr)
      - -
      - -
0399  (end itr)
0299  (end select)
0199  (end seq)
```

DO in Fortran has not the same effect as iteration (as earlier mentioned) since the DO condition test is performed in the end. The DO component will consequently be performed at least once. An iterated part must be able to be performed zero times so that all combinations of data will be correctly processed.

You will certainly have noticed that JSP doesn't deal with GO TO-less programming. But the GO TO's which are used are *controlled* GO TO's in contrast to "wild" GO TO's. You can consider the use of GO TO-statements as a compilation of PERFORM — — — UNTIL or DO UNTIL and IF — — — THEN ELSE by hand.

Sometimes code readability is discussed very extensively. As a matter of fact, coding is merely a way to communicate with the computer. The schematic logic, detailed down to statement level, is the final solution. Translating a schematic logic into code is a mechanical process. Nevertheless, here are a few comments on code readability: the choice of component names is important as well as frequent comments. Stick to the entity names in the program specification. If a specification name is inadequate or misleading, choose a better name in cooperation with the specifier! And the comments must be informative.

Now, some exercises:

The schematic logic in exercise 1.15 and 1.16 is to be coded in Cobol, Fortran or Algol.

Exercise 1.15

```
P seq
    IE := 0;
    KA := 1;
```

```
        BP itr until (KA>10)
            BB seq
                LFLT := 10;
                BT sel (cond = N)
                    LFLT := LFLT-1;
                    MT := IE+2*KA;
                    IE := IE+2;
                BT alt
                    IE := IE+1;
                BT end
                KA := KA+1;
            BB end
        BP end
        stop;
P end
```

Exercise 1.16

```
A seq
    B sel (type=T1)
        E sel (class=C1)
            exec J;
        E exec;
            exec K;
        E end
    B alt
        exec F;
    B end
    C itr until (not type=T3)
        G itr until (not class=C3)
            L seq
                exec M;
                exec N;
            L end
        G end
        exec P;
    C end
    D sel (class=C1)
        exec H;
    D alt
    D end
A end
```

1.5. Physical Data Structure, Logical Data Structure and How to Combine Data Structures into One Program Structure

By physical data structure we mean a structure which exhaustively describes all possible orders, groups and categories as seen by any program. Several different logical data structures may be extracted from the same physical data structure. Why? Well, a data structure must also be looked upon from the problem point of view.

Let's consider an example, figure 1.20.

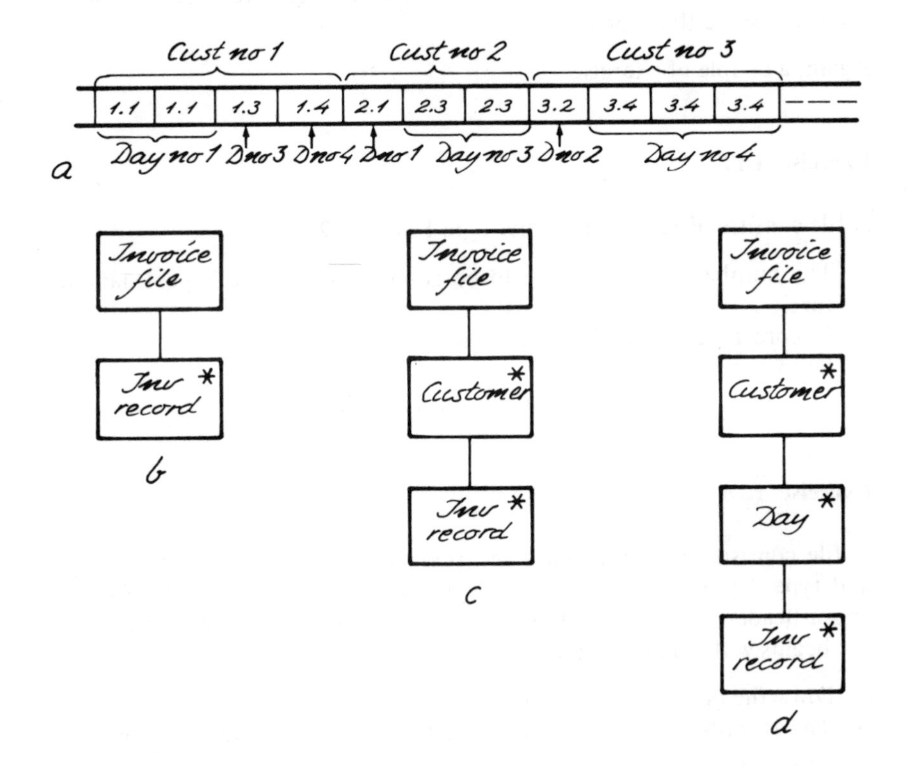

Fig 1.20

Here is an invoice file with its records sorted according to customer number as the first key, and day number as the second key, fig 1.20a. If the problem is only to count the number of invoices, then we can draw a logical data structure as in figure 1.20b. If instead the problem is to calculate the invoice total per customer, then we can draw a data structure according to figure 1.20c. We can also consider a task where invoice totals shall be calculated per customer *and* day. Then a data structure has to be drawn as in figure 1.20d.

You may very well get the impression that a data structure could look like just about anything. This is fortunately not the case. Figure 1.20d describes exhaustively the data as seen by any program, that is the physical data structure. It also provides a logical data structure for our last task. However, you can't draw a logical data structure which violates the physical data structure. You can't for instance, in our example, draw the day group as an iteration of the customer group. On the other hand, you can draw a logical data structure, where no more components are included than are needed to solve the problem.

Again, a couple of exercises:

Exercise 1.17

A file consists of records of either type 1 or type 2.

a) The number of records are to be counted. Draw the logical data structure.
b) Record type 1 shall be processed in one way, record type 2 in another. Draw the logical data structure.
c) What does the physical data structure look like?

Exercise 1.18

A file consists of type 1 and 2 records. The records are grouped in type 1 and type 2 groups. Every group begins with a header record-1 for type 1 and a header record-2 for type 2. The groups can occur in any order. The file begins with a main header.

a) Draw the physical data structure.
b) The records within each group are to be counted. Draw the logical data structure.

In the exercises above the components were given. But how detailed should a data structure be in practice? One main rule can be stated: the leaves in the data structure shall consist of the greatest possible data set which can be accessed by the program by means of one input operation (read) or can be output by one output operation (write). When these data sets are stored in the primary storage, parts of the sets are accessible and "storeable" in any order and frequency. However, string manipulation for instance can require data structures detailed down to and including character level.

Now, let's discuss how to combine two or more data structures into one basic program structure.

Example

An input file consists of a number of records. A report is to be produced with one report header followed by two report lines per input record. Draw the data structures and combine them into one basic program structure.

The data structures should not cause any difficulties, figure 1.21.

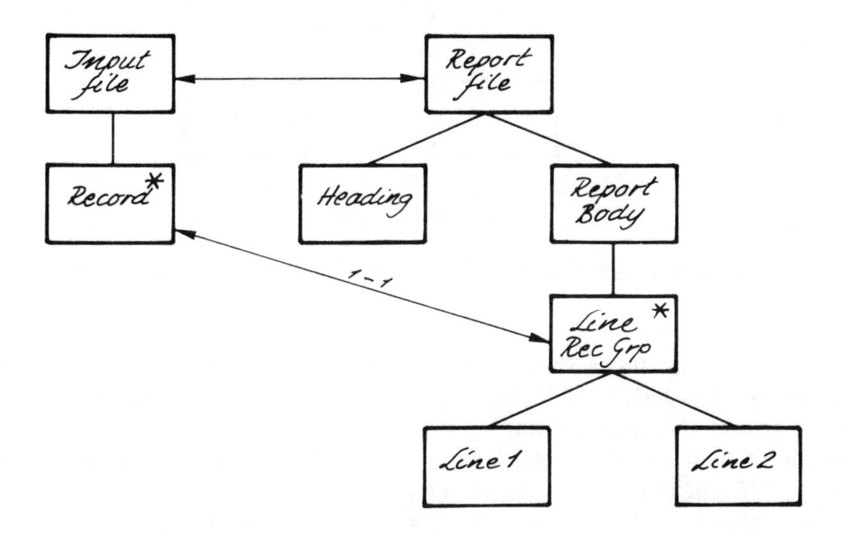

Fig 1.21

Now we have got to create one program structure with the data structures as a basis. A program structure should be static. It should mirror the components of the data structures. Those components which occur the same number of times and in the same order in the involved data structures we shall combine into *one* component in the program structure. Components like this have a so called 1—1 correspondence. In our example "Record" occurs the same number of times in the input file as "Line Record Group" in the output file and in the same order. These components should be combined into a single component in the basic program structure: PREC/

LRECGRP in figure 1.22 (P=process). The correspondence "Input File" — "Output File" is trivial: one "Input File" corresponds to one "Output File".

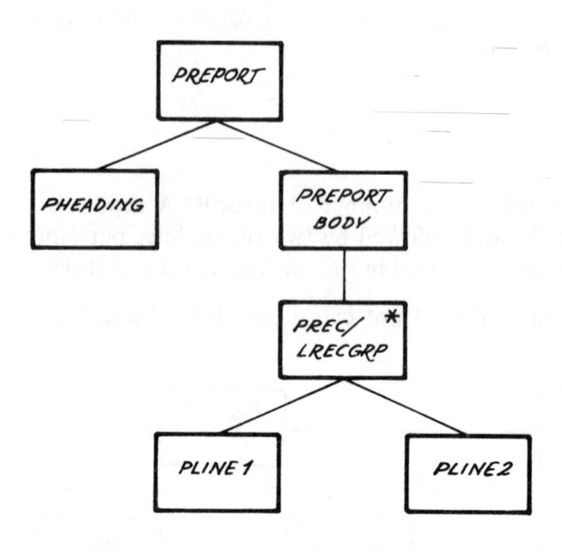

Fig 1.22

You may very well ask yourself whether the input record shouldn't be read before the line record group can be written. Well, of course, but this will be expressed later, when we allocate the operations to the program structure: How many times shall an input record be read? — Once per the header PREC/LRECGRP. — In the beginning, in the middle or etc. (Don't try to answer this question until you have read about "read ahead", unless you don't read ahead). — How many times shall a line record group be processed? Once per the header PREC/LRECGRP etc. You will find obvious places to allocate the operations in the program structure because PREC/LRECGRP has a frequency which corresponds to the operations. The component PREC/LRECGRP consumes one input record and produces one line record group.

PHDR and PREPBODY are placed in the level above PREC/LRECGRP. This doesn't cause any conflict. On the other hand, if "Record" in the input file had appeared under a header "Invoice" and "Line Record Group" under a header "Page" and there was no correspondence or relationship between "Invoice" and "Page", then the structures would be incompatible. But more about this difficulty later on in chapter 2.

The components "Line 1" and "Line 2" go along with "Line Record Group".

The basic program structure turns out to be the same as the report file structure. We have only changed the component names.

Example

A file contains records of type 1 and type 2. The records are not sorted by type. An output file is to be produced with records of type 1 only. Furthermore, a report shall be printed. The report is simple: the contents of the type 2 records shall be printed (one line per record). Draw the data structures and combine them into one basic program structure.

Here we have to combine three data structures, figure 1.23.

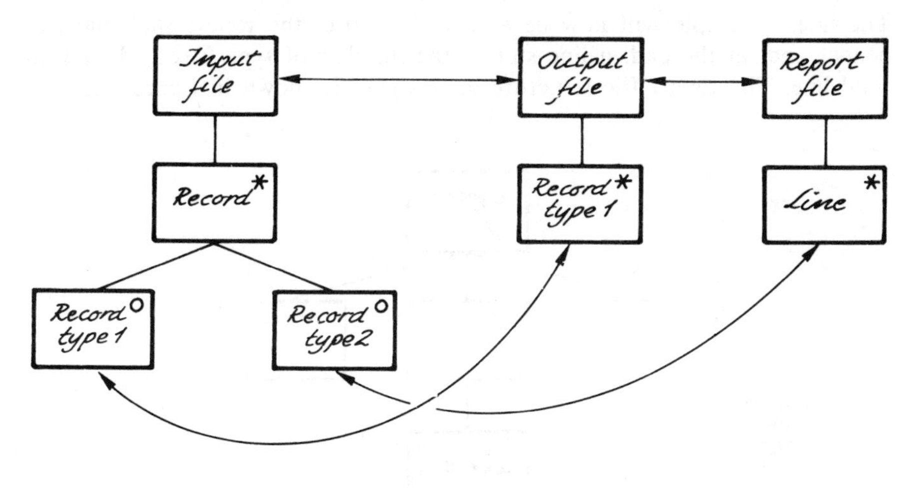

Fig 1.23

There are as many records of type 1 in the input file as in the output file and in the same order (nothing is said in the program specification about any other order in the output file). Note that here we have a 1—1 correspondence, though the one component is a selection part and the other an iterated part! In the same way we can identify a 1—1 correspondence between Record type 2 and Line. All components "find their place" in the input file structure, so we can use this structure as a basic program structure, figure 1.24.

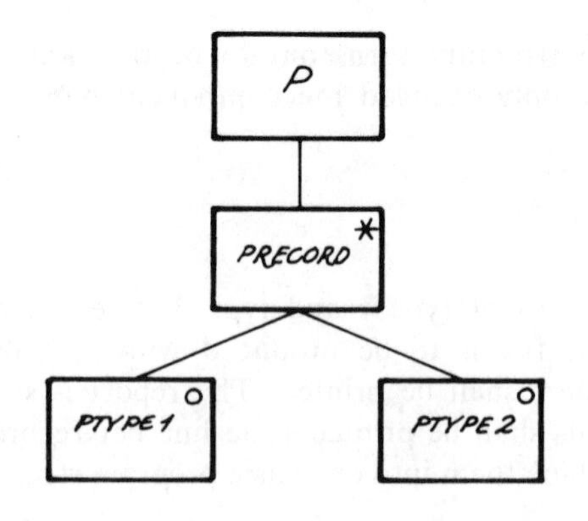

Fig 1.24

The latest example will now be extended a little: the report shall have a header and, at the end, a line stating the number of type 2 records, i.e. a total line. The report file structure in this case is shown in figure 1.25.

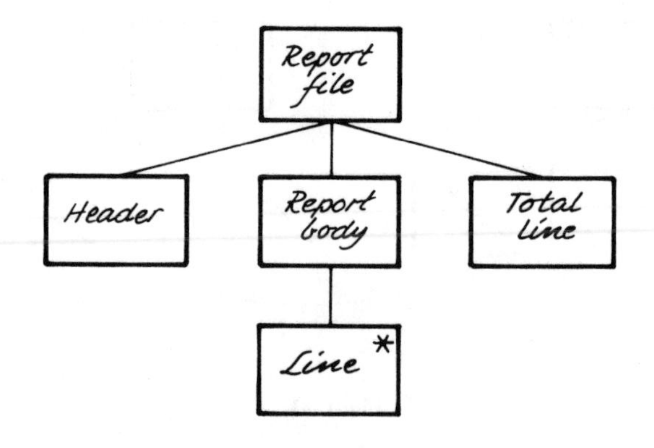

Fig 1.25

The program structure will now be a combination of the input file and the report file structures. The sequence parts Header, Report body and Total Line must have corresponding components in the basic program structure on the second level, figure 1.26.

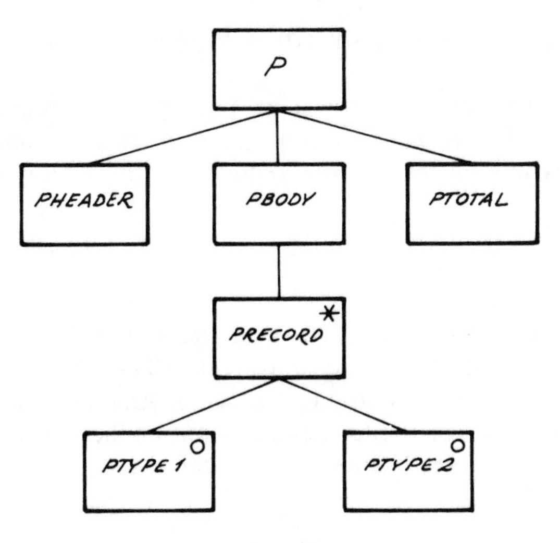

Fig 1.26

Sequence parts are "kind" in connection with structures. They can easily be inserted, provided they are not given incompatible headers or they themselves do not constitute incompatible headers.

Exercise 1.19

A program is to process a file with records and write a new record per input record. At the end of the output file, a special trailer record shall be written. Draw the data structures, search for 1—1 correspondences and draw the basic program structure.

Exercise 1.20

A stock file consists of article records with group number, article number, quantity and the value of each article in stock. The file is sorted according to group number. With this file as input, two files are to be produced. One output file shall have records corresponding to the records in the input file. At the end of each group the total value of the group in stock shall be stored (group total). The other output file is a report file with a report header and group headers. Two lines per group are to be printed. At the end of the report a total value of the articles in stock shall be printed (final total). Draw the data structures etc.

1.6. Some Good Programming Habits

In this section we will deal with some principles of programming which are probably familiar to most of you. We want to give some attention to these principles anyway as we intend to apply them later on.

Read Ahead

Read ahead enables data to be made available to the program, more specifically from sequential files or the equivalent. Where should the read operation be allocated in the program structure? Answer: *once* immediately after opening the file (or if file opening is not applicable: in the beginning of the program) and *once* immediately after a record in the file is consumed, figure 1.27.

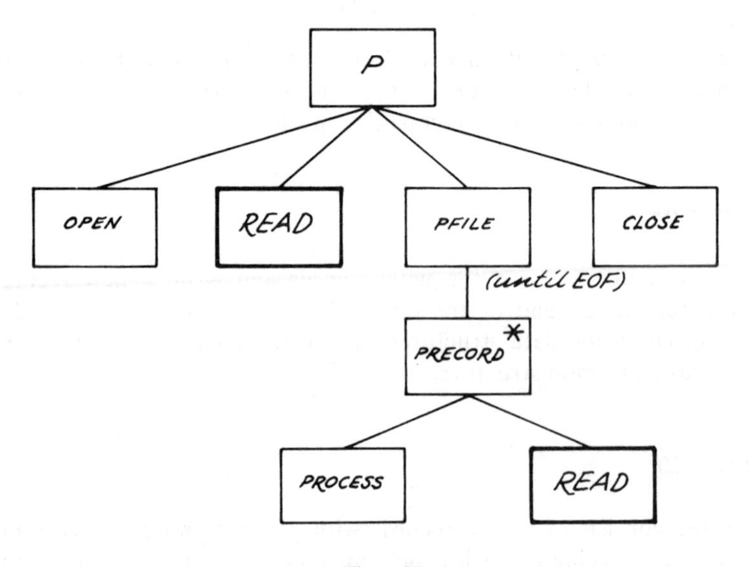

Fig 1.27

Here are the reasons why you should apply read ahead. The iteration PFILE must be terminated at end of file. If the program processes an empty file, then end of file will be found *before* the iteration PFILE is started. The introductory terminating condition test causes the PFILE not to be executed at all and the program will close the file neatly. Of course, empty files are not the most common case. More common is the appearance of end of file after a number of records has been processed.

If the lowest level in figure 1.27 had the order READ-PROCESS instead, then what would happen when end of file is reached? In this case, PROCESS would be executed with those data which happen to be stored in the input record area (if they are accessible at all in this situation — this is computer system dependent). This is apparently erroneous. Now, in figure 1.27 READ is allocated after PROCESS. If end of file is found at this level, then the iteration will be terminated. Iteration is as we know concluded by a return to the beginning of the iteration, where the terminating test is executed. The benefit of reading ahead is not restricted to the iteration case. We could for instance be forced to process two record types, REC-T1 and REC-T2, in different ways. The program structure must then contain a selection with selection conditions. A record must have been read *before* the selection is executed. Otherwise the selection condition test is not possible to execute. If you then read immediately after a record is consumed, a new record (or end of file label) becomes available for new condition tests (terminating and selection tests).

Exercise 1.21

Allocate the operations Open, Read, Close in the program structure, figure 1.28. The program reads one input file and writes one output file.

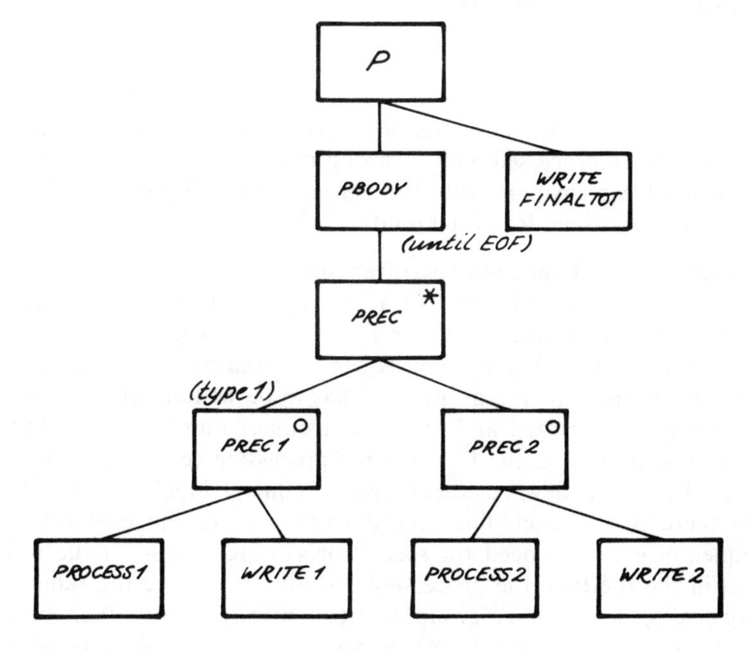

Fig 1.28

To Handle END OF FILE

First of all let's establish that end of file can be detected by a read operation only. How end of file is reported to the program is language or computer system dependent. In Cobol programs (independent of computer system) end of file behaviour is connected to the read statement: READ input file AT END . . . What the programmer writes after AT END will be executed at end of file. Quite often AT END GO TO CONCLUSION or something like it is used. Don't! Apart from having used a wild GO TO, we haven't used a correct terminating test at the beginning of the iteration. We must create a variable to be tested. Let's call that variable EF, end of file flag. EF is set=0 in the beginning of the program and *all* read statements shall then look like this: READ input file AT END MOVE 1 TO EF. The terminating condition can now be expressed: IF EF=1 GO TO AITEREND.

Sometimes a search key value is given HIGH VALUE (Cobol, places ones in all binary positions) at end of file. This is a less general solution as there are computer systems that do not allow access to the record area at end of file.

BREAKS without IF and BUT

As you know, records are often sorted into groups according to some common property, for example invoice records sorted according to customer number. Quite often the contents of a specific item of each record within a group are to be processed with a "group result" as a product, for instance invoiced total per customer number (group total). A total of all invoices is also commonly asked for (final total).

A problem of the kind above is often solved according to the following internal dialogue: either I have got a record with the same customer number as before (no control break) or I have got a record with a new customer number (control break), consequently a selection. If I have to execute a control break then a group total has to be written, at least one accumulator must be zeroized and the new customer number saved. *But — if* the record is the first in the file then the processing certainly should be the same as that for a new customer group (control break) — *but* then of course there is no concluding record from a preceding customer group, consequently here is a need for special processing. *But — if* the record is the last in the file then the processing certainly should be the same as that for concluding a customer group (control break) — *but* then of course there is no following record with a new customer number, consequently here is a need for more special processing.

The whole discussion above is absolutely unnecessary. It is based upon the *transition between* the records, control break — no control break. It is far better to consider the *records proper.* And after all, every group in the file shall be processed in the same way. Furthermore, the entity *customer group* has a corresponding entity in the data. The break mechanism will function perfectly if we base the program structure upon the data structures, apply read ahead and handle end of file in the way described above. In addition, we have to save the key which is common to the group, e.g. customer number. Desk test the example in figure 1.29. If you prefer to desk test a schematic logic then you had better try exercise 1.22.

Exercise 1.22

Write the schematic logic of the program in figure 1.29b.

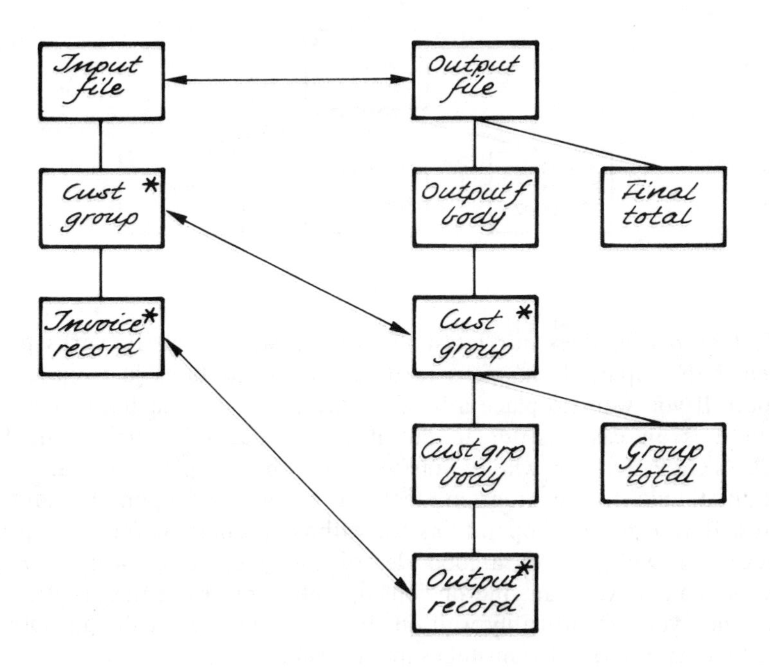

Fig 1.29a

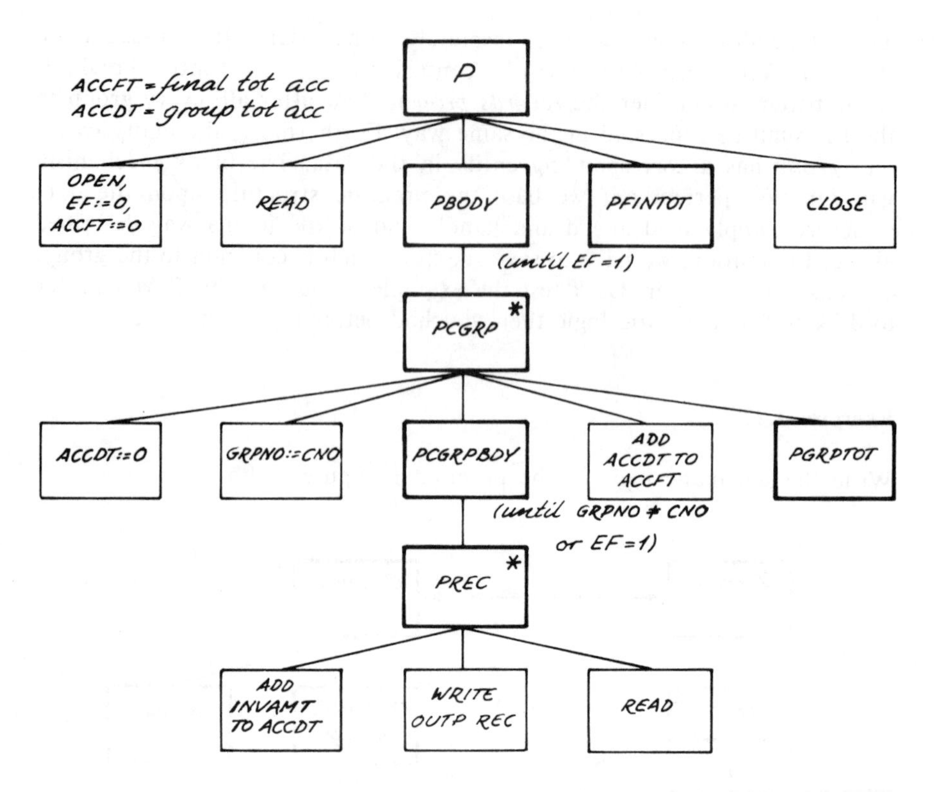

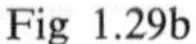

Fig 1.29b

What properties does our latest program design have? It works perfectly even if the input file happens to be empty or contains just one customer group. If you want to place a header record ahead of each customer group then it is an easy matter to put it in the beginning under the header PCUSTGRP. On the whole, you will find obvious places for all the operations thanks to the program structure being based upon the data structures. If you make an operations list without peeping at the basic program structure it will give you a good idea of how your design work is progressing. As long as you can find obvious operation places in the program structure then you are probably well on the way to a correct design. Otherwise you had better check for mistakes in an earlier step.

Exercise 1.23a

In a department store there are cash registers recording transactions containing, among other data, article number and quantity of each article sold.

In the stock department, article number and quantity of received articles are recorded in another way. The transactions are stored on tape periodically and sorted according to article number. The cash register transactions are marked I (issued) and those from the stock department are marked R (received). Design a program which reads the sorted tape file and produces a stock report with a report header and one line per article number. The line shall consist of an article number followed by 'NET MOVEMENT followed by the net movement quantity.

Single article transactions can look like this:

Article number	Trans type	Quantity
10445	I	15
10445	I	22
10445	R	100
10445	I	5

These transactions give rise to the following report line:

10445 NET MOVEMENT 58

You need not consider paging etc.

Now:

— draw data structures and look for correspondences
— draw the basic program structure
— make an operations list and allocate the operations
— write the schematic logic.

Remember read ahead and end of file handling!

And one more point: always ask "how many times . . .?" "in the beginning, in the middle or at the end?" when you allocate an operation!

Exercise 1.23b

Let us extend the preceding exercise. An asterisk is to be printed at the end of each article line when this article has had R transactions only. Make the necessary additions to the preceding solution, i.e. operations list, program structure and schematic logic.

1.7. Collating

To illustrate the collating problem we will use an example, based on a remote measurement system. A system like this can use a radio transmission to transfer measurement readings. In this example, a series of measurement readings is transferred from an aircraft to a ground station twice per second. Each flight produces exactly 5000 measurement series. When a measurement series is transmitted the number of the series (1—5000) is recorded on a special tape in the aircraft. At the ground station the number of the series is recorded too, together with the measurement readings. During some recent flights the number of series received has gradually decreased and the number of series recorded on the airborne tape is less than 5000. Now a detailed report is to be produced, indicating the four possible cases:

C1 — record in aircraft and in ground station
C2 — record in aircraft, but not in ground station
C3 — no record in aircraft, but record in ground station
C4 — no record in aircraft, no record in ground station

The report is to be used as a help in diagnosing the source of the error.

We draw the most obvious data structures, figure 1.30.

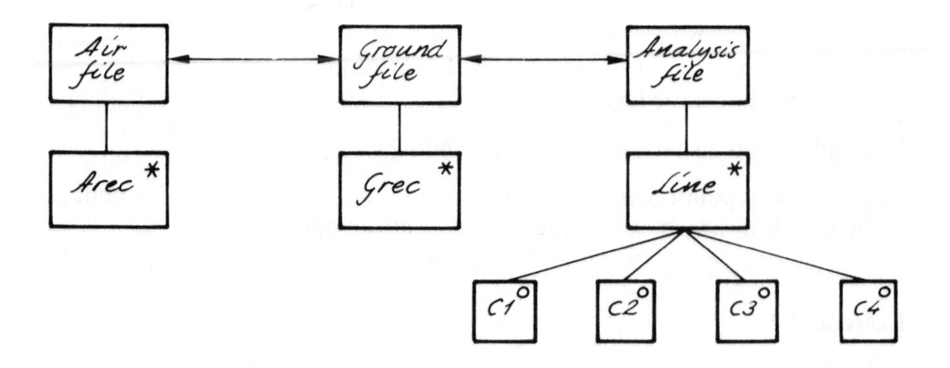

Fig 1.30

The uppermost level is trivial. But what then? We can't state that both files contain the same number of records. Can we find any more correspondences? Let's try. This is a collating problem. The aircraft file and the ground station file are to be compared. A record in each file is either matched or unmatched, figure 1.31.

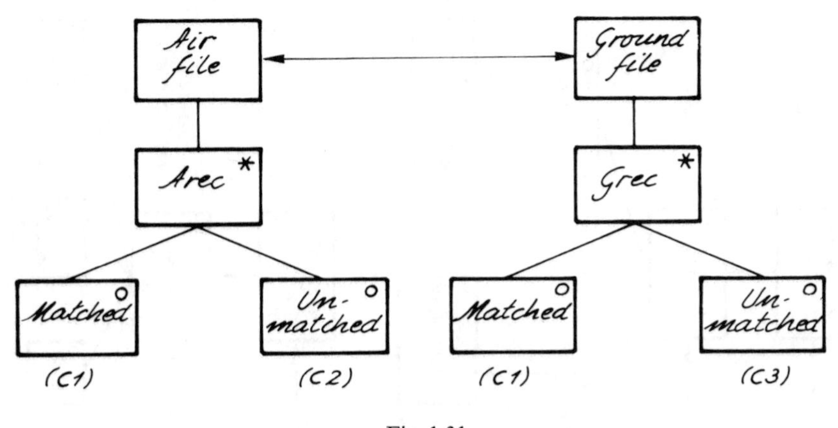

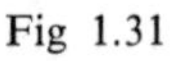

Fig 1.31

But still, we can't state that there is the same number of records in the files. Apparently there is something missing which causes the C4 case. It seems as if we have to study a specific constellation of records, figure 1.32.

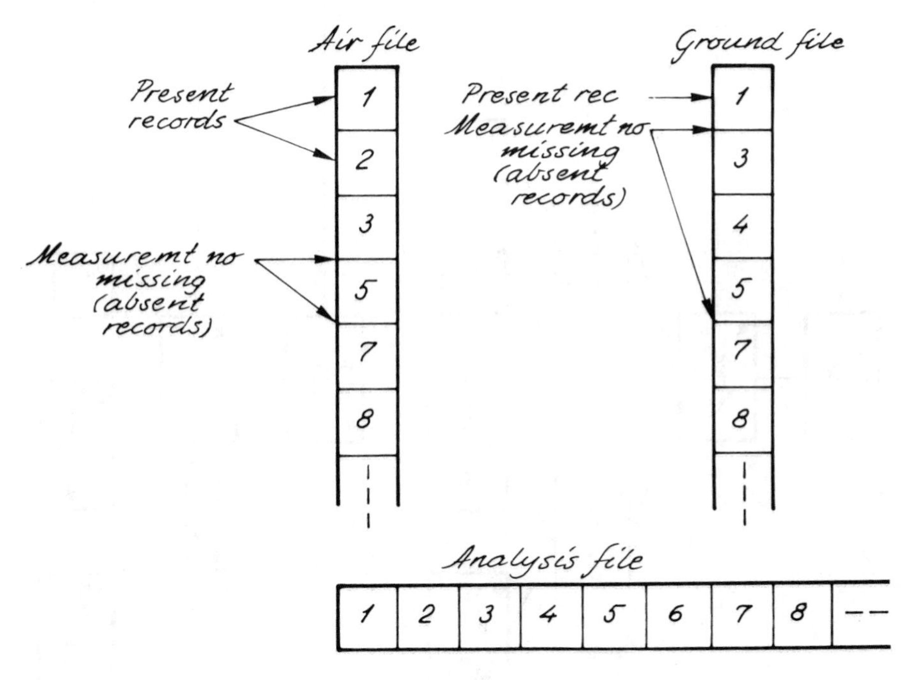

Fig 1.32

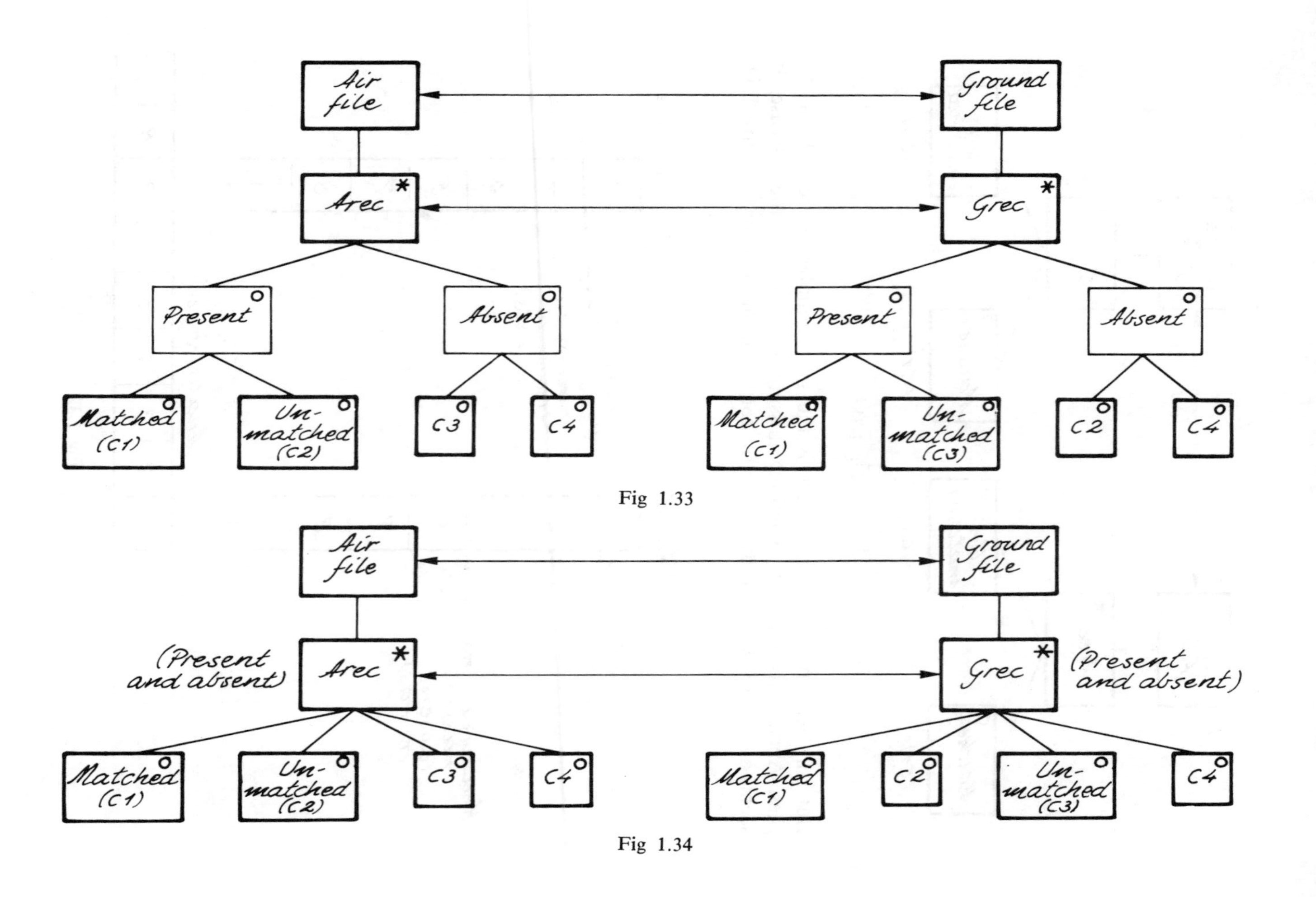

Fig 1.33

Fig 1.34

Our constellation was very revealing As a matter of fact, the missing record can be discovered thanks to our ability to count the measurement series numbers 1—5000. The missing *data* of, for instance, record number 4 in the aircraft file gives us the *information* that record number 4 is an absent record. In figure 1.32 record number 1 belongs to C1, 2 to C2, 3 to C1, 4 to C3, 5 to C1, 6 to C4, 7 to C1 and 8 to C1. Check!

If we add the concept absent record to the data structures then we can also include all matching cases, figure 1.33.

We can furthermore state that both files contain the same number of Arec as Grec and in the same order. Consequently we have 1—1 correspondence.

We can, without violating logic, draw structures of the Air file and Ground file simpler than those in figure 1.33. Then we include both present and absent records in Arec and Grec, figure 1.34.

The basic program structure in now evident.

Before we proceed to design the program, we had better consider the collating problem a little more closely. In figure 1.35 you will find a set diagram, depicting the total set of keys (measurement series numbers) and present keys in the air and ground files.

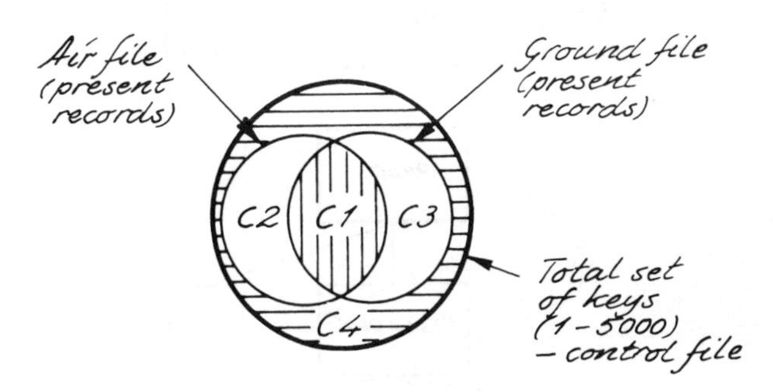

Fig 1.35

The absent records can be discovered thanks to the control file. This file includes the total set of keys. As a control file we can use in this case a counter which counts the measurement series numbers 1—5000 simply by starting at 1 and incrementing by 1. A file comprising the total set of keys is necessary if all matching cases are to be processed.

Let's have a look at the operations needed:

1. Open files
2. Read Air file
3. Read Ground file
4. Measurement series number := 1
5. Add 1 to Measurement series number
6. Process line C1 (edit and print)
7. Process line C2
8. Process line C3
9. Process line C4
10. Close files

If we now assiduously ask ourselves "how many times . . . in the beginning, in the middle or at the end" and apply unswervingly the read ahead rule then we will allocate the operations as in figure 1.36.

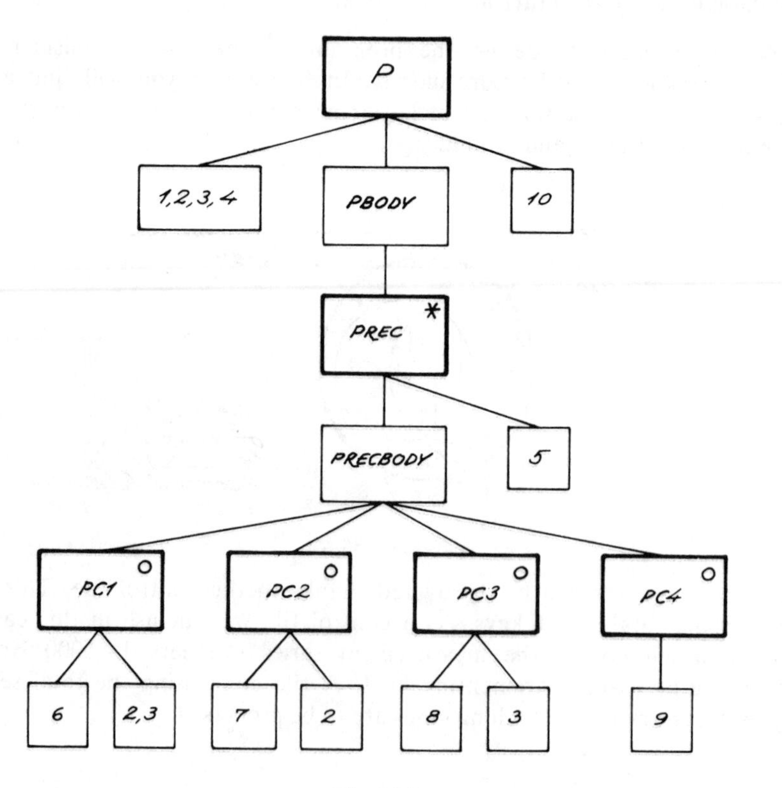

Fig 1.36

From figure 1.36 we can write the schematic logic (M S No = measurement series number).

```
P seq
    Open files;
    Read Air file;
    Read Ground file;
    M S No := 1;
    PBODY itr until (M S No>5000)
          PREC seq
               PRECBODY sel (Air M S No=M S No and
                                 Ground M S No=M S No)
                     Process line C1;
                     Read Air file;
                     Read Ground file;
               PRECBODY alt (Air M S No=M S No)
                     Process line C2;
                     Read Air file;
               PRECBODY alt (Ground M S No=M S No)
                     Process line C3;
                     Read Ground file;
               PRECBODY alt
                     Process line C4;
               PRECBODY end
               Add 1 to M S No;
          PREC end
    PBODY end
    Close files;
P end
```

This collating program structure is general: an iteration of a selection. Now the question is: is our solution general in all details? How does the program work for instance at end of file (one or both) before Measurement series number > 5000? This could very well happen. Unfortunately computer systems behaviour at end of file is not standardized. There are at least three cases we must consider.

End of file behaviour type 1: End of file signal is given, last read record remains in the input record area and is accessible.
End of file behaviour type 2: End of file signal is given, the input record area is not accessible.
End of file behaviour type 3: End of file signal is given, the input record area contains other data (system data) than the last read record *and* is accessible.

If end of file behavior type 1 is valid, then our solution works. When one end of file is reached the measurement series number of that file "stops" at the last value and the selection conditions work neatly. If, for instance, both files reach end of file before Measurement series number > 5000, then the selection conditions pass control to the selection part C4 during the rest of the processing.

End of file behaviour type 2 prevents the program from performing comparison test on fields in the input record area. What will happen exactly depends on the computer system. Anyway our solution doesn't work in this case.

The worst case is end of file behaviour type 3. In this case anything could happen!

If we want to have a general solution then we have to take care of end of file in the selection conditions. So we zeroize end of file flags of both files in the beginning of the program, EFA := 0 and EFG := 0. The flags will be set to 1 in read operations when end of file is reached. The selection conditions can now be written:

```
PRECBODY sel (EFA=0 and EFG=0 and Air M S No=M S No=Ground
M S No)
---
PRECBODY alt (EFA=0 and Air M S No=M S No)
---
PRECBODY alt (EFG=0 and Ground M S No=M S No)
---
PRECBODY alt
---
```

A simpler solution — but not quite as general — is to set Air M S No and Ground M S No to absurdly high values at end of file for the file in question. An absurdly high value today may perhaps be a relevant value in a future system, a factor which we must bear in mind.

Let us now restrict the problem to cases C1, C2 and C3. This is a commoner situation. The simplest amendment is to make the fourth selection part empty. A program like this will run through *all* measurement series numbers even when not necessary. Can this be avoided? Yes, if we initiate M S No like this: M S No := min (Air M S No, Ground M S No) instead of M S No := 1. Put another way this means the M S No is set to the least of the values of Air M S No and Ground M S No. In addition, we replace Add 1 to M S No by M S No := min (Air M S No, Ground M S No). At least one file is read in that spot in the program. The schematic logic looks like this (we have chosen the simplest end of file handling and presumed that the input record area is accessible at end of file):

```
P seq
    Open files;
    Read Air file; Note: if end of file Air M S No := 4 000 000;
    Read Ground file; Note: if end of file Ground M S No := 4 000 000;
    M S No := min (Air M S No, Ground M S No);
    PBODY itr until (Air M S No=4 000 000 and
                     Ground M S No=4 000 000)
        PREC seq
            PRECBODY sel (Air M S No=M S No and
                          Ground M S No=M S No)
              Process line C1;
              Read Air file;
              Read Ground file;
            PRECBODY alt (Air M S No=M S No)
              Process line C2;
              Read Air file;
            PRECBODY alt
              Process line C3;
              Read Ground file;
            PRECBODY end
            M S No := min (Air M S No, Ground M S No);
        PREC end
    PBODY end
    Close files;
P end
```

Here the integrated set of keys in the Air file and in the Ground file works as a control file.

If we are asked to deal with cases C1 and C2 only then we had better store the ground file on a direct access storage, figure 1.37.

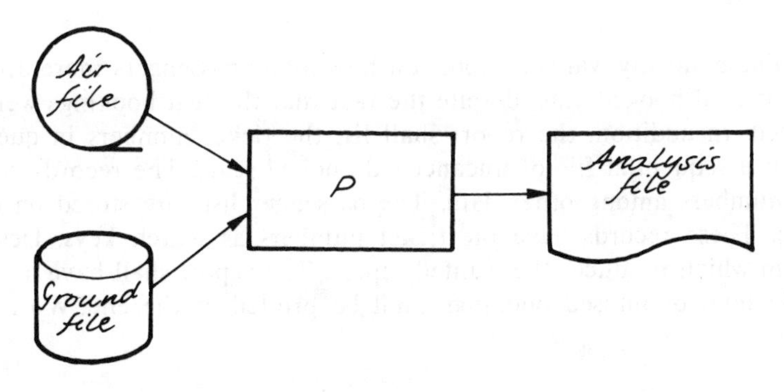

Fig 1.37

The program structure will still be an iteration of a selection but with the following schematic logic:

```
P seq
      EFA := 0;
      Open files;
      Read Air file;
      PBODY itr until (EFA=1)
            PREC seq
                  Read Ground file with key=Air M S No;
                  PRECBODY sel (found)
                        Process line C1;
                  PRECBODY alt
                        Process line C2;
                  PRECBODY end
                  Read Air file;
            PREC end
      PBODY end
      Close files;
P end
```

Here the Air file works as a control file. As the ground file is stored on a direct access storage there is no end of file problem. It's sufficient to read the file immediately before the selection PRECBODY.

Exercise 1.24

If three files are to be collated, how many cases will appear? (We presume the use of a control file).

Exercise 1.25

An airline company wants a report on how many passengers there are who have not used booked seats despite the fact that the seat bookings were not cancelled. In addition, the report shall list the ticket numbers in question. There is a sequential file of uncancelled booked seats. The records contain ticket numbers among other data. The passenger lists are stored on direct storage. These records have the ticket numbers as search keys. Design a program which produces the wanted report. The report shall have a header and the total of unused bookings shall be printed at the end. Work step-by-step:

- draw the data structures and look for correspondences
- draw the basic program structure
- make an operations list and allocate the operations to the program structure
- write a schematic logic

You need not take page breaks etc. into consideration.

Exercise 1.26

A company has a sequential stock file. The file consists of records sorted according to article number. Issue transactions are stored on a tape, also sorted according to article number. There may be several issue transactions for the same article. There may also be articles, having no transactions at all. A report shall be printed with a header and one line per article having no transaction. Design a program which prints such a report, figure 1.38.

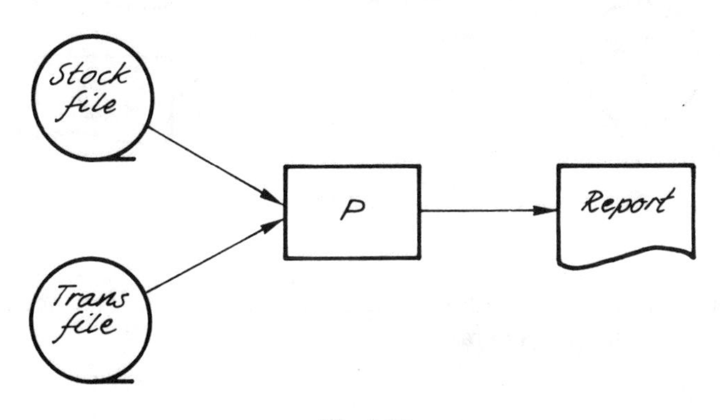

Fig 1.38

This is a combination of record group and collating problems. Work step-by-step, applying the design rules. You need not take page breaks etc. into consideration.

Exercise 1.27

A transaction file is to be used to update a stock file. The article records are sorted according to ascending article number. The records in the transaction file are sorted in the same way. Several transactions can deal with the same article number. Each issue transaction has a negative transaction quantity, each receipt transaction has a positive transaction quantity. The stock quantity balance of the article records shall be updated. In addition, an inventory shall be printed with a header and one line per article record in the stock file: ARTICLE NO nnnnn QUANTITY BALANCE sssss. An error list shall also be printed with a header and one line per article number in the transaction file where this number is not found in the stock file: ARTICLE NO nnnnn MISSING. All quantity values have either a plus or a minus sign (checked during the preceding sorting).

Design a program according to the specification above. The files are shown in figure 1.39.

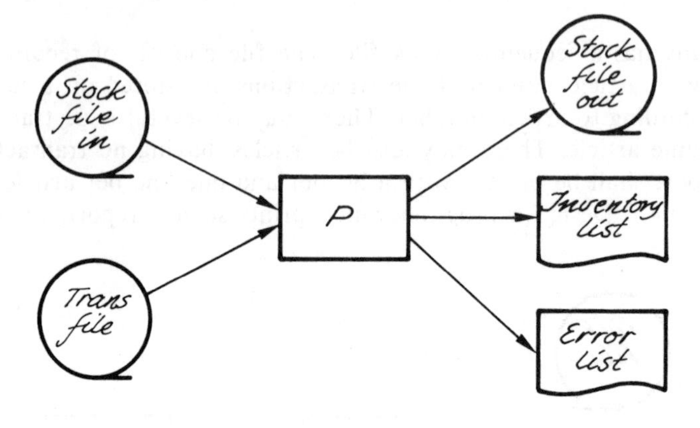

Fig 1.39

This is also a combination of record group and collating problems. Here we have to consider the collating cases C1, C2 and C3. You need not take page breaks etc. into consideration.

1.8. To Test or Not to Test

Of course you have to test before the program will be used in production runs. But let's consider for a moment what we can achieve by testing.

The following intellectual experiment is sometimes used during test discussions. The Timbuktu data processing subsidiary of our company has been destroyed by fire. All the twelve employees have been dispersed and are unavailable. The only remnant of the subsidiary is a program tape. (This was the sole tape in the fireproof cupboard . . .) Fortunately, we have by chance been able to determine by the volume number that the tape contains a program which was the pride of the subsidiary. Unfortunately, it was not the source code but the object code which survived. We happen to know that the program updates a register file from records in a transaction file, figure 1.40.

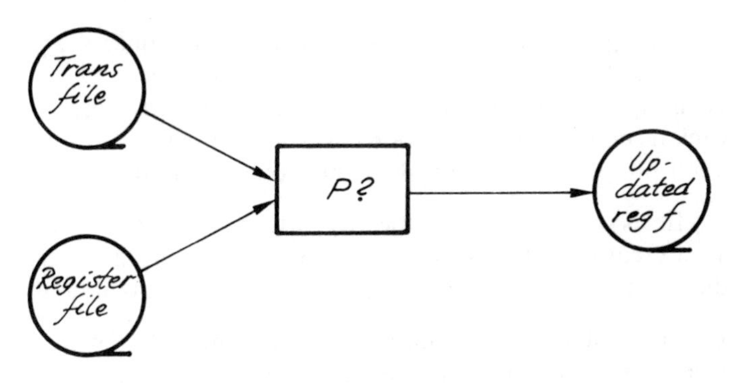

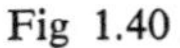
Fig 1.40

We also know that the transaction records are 16 bits long and the register records are 35 bits long. But, sorry to say, this is all. There is no program documentation, it has gone up in smoke. (Sometimes, you don't need a fire to "lose" program documentation!) What can we do to find out what the program does? Well, we can test the program. How many test cases are necessary? We must test all combinations of input data, i.e.

$$2^{16} * 2^{35} = 2^{16+35} = 2^{51} =$$

= (about) 2 000 000 000 000 000 combinations or test cases.

If each test case is processed in 1 μs, then a program test would take about 60 years to run (continuous twice around the clock processing).

The records are not long at all and still we need an unreasonably long test run. What is the conclusion? Well, we can *in practice never prove that a program is correct,* only discover any errors appearing when a data combination is input.

How, then, can we convince ourselves that a program is correct? Only by designing the program according to strictly logical principles can we hope to arrive at a solution, which is correct regardless of which data combinations are input. By proceeding in small steps during the design work as dealt with in the preceding sections, you have a pretty good chance of knowing that your solution is correct.

From the above it could very well follow that testing is superfluous. No, we have to test anyway. It could for instance happen that a mispunching doesn't cause a syntax error but causes a logical error. The operator could drop a source code card. You can probably make yourself a list of possible calamities in a computer installation.

Test, consequently, but what to test? Here is a demanding list:

- that each program statement is performed at least once
- that each type of input data has been read at least once
- that each type of output data has been written at least once
- that each terminating and selection condition is used
- that each program statement gives the expected result

The list reflects a demanding objective which however is feasible. It's feasible to a great extent thanks to the fact that the terminating and selection of different components need not be tested in combinations.

In this connection it's perhaps appropriate to tell the wellknown story of the ballpoint pen. In a little book shop a customer catches sight of the Bargain of the Week; ballpoint pens in attractive colours, only 15 pence each. This is exactly what this customer needs — the day before he had lost his ballpoint pen. He selects a pen in his favorite colour and tests it:

1. He presses the knob (the ballpoint protrudes).
2. He writes his name and address (it works alphanumerically).
3. He writes his telephone number (it works numerically).
4. He presses the knob (the ballpoint retracts).

Nice, he says, I'll take this one, pays and returns home. In the evening he wants to write a postcard to his old aunt in Brighton. He takes his new ballpoint pen out of his pocket and presses the knob. Nothing happens. He presses and presses the knob. Still nothing happens. What to do in a situation like this? Dismantle the pen of course. Out comes a plastic knob and a small piece of plastic originating from the plastic knob. By studying the plastic knob carefully all becomes clear. The knob turns 90° when the ballpoint protrudes and another 90° when in retracts. The mechanism was consequently in that position where the little plastic piece was missing, so it couldn't work when he tried to make the ballpoint protrude the second time.

Where did our would-be postcard writer make his big mistake? Well, he tested the pen without knowing anything about the internal design or number of possible internal states of the pen. A complete test should have comprised *four* depressions of the knob instead of two. The knowledge of this would have saved him vexation and 15 p.

A program can, like the ballpoint pen, have different internal states. The more internal states, the more surprisingly the program can behave.

A program with switches can have several internal states. If it has for instance six switches (two values: 0 or 1) 64 combinations are possible. If you state this you will very often be contradicted, like this for example: when switches 1 and 2 are on, 3 and 5 can't be on and when switch 6 is off, 1 and 4 are on etc. So there are only five combinations of interest left. Is your opponent right? Well, at least he *thinks* he is until half a year has passed after the first production run. Then the telephone rings at our opponent's home at 2 o'clock in the morning. A distressed and impatient voice tells him that the program has blown into pieces and it *has* to be executed right now. There is only one thing a responsible programmer can do. Toddle off to look at the program and the dump. And behold! There has apparently appeared a combination of data causing the sixth (unexpected) combination of switches. The problem is a little complicated — our drowsy programmer adds another switch to enable a short-cut in the program. This amendment gets the program to work — this time — but as a matter of fact the program has now 128 different internal states!

Avoid switches!

2 Structure Clashes, their Solution and Program Inversion

2.1. Structure Clashes

When there are no correspondences in two data structures we have a structure clash. Let's explain that a little more by some examples.

A card file contains a number of football match results, figure 2.1.

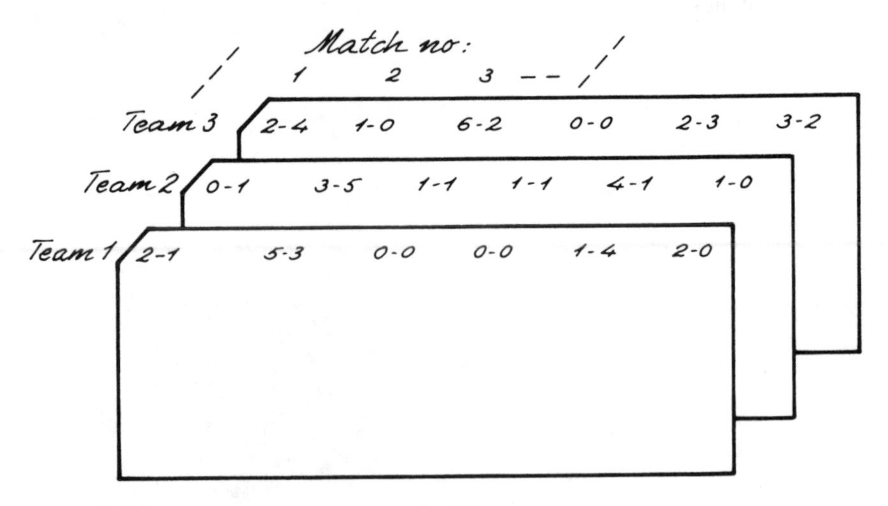

Fig 2.1

The first card contains all match results of football team no 1, the second the results of football team no 2 etc. We want a program which prints a result table. This table shall contain the match results of each team in columns, figure 2.2.

	Team 1	Team 2	Team 3	— — —
Match 1	2 - 1	0 - 1	2 - 4	— — —
Match 2	5 - 3	3 - 5	1 - 0	— — —
¦	¦	¦	¦	

Fig 2.2

What do the data structures look like? Figure 2.3 shows these structures. How about the correspondences?

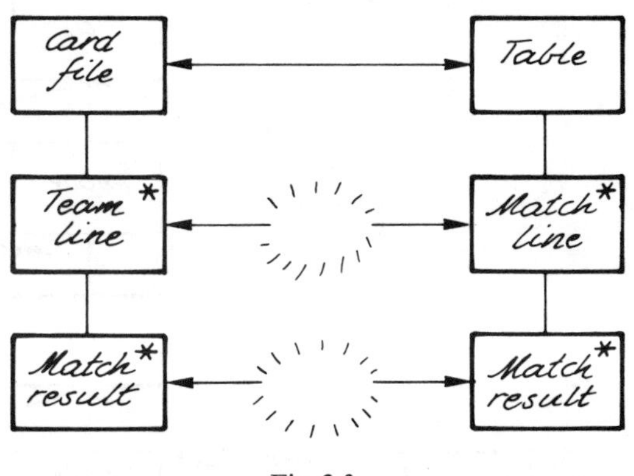

Fig 2.3

Team line and match line are quite different entities so there is no correspondence. Match results in both files are certainly of the same number, but they don't occur in the same order so there is no correspondence here either. This is an example of a structure clash called *ordering clash*. The fundamental solution is evident: first we have to sort the card file using match number as a primary key and team number as a secondary key, figure 2.4.

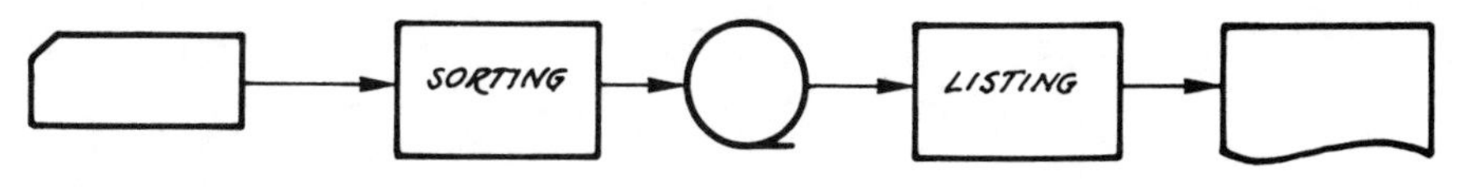

Fig 2.4

The figure doesn't include the work files of the sorting program. Note that the card file and the table structures are separated when being processed by separate programs.

Ordering clashes have been fought against in data processing since time immemorial, or rather since the Hollerith machine era. Between different types of processing, the card decks often had to be sorted by different entities.

Before discussing another type of structure clash we will look at some typical cases of corresponding structures. Imagine a file containing unblocked records. The file is to be input to a program which shall output the records by block, where one block contains an integer number of records. The program structure is simple, figure 2.5.

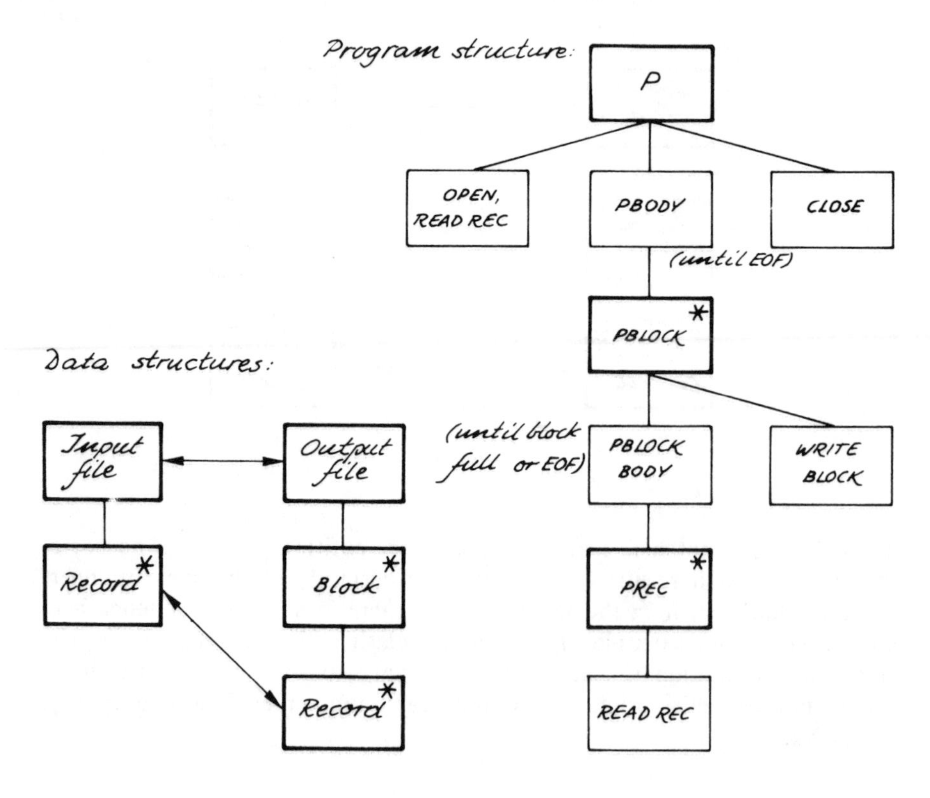

Fig 2.5

Since a block consists of an integer number of records, it can be described as an iteration of record. Consequently, the program structure will include both the component PBLOCK and PREC. We can allocate the operation "write block" to PBLOCK. The same is true for "read record" and PREC.

A similar situation occurs if the records are so large that they span an integer number of blocks (overblocked records), figure 2.6.

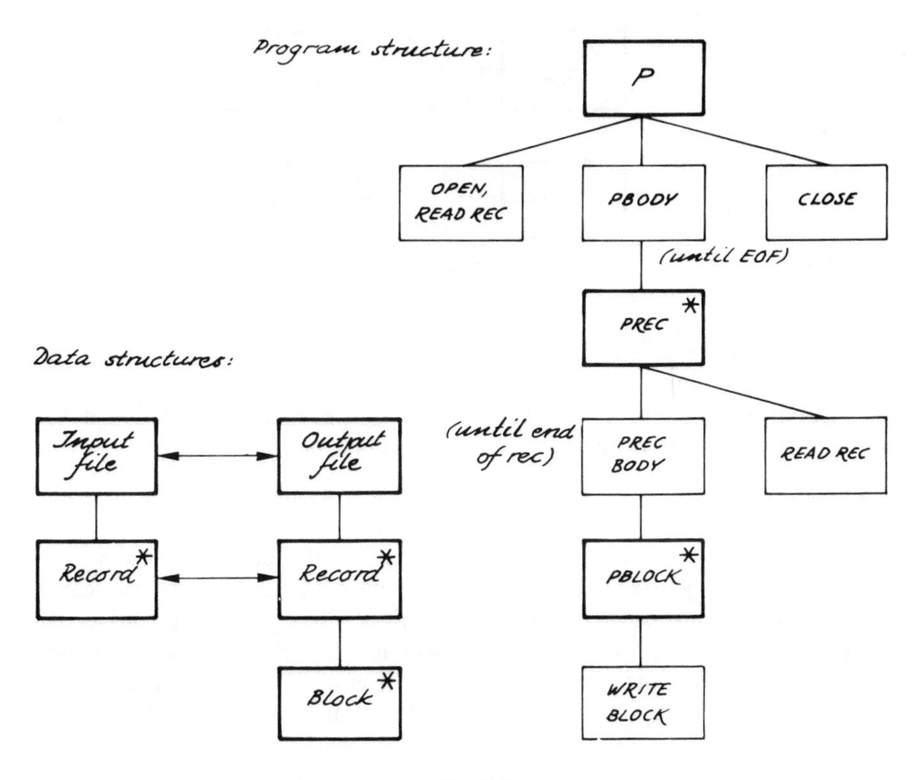

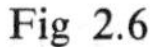

Fig 2.6

Here the records can be described as an iteration of block. In this program too there are obvious places in which to allocate the operations "read record" and "write block".

Now it's time to present the previously mentioned structure clash. This will occur if you want to produce a file with so called "spanned records". In this case you have to deal with records of variable length, as in figure 2.7.

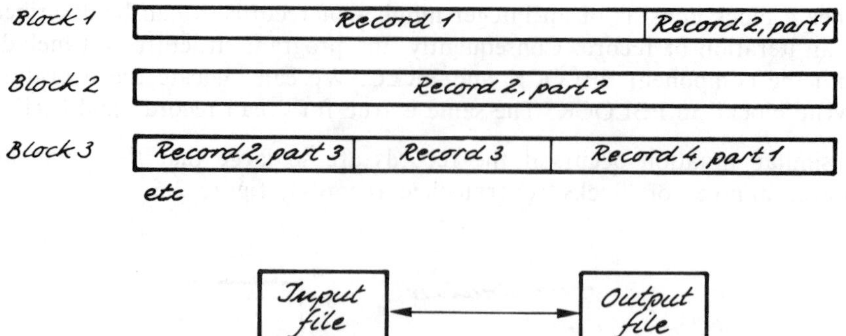

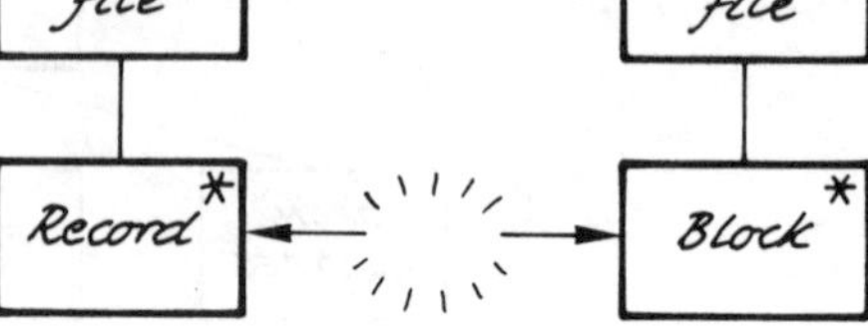

Fig 2.7

As you can see there is no definable block — record relationship. None of our three components, sequence, iteration or selection, is usable to describe the relationship. The record boundaries and the block boundaries don't coincide so this type of structure clash is called *boundary clash.*

If you try to ignore the difficulties in the latest example basing the program structure upon "block" and disregarding the component "record" then you have no component to allocate the operation "read record" to. Trying the reverse, i.e. basing the program structure upon "record", then we can't allocate the operation "write block" to any obvious place. Of course it's possible to solve the problem by using switches. But in that case the structure is violated and the program will be difficult to understand. Furthermore, we have agreed to avoid switches. If you ask yourself why, we refer you to section 1.8.

A case of boundary clash occurs often between an input file and a print file. The reason is that the pages seldom can be related to the input file.

A third type of structure clash can be defined. Here is an example: the structures of a job log file and of a job log printout. A job log file is written chronologically. It can of course include a lot of different record types, but it's enough to look at the records of job start and job termination, program start and program termination. These records reflect the order and duration of the jobs and the programs, figure 2.8.

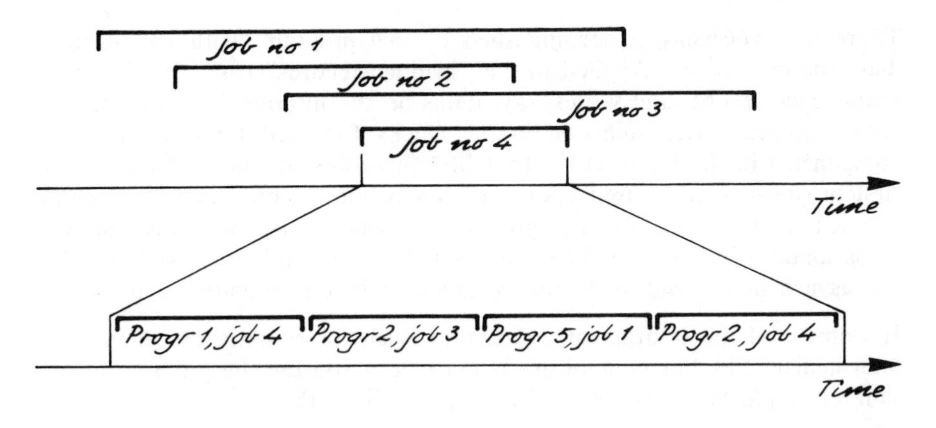

Fig 2.8

The job log printout shall include among other things start and stop times *by job*. The data structures are shown in figure 2.9.

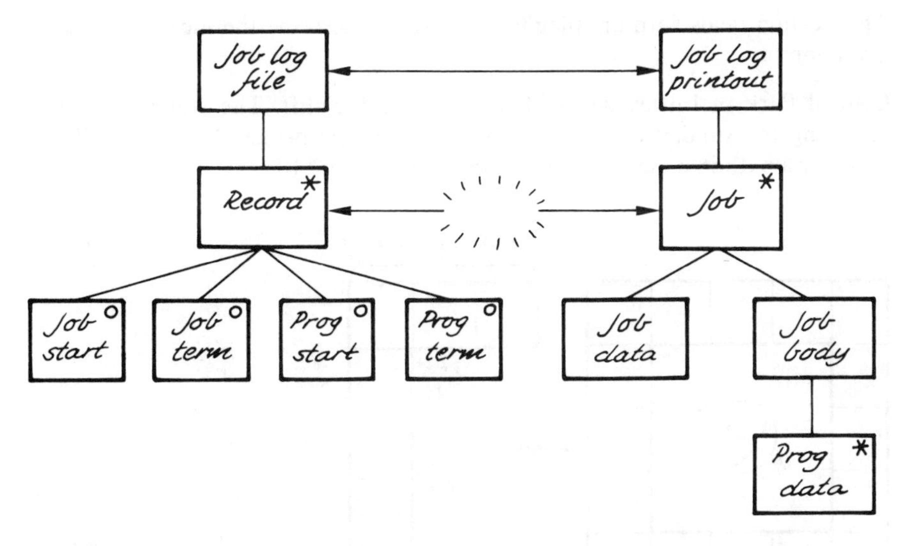

Fig 2.9

Apart from the uppermost level, there are no correspondences. This type of structure clash is called *interleaving clash*. It can be considered as a special case of ordering clash and can be solved by sorting, if you don't want job statistics in real time. Sorting is too slow in real-time processing.

The fundamental solution of a structure clash is based upon the same principle as the solution of the ordering clash, consider figure 2.4 once again.

There the processing is accomplished by *two* programs with an intermediate file in between. Applied to the "spanned records" case, the first program reads records and writes, say, items on the intermediate file and the second program reads items and writes blocks. Provided items are common components in the input and output files this solution will be correct. The first program is now based upon the component "record" and the second is based upon "block". The two programs are *independent* which is a matter of paramount importance. The operations "read record" and "write block" are asynchronous and shall not be included in one monolithic program.

It seems as if the solution of a structure clash forces us to use a physical intermediate file. Fortunately this is not true if you use the program inversion technique which the rest of this chapter deals with.

2.2. The Pieceworkers and the Rosegarden Path

This section deals with an allegory in order to describe the idea of program inversion.

Central Park in Littletown is about to get a face-lift. The stone slabs surrounding the sundial are to be replaced by a yew hedge. The slabs will be used for a path in a new rosegarden instead, figure 2.10.

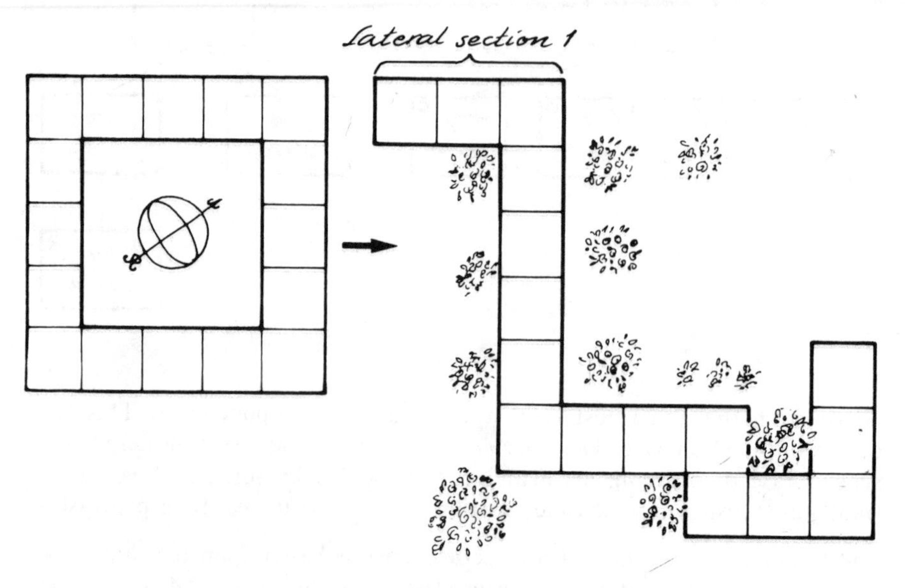

Fig 2.10

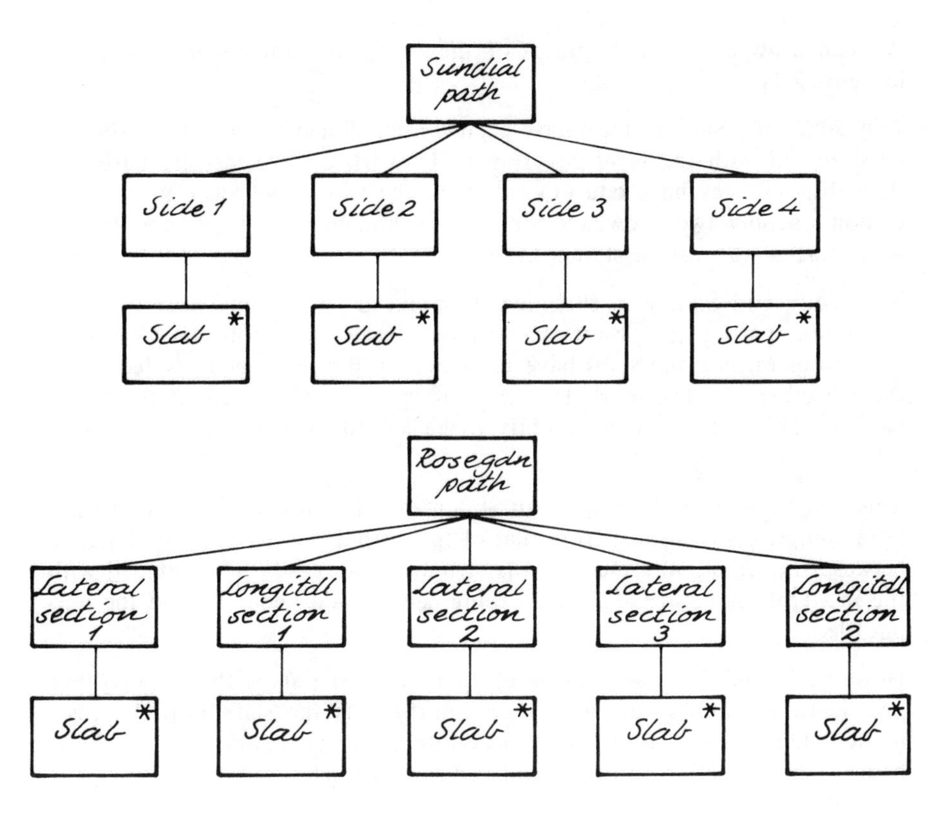

Fig 2.11

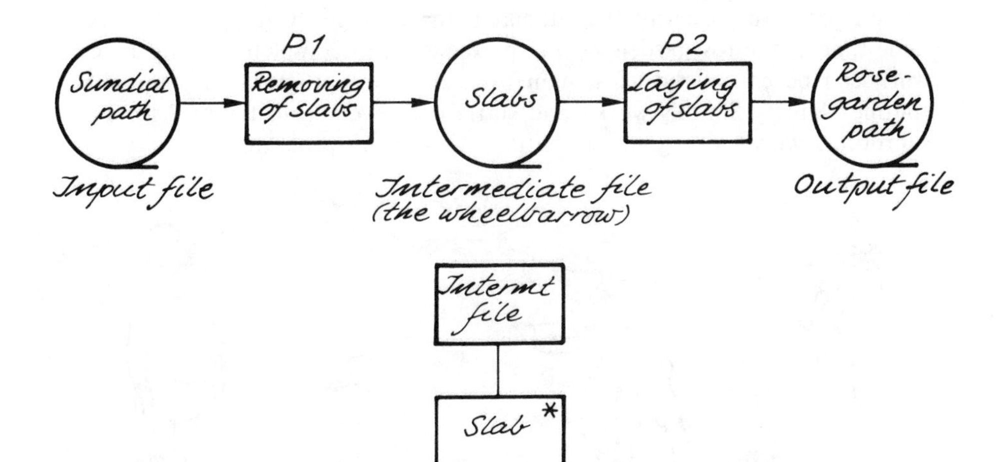

Fig 2.12

We can draw structure diagrams of the two slab arrangements as shown in figure 2.11.

Jolly Jones and Snuffy Smith have been commissioned to move the slabs and have agreed with the local government to work on a piece-rate basis. At their disposal they have one (1) crowbar (the Littletown local government couldn't supply two crowbars for reasons known only to themselves), a wheelbarrow and a stone stamper.

Now Jolly and Snuffy discuss how to proceed. It is impossible to move the sundial path as it is, there is a structure clash apart from the pure practical problem. No, the slabs have to be removed one by one, loaded on to the wheelbarrow, transported to the rosegarden and placed in their new pattern. The task has consequently to be solved by *two* programs. figure 2.12.

This is a fundamentally important statement. The input file structure has been completely separated from that of the output file. P1 is easily designed because the simple intermediate file structure can easily be combined with the input file structure. The same thing can be said about P2 and the output file.

However, if Jolly uses the crowbar to remove the slabs then Snuffy has practically nothing to do, and when Snuffy puts the slabs into the rosegarden then Jolly is idling. The piece-rate could be better utilized. Jolly, being a shrewd fellow, hit on a smarter solution. The distance between the sundial and the rosegarden is not longer than it is possible to throw the slabs between these places. As soon as Jolly has removed a slab he throws it to Snuffy shouting: "Slab coming!" Snuffy places the slab into the rosegarden path. In this way the sundial path successively disappears at the same time as the rosegarden path is approaching its completion. Jolly Jones' work can be considered as a main program. This program calls the subroutine (Snuffy Smith's work) and starts it at every call, figure 2.13. The subroutine works as an output routine of the main program.

Fig 2.13

The solution could very well be the reverse, particularly if Snuffy Smith is the more dominant. In that case Snuffy would shout:

"I want a slab' ", and Jolly would comply. Here Snuffy's work functions as a main program. What Jolly does now corresponds to a subroutine, an input routine.

2.3. The Principle of Program Inversion

The principle of program inversion is probably nothing new to most of you. What could be new is the reasoning about the problems in connection with program inversion.

Let's remind ourselves of the structure clash solution. Look at figure 2.14.

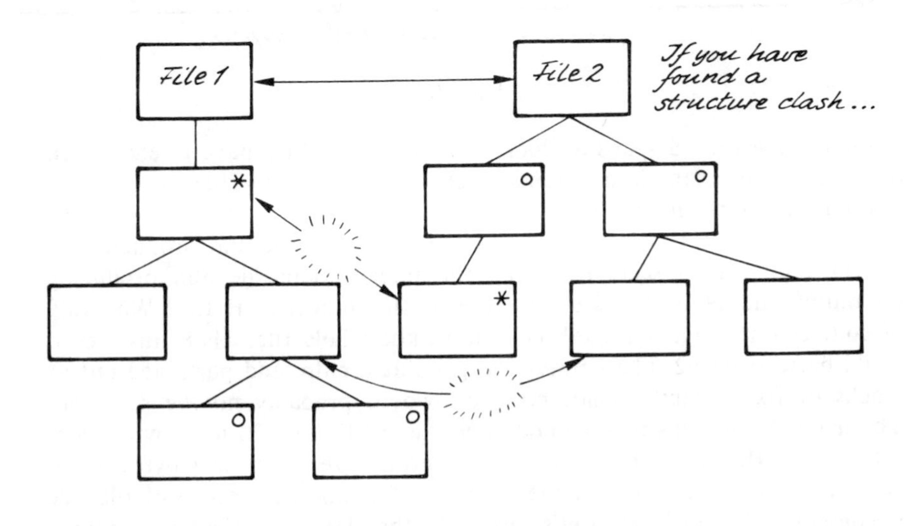

... don't solve the problem in one program! Divide the program into two instead:

Fig 2.14

The physical intermediate file is mostly unwanted. Creating a single program forces us to use wild switches and wild GO TO's. Still, it is possible to arrive at a solution without an intermediate file. This is achieved by program inversion. Nevertheless, the intemediate file has to be taken into account in the beginning of a structure clash solution. Here, one of the first questions is: What to store on the intermediate file? The answer will be given in the following discussion concerning a structure clash problem.

An input file contains records of variable length. The records are unblocked. They shall be written on a file with fixed block length (the "spanned records" case). The physical appearance is shown in figure 2.15.

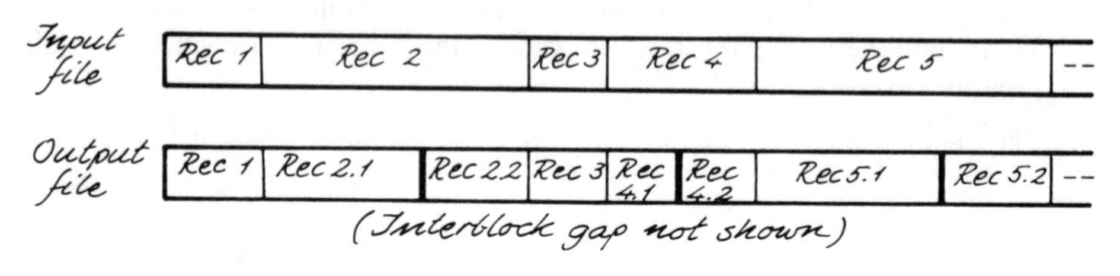

Fig 2.15

No item of a record spans a block boundary. The files have already been discussed as an example of boundary clash (figure 2.7). There is no fixed relationship between record and block. Accordingly we have to solve the problem with two programs, one reading the input file and producing an intermediate file, a second reading the intermediate file and producing the output file. However, what to store on the intermediate file? We could of course store a giant record, containing the whole file. Then this record could be read by P2, like emptying a glass at a gulp, and portioned out as blocks of fixed length. That, however, would probably not be practical. The main storage has to accomodate a whole file, say, 20 megabytes from a tape reel. But, as you know, a main storage size of 20 megabytes is not very common, at least not at the moment of writing! A record of file size is consequently too large. Let's moderate the size. The input file records can't be used, these have no correspondence in the output file structure. How about items? Maybe. Could we use still smaller components? Well, in that case we should use characters. Characters as well as items are components in the input and output file structures. But what will happen if characters are used as records in the intermediate file? Well, after inversion the main program has to call the subroutine every time a character is to be transferred. A lot of calls will occur. The situation would like Jolly Jones breaking the slabs into very small pieces and crying: "Herecomesapieceherecomesapiecehere . . . !" Probably Snuffy whould spit out his fag and go away leaving Jolly to get on with it!

Let's return to item. This component exists in the input file as well as in the output file (no item spans a block boundary). An item does not demand absurdly large main storage space and gives considerably fewer calls for the subroutine compared with the character case. So let us decide to use items as records in the intermediate file. We can put it like this:

> Store in the intermediate file an entity which is common to the clashing structures and is as large as possible taking the main storage space into consideration.

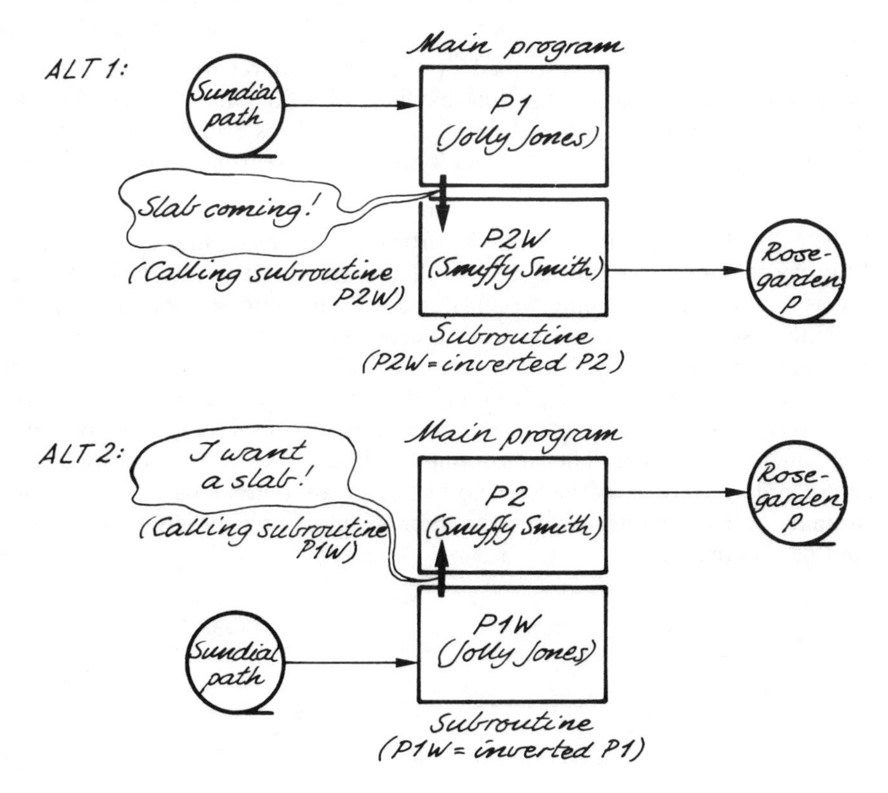

Fig 2.16

To use a physical intermediate file is, as said before, a waste of resources. We have to think like Jolly Jones: is it possible to avoid loading the wheelbarrow, move it and unload it? Yes it is if we convert one of the programs into a main program and the other into a subroutine. So there are two alternatives illustrated in figure 2.16, based upon Jolly Jones' and Snuffy Smith's situation.

The intermediate file has disappeared. At every call a slab is transferred between the programs. After sixteen calls all slabs have been transferred (cf. figure 2.10). These successive transfers replace the intermediate file.

Program inversion can be used everywhere an independent subroutine is to be made. In the following description we presume that the reason for inversion is a structure clash problem.

1. Decide what to store in the intermediate file.
2. Design and *code* P1 and P2 as if the intermediate file were to be used.
3. Modify (invert) one of the source programs to a subroutine.
4. Modify the other source program to a main program calling the subroutine.

Step 1 has already been discussed in the "spanned records" case. There, items should be stored in the intermediate file. Step 2 is carried out as usual, as described in chapter 1, Fundamentals. Steps 3 and 4 will now be described in rough outline. The details will be clarified in the next section.

Step 3 deals with converting a program into a subroutine. It shall be able to be called by CALL in Cobol and Fortran and by procedure call in Algol. Why waste time explaining such a well known programming task? There are as a matter of fact some circumstances to take into consideration when making a subroutine which is truly independent, circumstances often not existing in connection with subroutines. We have to arrange things so that the subroutine is able to start from different places *and still have its control flow separated from the main program.* ENTRY POINTS in Cobol are consequently of no use. The subroutine has itself to keep the return addresses in order. Here is perhaps the right place to remind ourselves of the ordinary call mechanism in the direction from a main program to a subroutine, figure 2.17.

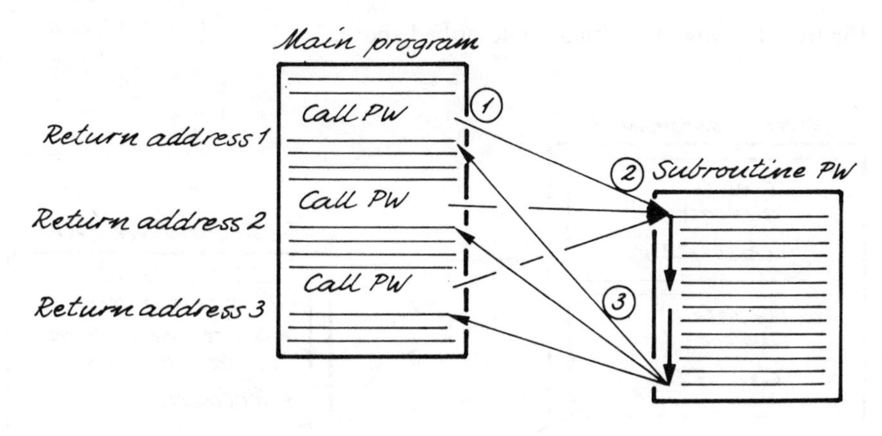

Fig 2.17

At each call the following happens:

1. The return address is stored.
2. Jump is carried out to the first statement of the subroutine and the subroutine is executed.
3. Return is carried out to the stored address and the main program starts from and including the statement immediately after the call.

Let us now explain why an inverted program often needs many restart places. Before inversion we have designed and coded the program as if the intermediate file were to be used. Presume that we are going to invert the program which reads the intermediate file. Then, of course, we apply the read ahead rule. This implies that "read intermediate file" will occur twice, perhaps more times, in the program. The read operation enables the program to access one record. When this record is processed the program has to read another intermediate file record. When we invert the program with respect to the intermediate file then this file is no longer needed, it "disappears". The records are created by the main program. As soon as a record is created the main program calls the inverted program. The call statement has the record as an argument or a parameter. The inverted program processes the record and when this record is processed the program would normally read another record from the intermediate file. But the intermediate file doesn't exist! What then, does the inverted program have to do? Well, it has to store a return address and hand over the CPU control to the main program. The return to the main program is executed by EXIT PROGRAM in Cobol, **go to** the last **end** in Algol and RETURN in Fortran, but storing the return address to the inverted program must be carried out by the inverted program itself.

Figure 2.18 shows the situation described above.

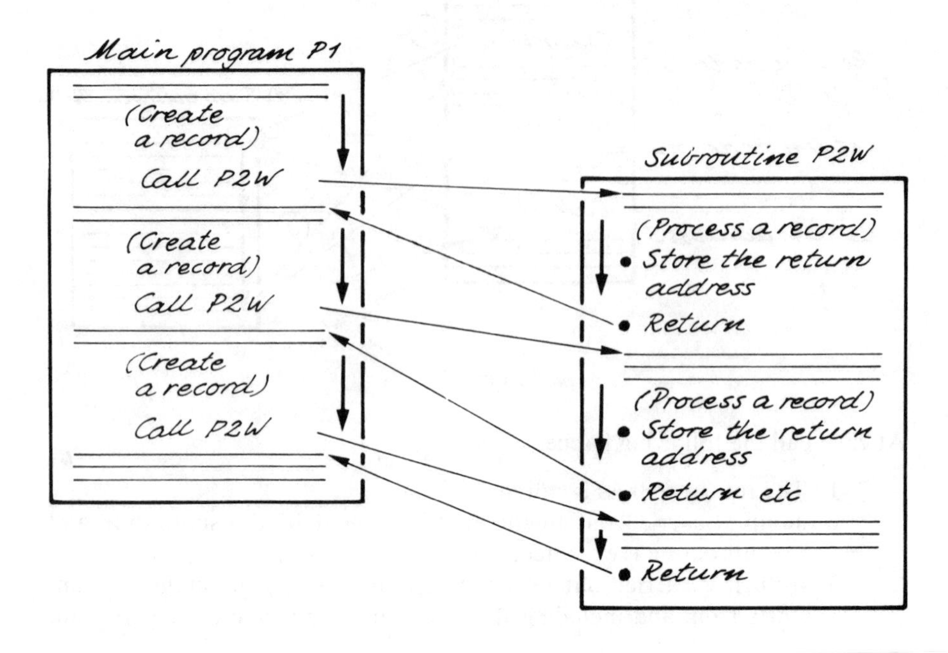

Fig 2.18

Figure 2.19 shows how a main program and a subroutine are derived from the two original, separate programs.

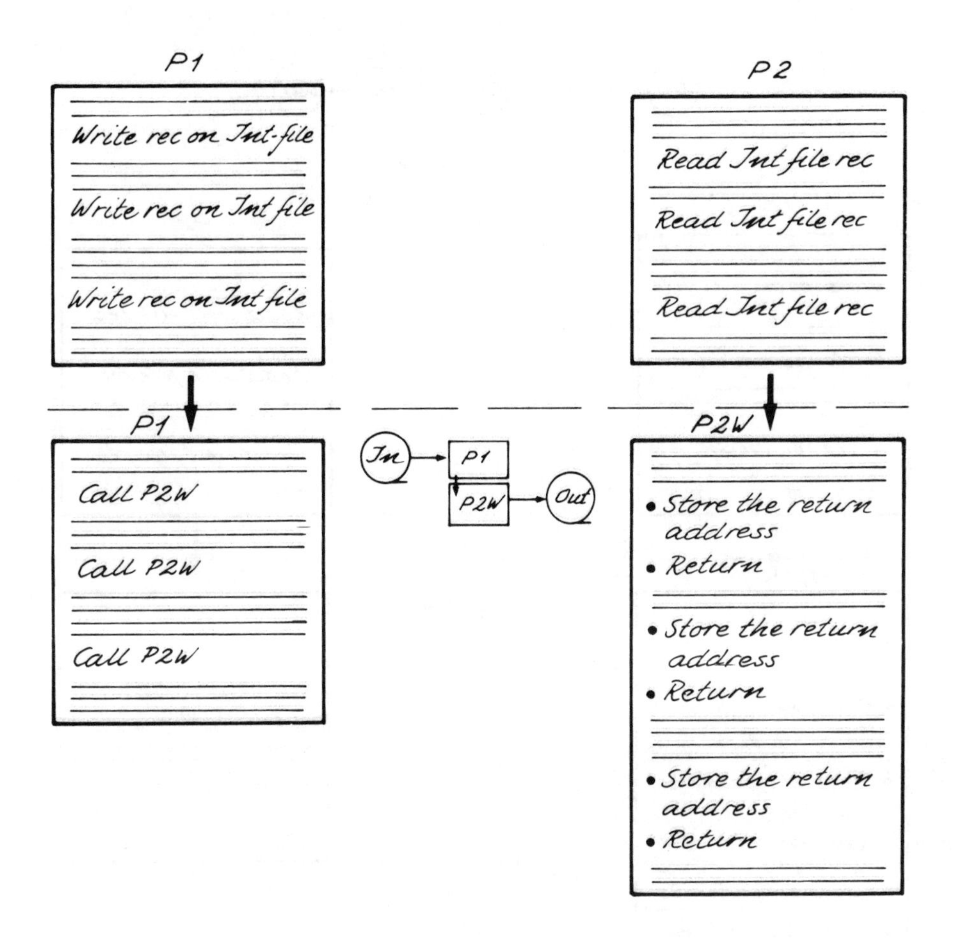

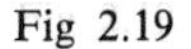
Fig 2.19

In the main program (P1) all statements of writing on the intermediate file are replaced by calling the subroutine (P2W). In P2W, statements of reading the intermediate file are replaced by storing the return address and exit. The details will be discussed in the next section.

You could perhaps by now draw a picture showing the principle of inverting P1 and converting P2 into a main program. Anyhow, figure 2.20 is included in the book.

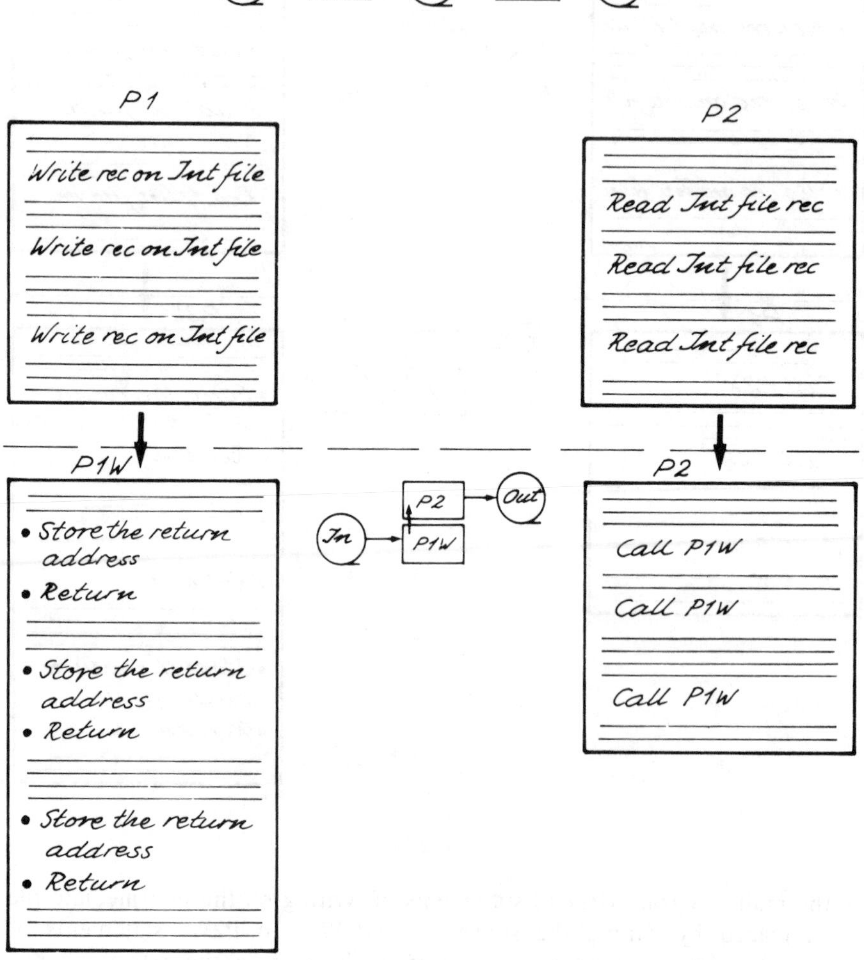

Fig 2.20

Here all P1 statements of writing on the intermediate file are replaced by storing a return address and exit. In P2 all statements of reading the intermediate file are replaced by calling the subroutine (P1W).

Figure 2.19 shows how P2 is inverted with respect to the file Int into P2W and figure 2.20 how P1 is inverted with respect to the file Int into P1W. Both the alternatives are in principle equivalent.

Anyone who has dealt with co-routines will recognize the principle described above and can easily apply this type of "mutual call".

Below, some exercises follow concerning structure clashes and intermediate files.

Exercise 2.1a

A card file contains part numbers for batch production orders, figure 2.21. An order can start anywhere on the card and span many cards. Each order is finished by an item which consists of eight &-characters. This character appears neither in the order numbers nor in the part numbers which contain eight digits each. After the ending &-characters of the last order, an additional eight &-characters appear. No item can, as you see,

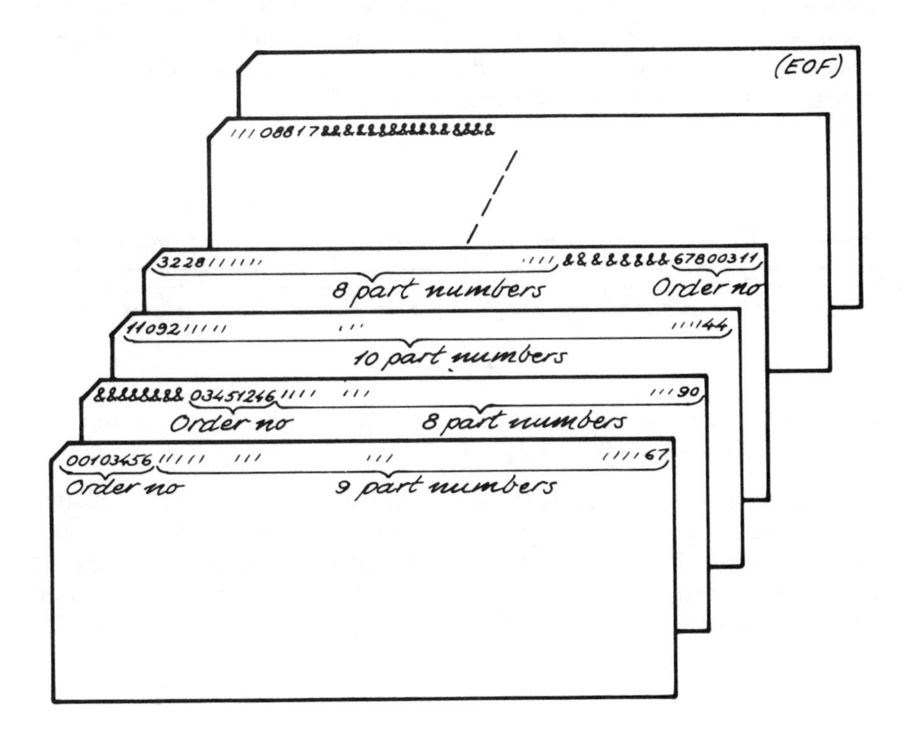

Fig 2.21

span from one card to another. No order contains more than 30 part numbers. With the card file as input a sequential file is to be produced with the orders as variable length records. Draw the data structures, identify the structure clash and decide what to store in the intermediate file.

Exercise 2.1b

Draw the structure of the intermediate file as it is seen on the one hand by P1, on the other by P2 in exercise 2.1a.

Exercise 2.2a

During tests of a process control system, digital data are recorded on tape. Each measurement value is represented by a real item corresponding to 6 integer digits and two decimals with a leading sign (+ or —). Maximal and minimal values are however limited to ± 900 000.00. The interval above +900 000.00 is used for numbering the measurement positions. +900 001.00 = position no 1, +900 002.00 = position no 2, and so on. Each measurement position is recorded via one recording channel and each measurement consists of a value pair: reading and time. The measurement recordings are concatenated on one measurement data tape, where one record consists of all measurement values of one position, figure 2.22.

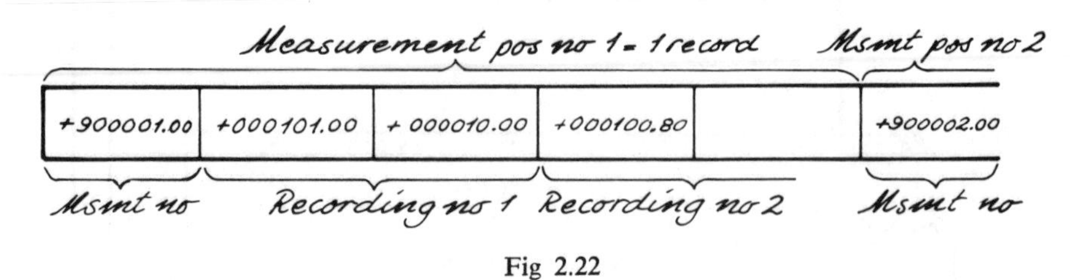

Fig 2.22

A record has variable length depending on the length of the test run but includes a maximum of 100 value pairs.

The measurement data tape is to be read (record by record) and a plotter tape is to be produced. The plotter can produce time diagrams of a maximum length which is considerably shorter than the maximum length of the test runs when the wanted time scale is used. A measurement position record may consequently be presented on many time diagrams, figure 2.23.

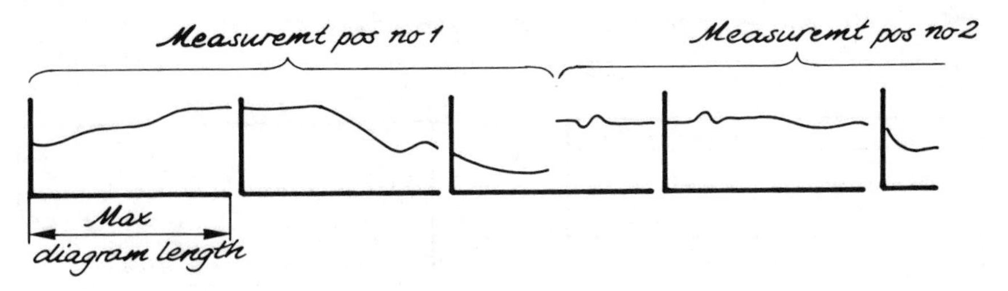

Fig 2.23

Each diagram begins with a header containing measurement position number. Draw the data structures of the measurement data tape and the plotter tape. Look for correspondences. Tick off where structure clashes appear and state the reasons. The problem is to be solved by two programs, but what should we store in the intermediate file?

Exercise 2.2b

Draw the intermediate file structure as it is seen on the one hand from P1, on the other from P2.

2.4. The Program Inversion Technique

When a program is inverted the intermediate file is replaced by data transfer via the main storage. This implies modification of all statements concerning the intermediate file. How this is done in alternative 1 is shown in Cobol in figure 2.24. Fortran and Algol programmers have probably no difficulties following the presentation in this figure. We will return to the Fortran and Algol specialities later on.

We have to consider carefully the end of file situation also when dealing with P1—P2 in a structure clash solution. P1 reads at least one input file and will sooner or later arrive at end of file. Then P1 has no more records to write into the intermediate file I-FILE so P1 closes it. If we choose a solution without program inversion, i.e. production of a (sequential) intermediate file on a secondary storage, then the operating system will neatly write an end of file label on the intermediate file when executing the statement CLOSE I-FILE. This end of file label can later be used by P2 to make, for instance, termination of iterations possible. But, as you know, in program inversion the intermediate file "disappears", and P2 has to be in-

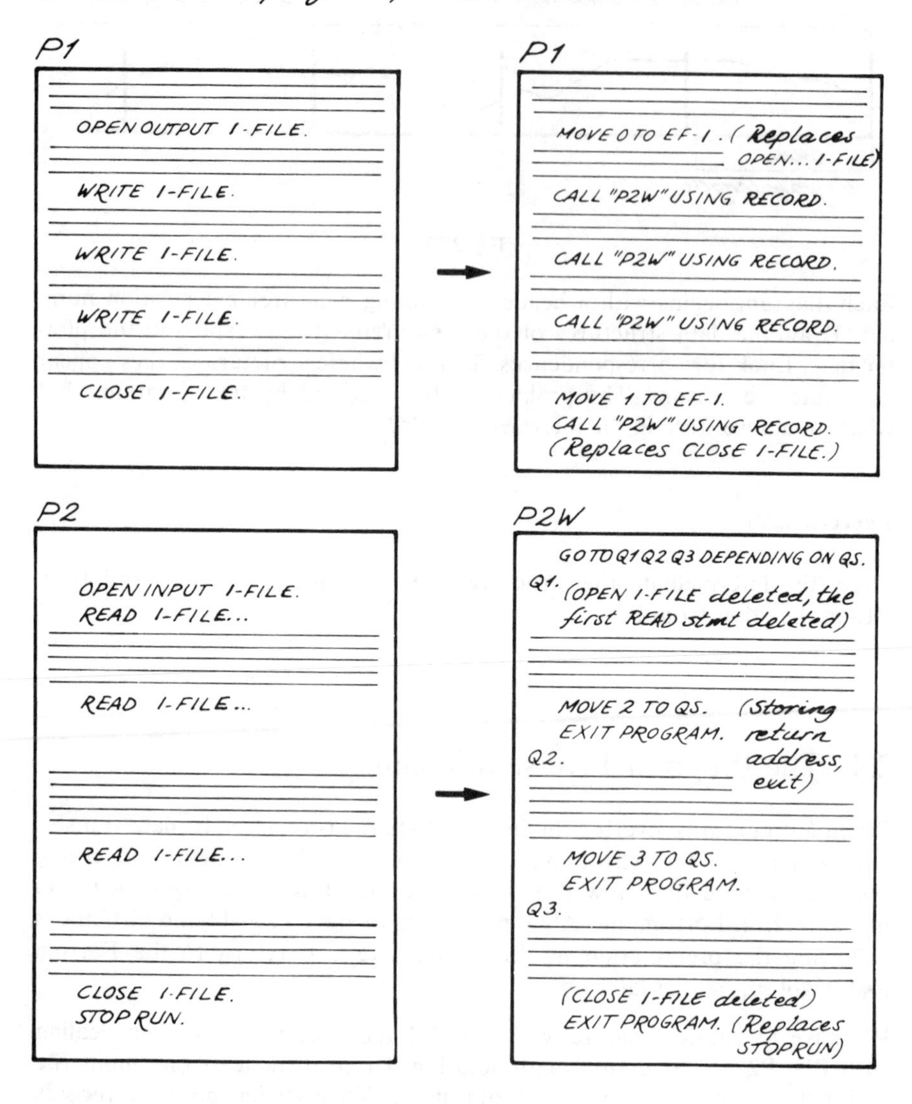

Fig 2.24

formed in some way that no more records will be delivered. We can do this by having an end of file flag, for instance, among the record items. So we replace OPEN OUTPUT I-FILE with MOVE 0 TO EF-I and CLOSE I-FILE with MOVE 1 TO EF-I and CALL "P2W" USING RECORD. At this last CALL, P2W has the opportunity to discover that EF-I is set to 1, i.e. no more records will be delivered by P1. Moreover all WRITE I-FILE statements are replaced by CALL "P2W" USING RECORD.

In P2 the first READ statement is deleted. The first READ would be executed to make the first I-FILE record available to P2. When P2W is called the first time the first record is already created in the RECORD parameter area ready to be processed.

The first record is consequently processed by P2W. When P2W needs record number two P1 must first continue its processing to create this number two record. Then P2W must exit instead of executing its second READ. But as soon as P1 has created record number two, P2 shall be called again. This time P2W has to start executing the statement immediately after the second (original) READ. The return address has been stored in a so called status variable, as shown in figure 2.24. READ I-FILE is replaced by

```
        MOVE n TO QS.
        EXIT PROGRAM.
    Qn.
```

The GO TO . . . DEPENDING statement executes the return to the correct address. Note that ENTRY points must not be used. If ENTRY points were used P1 would have to manipulate them. But P1 must *not know anything at all* about what P2W does and vice versa. The programs shall be completely separated. Some operations in P1 are asynchronous to some operations in P2W. Using ENTRY points means that the two program structures will be tied together which gives rise to difficulties and a program hard to understand. Because of this P1 must not manipulate QS either. When P2W is separately compiled this is prohibited by declaring QS in the WORKING-STORAGE SECTION of the subroutine. QS shall have 1 as initial value.

You may very well call GO TO Q1 Q2 . . . DEPENDING ON QS a switch. It is anyway a standardized one or a controlled switch. It is used to fill up the lack of co-routines in Cobol. The statement shall have as many paragraph names (labels) as the number of original READ statements.

In principle, we could as well invert P1 and convert P2 into a main program, as earlier mentioned. Then *each* READ I-FILE . . . in P2 shall be replaced by CALL "P1W" USING RECORD and OPEN INPUT I-FILE, and CLOSE I-FILE shall be deleted. P1W begins with GO TO Q1 Q2 . . . DEPENDING ON QS with *one paragraph name (label) more* than the number of original WRITE I-FILE statements. At the beginning we also include zeroizing EF-I. Each WRITE I-FILE is replaced by

```
        MOVE n TO QS.
        EXIT PROGRAM.
    Qn.
```

Instead of CLOSE I-FILE we write MOVE 1 TO EF-I and instead of STOP RUN we write EXIT PROGRAM.

The technique described above can of course be used in all situations where an independent subroutine is needed.

Below, a summary follows containing the steps of the inversion technique applied to structure clash problems. Cobol, Fortran and Algol varieties are described separately.

Cobol

1. Decide what to store in the intermediate file.
2. Design and code P1 and P2 as if the intermediate file were to be used.
3. Alternative A (P1 main program, P2 subroutine).

P1→P1 as a main program:

- OPEN OUTPUT I-FILE.→MOVE ZERO TO EF-I.
- Each "write intermediate file"→call for subroutine P2W, i.e.
WRITE I-FILE.→CALL "P2W" USING RECORD.
- CLOSE I-FILE→ {MOVE 1 TO EF-I.
CALL "P2W" USING RECORD.

P2→P2W:

Declare a status variable QS and give it the initial value = 1.

- PROCEDURE DIVISION USING RECORD.
GO TO Q1, Q2, . . . DEPENDING ON QS.
Q1. — — —
(As many paragraph names as original READ I-FILE . . . statements)
- OPEN INPUT I-FILE.→deleted
- The first READ I-FILE . . .→deleted
- Each remaining READ I-FILE . . .→ { MOVE n TO QS.
EXIT PROGRAM.
Qn. (n = 2, 3, 4 . . .)

(If you have PERFORM within PERFORM the return addresses will be lost in some computer systems. Because of this, nest-free code should be used.)

- CLOSE I-FILE.→deleted
- STOP RUN.→EXIT PROGRAM.

Alternative B (P1 subroutine, P2 main program).

P1→P1W:

- Declare a status variable and give it the initial value = 1.
- PROCEDURE DIVISION USING RECORD.
  GO TO Q1, Q2, . . . DEPENDING ON QS.
  Q1. — — —
  (As many paragraph names as original WRITE I-FILE statements + *1*)
- OPEN INPUT I-FILE.→MOVE ZERO TO EF-I.
- Each "write intermediate file"→store the return address + exit, i. e.

```
                 {      MOVE n TO QS.
WRITE I-FILE.→   {      EXIT PROGRAM.
                 {Qn.      (n=2, 3, 4 . . .)
```

- CLOSE I-FILE.→MOVE 1 TO EF-I.
- STOP RUN.→EXIT PROGRAM.

P2→P2 as a main program:

- OPEN INPUT I-FILE.→deleted.
- Each "read intermediate file"→call for subroutine P1W, i.e.
  READ I-FILE . . .→CALL "P2W" USING RECORD.
- CLOSE I-FILE.→deleted.

Fortran

1. Decide what to store in the intermediate file.
2. Design and code P1 and P2 as if the intermediate file were to be used.
3. Alternative A (P1 main program, P2 subroutine).

P1→P1 as a main program:

- (At the beginning)→IEFI = 0
- Give a subroutine label (Lnn) the initial value = 1 immediately before the first subroutine call. Note carefully that *this is the only occasion* the main program is allowed to manipulate Lnn! (There is a better solution: use a communication area, cf. section 4.1).

- Each "write intermediate file"→call for the subroutine P2W, i.e.
  WRITE(3)(IEFI, ITEM(I),I=1,N)→
  →CALL P2W (IEFI,ITEM (I),I=1,N)

- ENDFILE 3→ {IEFI=1 / CALL P2W(IEFI, ITEM(I),I=1,N)}

P2→P2W:

```
•         SUBROUTINE P2W(IEFI, ITEM, N)
          — — —
          GO TO(nn001, nn002, . . .), Lnn
nn001     CONTINUE
```

(As many labels as original "read intermediate file" statements).

- The first "read intermediate file"→deleted.
- Each remaining "read intermediate file"→
  →store the return address+exit, ie.

```
          Lnn=2     }
          RETURN    } replacing the second "read . . ."
nn002     CONTINUE  }
          — — —
          Lnn=3
          RETURN
nn003     CONTINUE
          — — —
          etc.
```

```
•         END→ {RETURN
               {END
```

Alternative B (P1 subroutine, P2 main program).

P1→P1W:

```
•         SUBROUTINE P1W(IEFI, ITEM, N)
          — — —
          GO TO (nn001, nn002, . . .), Lnn
nn001     CONTINUE
```

(As many labels as original "write intermediate file" statements *+1*).

- (At the beginning)→IEFI=0

- Each "write intermediate file"→store the return address+exit, i.e.

```
         Lnn=2     }
         RETURN    }  replacing the first "write . . ."
nn002    CONTINUE  }
         — — —
         Lnn=3
         RETURN
nn003    CONTINUE
         etc.
```

- END→
```
{IEFI=1
 RETURN
 END
```

P2→P2 as a main program:

- Give the subroutine label (Lnn) the initial value=1 immediately before the first subroutine call. Note carefully that this is *the only occasion* the main program is allowed to manipulate Lnn. (There is a better solution: use a communication area, cf. section 4.1).
- Each "read intermediate file"→call for the subroutine P1W, i.e.

  CALL P1W, (IEFI, ITEM(I),I=1,N)

Algol

1. Decide what to store in the intermediate file.
2. Design and code P1 and P2 as if the intermediate file were to be used.
3. Alternative A (P1 main program, P2 subroutine).

P1→P1 as a main program:

- (At the beginning)→EFI := 0;
  Give the subroutine status variable QS the initial value=1 immediately before the first subroutine call. Note carefully that this is *the only occasion* the main program is allowed to manipulate QS. (There is a better solution: use a communication area, cf. section 4.1).
- Each "write intermediate file"→call for the subroutine P2W, i.e.

  (The following procedure is presumed: writefile (<filename>))

  writefile (intermediate file)→P2W(EFI,RECORD);

- (After delivering the last intermediate file record)
  $\rightarrow\begin{cases}\text{EFI} := 1; \\ \text{P2W(EFI, RECORD);}\end{cases}$

P2→P2W:

-
```
        procedure P2W(EFI, RECORD);
        ———
        begin integer QS;
              switch S := Q1, Q2,...;
              go to S [QS];
        Q1:   ———
```
  (As many labels as original "read intermediate file" statements)

- The first "read intermediate file" statement→deleted
- Each remaining "read intermediate file"→store the return address+ +exit, i.e.

```
              QS := n;
              go to concl;
        Qn:   ———              (n=2, 3, 4,...)
              ———

   concl: end      (the last end)
```

Alternative B (P1 subroutine, P2 main program):

P1→P1W:

-
```
        procedure P1W(EFI, RECORD);
        ———
        begin integer QS;
              switch S=Q1, Q2,...;
              go to S [QS];
        Q1:   ———
```
  (As many labels as original "write intermediate file" statements *+1*).

- (At the beginning)→EFI := 0;
- Each "write intermediate file"→store the return address+exit, i.e.

```
              QS := n;
              go to concl;
        Qn:   ———              (n=2, 3, 4,...)
              ———

   concl: end (the last end)
```

• (At the end)

$$\textbf{end}\rightarrow\begin{cases}\text{EFI} := 1;\\ \textbf{end}\end{cases}$$

P2→P2 as a main program:

- Give the subroutine status variable (QS) the initial value = 1 immediately before the first subroutine call. Note carefully that this is *the only occasion* the main program is allowed to manipulate QS. (There is a better solution: use a communication area, cf. section 4.1).
- Each "read intermediate file"→call for the subroutine P1W, i.e.

P1W(EFI, RECORD);

So much for the rules. Let us apply them to the "spanned records" problem, figure 2.7. This is about reading a file of unblocked records of variable length and writing a file of fixed length blocks. There is no relation between records and blocks. A record contains a maximum of 600 items. Each item is an integer. At the end of a record, there is a final item with a value<—4 000 000. An item doesn't span a block boundary. A block contains 500 items. Including the items we get the data structures as in figure 2.25.

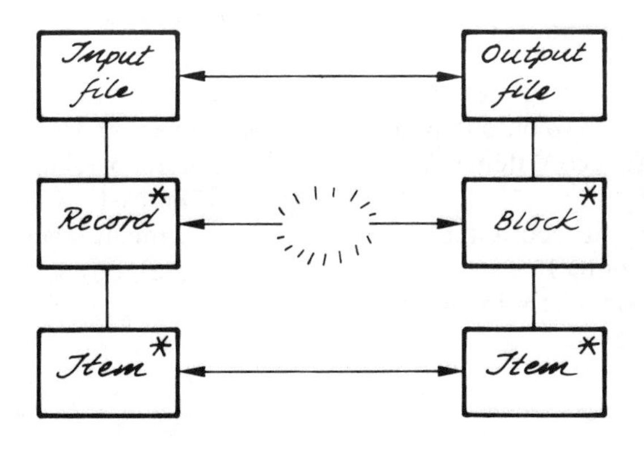

Fig 2.25

There is a boundary clash. There is certainly a 1—1 correspondence between the items but they occur in different connections. In the input file they are grouped by record, in the output file by block. As the items are the "greatest common denominator" we choose to store items as records in the intermediate file. Then we can give P1 the structure of the input file and P2 the structure of the output file, figure 2.26.

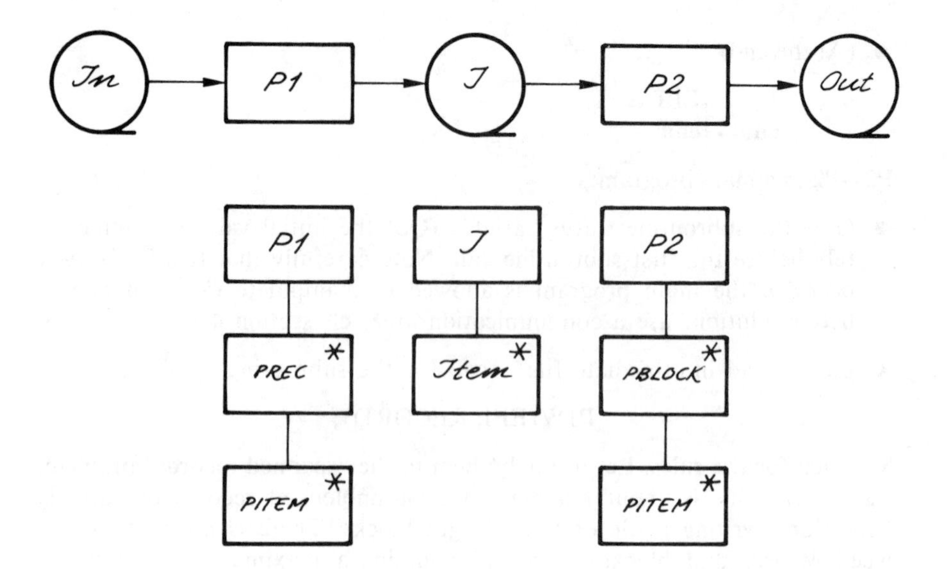

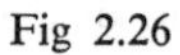
Fig 2.26

Firstly we will design and code P1 and P2 as if the intermediate file were to be used. Operations lists:

P1
1. Open files
2. Close files
3. Read input file
4. Write intermediate file
5. Move item to output area
6. Initiate record item subscipt by 1
7. Increment record item subscript by 1
8. Move final item to output area

P2
1. Open files
2. Close files
3. Read intermediate file
4. Write block
5. Move item to output area
6. Initiate block item subscript by 1
7. Increment block item subscript by 1

The operations are allocated in figure 2.27. As the final item serves as a "record-end-flag" that item too has to be moved and written (last in PREC) so the records can be identified in the blocked file.

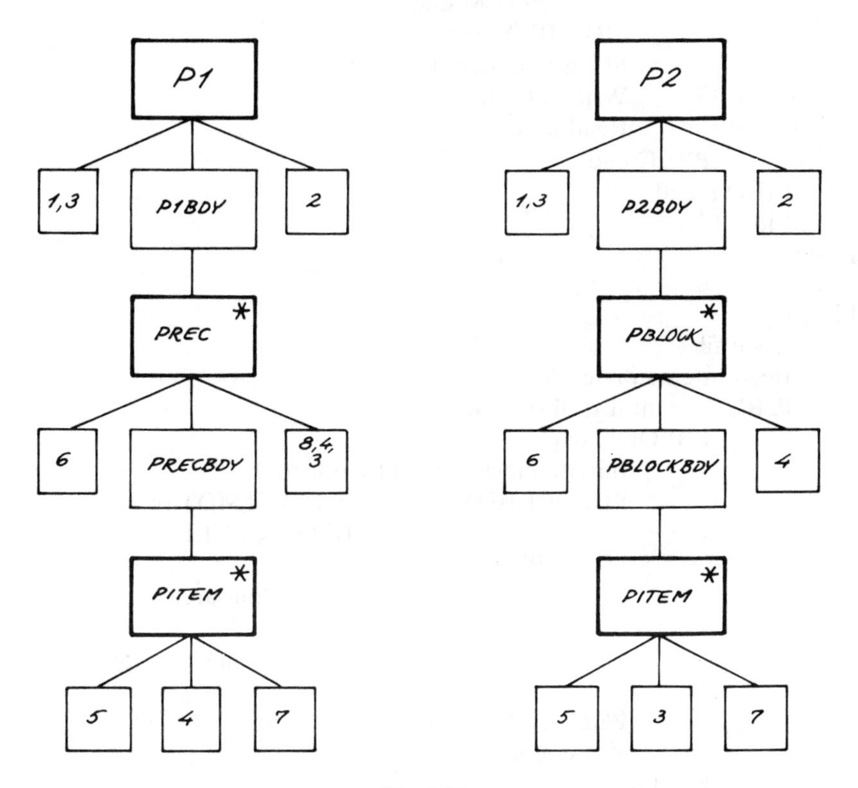

Fig 2.27

Note that "write intermediate file" implies writing a record which contains *one* item. The corresponding is true for "read intermediate file".

Schematic logic:

```
P1 seq
    Open files;
    Read input file;
    P1BDY itr until (EOF-INPUT)
        PREC seq
            Initiate record item subscript by 1;
            PRECBDY itr until (end of record)
                PITEM seq
```

```
                        Move item to output area;
                        Write intermediate file;
                        Increment record item subscript by 1;
                    PITEM end
                PRECBDY end
                Move final item to output area;
                Write intermediate file;
                Read input file;
            PREC end
        P1BDY end
        Close files;
P1 end

P2 seq
        Open files;
        Read intermediate file;
        P2BDY itr until EOF-INTMDT
            PBLOCK seq
                Initiate block item subscript by 1;
                PBLOCKBDY itr until EOF-INTMDT or
                                    BLOCK FULL
                    PITEM seq
                        Move item to output area;
                        Read intermediate file;
                        Increment block item subscript by 1;
                    PITEM end
                PELOCKBDY end
                Write block;
            PBLOCK end
        P2BDY end
        Close files;
P2 end
```

When coding we assume that there is a section WRITE-BLOCK available.

Cobol code:

```
IDENTIFICATION DIVISION.
       PROGRAM-ID. "P1".
       ———
DATA DIVISION.
       FILE SECTION.
       FD INPUT-FILE LABEL RECORD IS STANDARD
                     DATA RECORD IS INPUT-RECORD.
```

```
       01  INPUT-RECORD.
           02  ITEM COMPUTATIONAL-0 OCCURS 600
                      TIMES.
       FD  INTERMEDIATE-FILE LABEL RECORD IS
                   STANDARD
                   DATA RECORD IS INTERMEDIATE-
                   RECORD.
       01  INTERMEDIATE-RECORD.
           02  I-ITEM COMPUTATIONAL-O.
       WORKING-STORAGE SECTION.
       77  REC-ITEM-SUBSCR COMPUTATIONAL-O.
       77  EF-INPUT           PICTURE 9 VALUE ZERO.

PROCEDURE DIVISION.
       P1-SEQ.           OPEN INPUT INPUT-FILE OUTPUT
                         INTERMEDIATE-FILE.
                         READ INPUT-FILE AT END MOVE
                         1 TO EF-INPUT.
       P1BDY-ITER.       IF EF-INPUT = 1 GO TO
                         P1BDY-END.
       PREC-SEQ          MOVE 1 TO REC-ITEM-SUBSCR.
       PRECBDY-ITER.     IF ITEM (REC-ITEM-SUBSCR)
                         < -4000000
                         GO TO PRECBDY-END.
       PITEM-SEQ.        MOVE ITEM (REC-ITEM-SUBSCR)
                         TO I-ITEM.
                         WRITE INTERMEDIATE-FILE.
                         ADD 1 TO REC-ITEM-SUBSCR.
       PITEM-END.
                         GO TO PRECBDY-ITER.
       PRECBDY-END.      MOVE. ITEM (REC-ITEM-SUBSCR)
                         TO I-ITEM.
                         WRITE INTERMEDIATE-FILE.
                         READ INPUT-FILE AT END MOVE
                         1 TO EF-INPUT.
       PREC-END.
                         GO TO P1BDY-ITER.
       P1BDY-END.
                         CLOSE INPUT-FILE
                         INTEMEDIATE-FILE.

       P1-END.           STOP RUN.
```

```
IDENTIFICATION DIVISION.
      PROGRAM-ID. "P2".
      - - -
DATA DIVISION.
      FILE SECTION.
      FD INTERMEDIATE FILE LABEL RECORD IS
          STANDARD DATA RECORD IS
          INTERMEDIATE-RECORD.
      01 INTERMEDIATE-RECORD.
          02 I-ITEM COMPUTATIONAL-0.
      FD OUTPUT-FILE LABEL RECORD IS STANDARD
          DATA RECORD IS BLOCK-REC.
      01 BLOCK-REC.
          02 B-ITEM COMPUTATIONAL-0 OCCURS 500
                          TIMES.
      WORKING-STORAGE SECTION.
      77 BLOCK-ITEM-SUSBSCR COMPUTATIONAL-0.
      77 EF-INTMDT              PICTURE 9 VALUE 0.
PROCEDURE DIVISION.
      P2-SEQ.             OPEN INPUT INTERMEDIATE-
                          FILE
                          OUTPUT OUTPUT-FILE.
                          READ INTERMEDIATE-FILE AT
                          END
                          MOVE 1 TO EF-INTMDT.
      P2BDY-ITER.         IF EF-INTMDT = 1 GO TO
                          P2BDY-END.
      PBLOCK-SEQ.         MOVE 1 TO BLOCK-ITEM-
                          SUBSCR.
      PBLOCKBDY-ITER.IF EF-INTMDT = 1 OR BLOCK-
                          ITEM-SUBSCR
                          > 500 GO TO PBLOCKBDY-END.
      PITEM-SEQ.          MOVE I-ITEM TO
                          B-ITEM (BLOCK-ITEM-SUBSCR).
                          READ INTERMEDIATE-FILE AT
                          END
                          MOVE 1 TO EF-INTMDT.
                          ADD 1 TO BLOCK-ITEM-SUBSCR.
      PITEM-END.
                          GO TO PBLOCKBDY-ITER.
      PBLOCKBDY-END.
                          PERFORM WRITE-BLOCK.
```

```
     PBLOCK-END.
                          GO TO P2BDY-ITER.
     P2BDY-END.
                          CLOSE INTERMEDIATE-FILE
                          OUTPUT-FILE.
     P2END.               STOP RUN.
```

P1 main program:

```
     - - -
     LINKAGE SECTION.
     01    L-REC.
           02 EF-INTMDT PICTURE 9.
           02 I-ITEM    COMPUTATIONAL-0.
PROCEDURE DIVISION.
     P1-SEQ.              OPEN INPUT INPUT-FILE.
                          MOVE ZERO TO EF-INTMDT.
                          READ INPUT-FILE AT END
                          MOVE 1 TO EF-INPUT.
     P1BDY-ITER.          IF EF-INPUT = 1 GO TO
                          P1BDY-END.
     PREC-SEQ.            MOVE 1 TO REC-ITEM-SUBSCR.
     PRECBDY-ITER.        IF ITEM (REC-ITEM-SUBSCR)
                          < - 4000000
                          GO TO PRECBDY-END.
     PITEM-SEQ.           MOVE ITEM (REC-ITEM-SUBSCR)
                          TO I-ITEM.
                          CALL "P2W" USING L-REC.
                          ADD 1 TO REC-ITEM-SUBSCR.
     PITEM-END.
                          GO`TO PRECBDY-ITER.
     PRECBDY-END.
                          MOVE ITEM (REC-ITEM-SUBSCR)
                          TO I-ITEM.
                          CALL "P2W" USING L-REC.
                          READ INPUT-FILE AT END
                          MOVE 1
                          TO EF-INPUT.
     PREC-END.
                          GO TO P1BDY-ITER.
     P1BDY-END.
                          CLOSE INPUT-FILE.
                          MOVE 1 TO EF-INTMDT.
                          CALL "P2W" USING L-REC.
     P1-END.              STOP RUN.
```

P2W subroutine:

```
       - - -
       WORKING-STORAGE SECTION.
       77 QS PICTURE 9 VALUE 1.
       - - -
       LINKAGE SECTION.
       01    L-REC.
             02 EF-INTMDT PICTURE 9.
             02 I-ITEM COMPUTATIONAL-0.
PROCEDURE DIVISION USING L-REC.
       P2SEQ.            GO TO Q1 Q2 DEPENDING ON
                         QS.
       Q1.               OPEN OUTPUT OUTPUT-FILE.
       P2BDY-ITER.       IT EF-INTMDT = 1 GO
                         TO P2BDY-END.
       PBLOCK-SEQ.       MOVE 1 TO BLOCK-ITEM-
                         SUBSCR.
       PBLOCKBDY-ITER.   IF EF-INTMDT = 1 OR
                         BLOCK-ITEM-SUBSCR > 500
                         GO TO PBLOCKBDY-END.
       PITEM-SEQ.        MOVE I-ITEM TO
                         B-ITEM (BLOCK-ITEM-SUBSCR).
                         MOVE 2 TO QS.
                         EXIT PROGRAM.
       Q2.
                         ADD 1 TO BLOCK-ITEM-SUBSCR.
       PITEM-END.
                         GO TO PBLOCKBODY-ITER.
       PBLOCKBDY-END.
                         PERFORM WRITE-BLOCK.
       PBLOCK-END.
                         GO TO P2BDY-ITER.
       P2BDY-END.
                         CLOSE OUTPUT-FILE.
       P2-END.           EXIT PROGRAM.
```

The problem above is solved by creating two programs, one based upon the INPUT-RECORD component, the other based upon the BLOCK component. If you solve the problem by designing one single program you will be forced to use wild switches which are to be avoided. However, a program language which reads item by item doesn't use the record concept in its input system. So in such a case you can certainly solve the problem by using one single program based upon the BLOCK component and without wild switches. But that is not a good solution with respect to the demand that the program shall mirror the real world of the user. In this real world the record entity does exist (*customer* record, *article* record, *measurement* record). The record entity must not be scattered in the program. Consequently there are reasons for applying program inversion even if the input or output system doesn't force you to apply it. A fundamental condition for an easy-to-modify program is, as said before, that the program mirror the real world of the user.

Exercise 2.3

In a terminal system there is standard software which among other things handles messages from the terminals. This message handling program calls different subroutines a number of times depending on what type of dialogue is initiated. The subroutines are to be written by the user. One of the dialogue types consists of three transactions: type 1, type 2 and type 3 in that order. The corresponding subroutine is called three times, once per transaction. At each call the subroutine is given "type of transaction" which can be correct or erroneous.

Use the program inversion technique to create a subroutine which puts 1 into an error flag if the transaction type is erroneous and moves an error message to a data field. (Guidance: consider the incoming transactions as records of a sequential file). The subroutine can be written in Cobol, Fortran or Algol.

(This exercise is perhaps considered by many as embarrasingly simple, but it is a pure application of the inversion technique so don't skip it!)

3 Backtracking – Error Handling with Uncomplicated Program Structures

3.1. An Introductory Example

Facing the task of designing an error handling program, you may be forced to use unnecessarily complicated structures. Backtracking is a tool to bring the data and program structures into order. We will demonstrate this in the following example:

A calculation system can be used via terminals. A so-called base transaction is to be used in the beginning of the calculation dialogue. This base

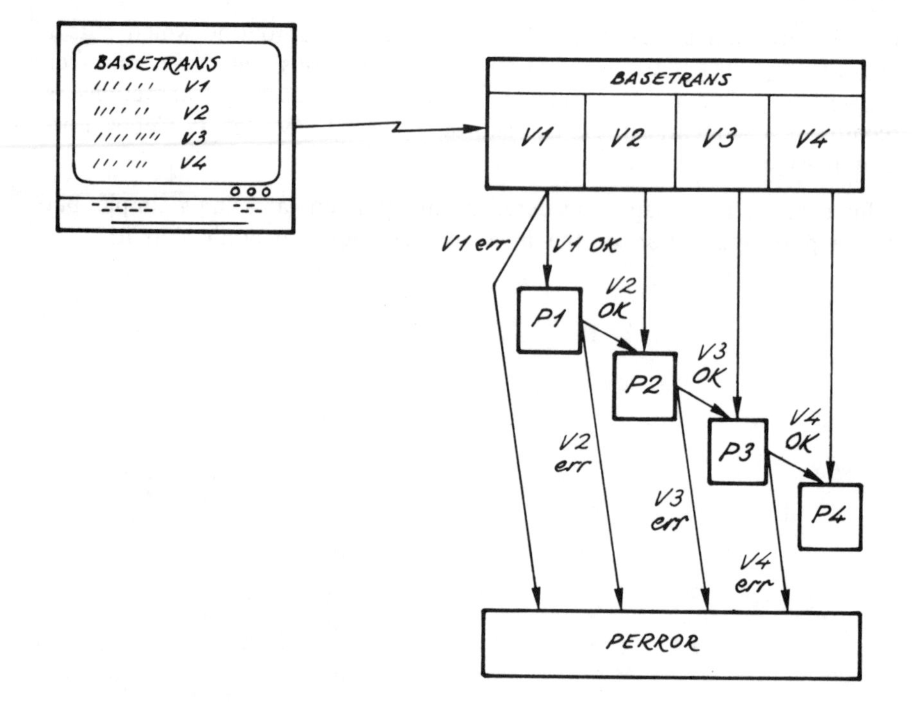

Fig 3.1

transaction contains four numbers, V1, V2, V3 and V4. Four different calculation programs P1, P2, P3 and P4 process these numbers one at a time. It is important that the numbers meet special conditions. V1 can be checked before P1 is executed. If V1 is erroneous the program ERROR has to be executed instead of P1 and the whole base transaction is rejected. V2 can't be checked until P1 has been executed because certain results from P1 are to be used when V2 is checked. If V2 is erroneous the program ERROR has to be executed instead of P2 and the whole base transaction is rejected. The same is true for V3, P3 and V4, P4, figure 3.1.

If any of the programs P1, P2, P3 or P4 were to be executed with erroneus V1, V2, V3 or V4 the data base of the terminal system would be ruined. All terminal users would get erroneous results.

The logical data structure this type of problem gives rise to is a little tricky. A schematic logic is perhaps easier to accept. Let's write a schematic logic:

```
PBASE sel (V1 OK)
        exec P1;
        PV2 sel (V2 OK)
              exec P2;
              PV3 sel (V3 OK)
                    exec P3;
                    PV4 sel (V4 OK)
                          exec P4;
                    PV4 alt
                          exec ERROR;
                    PV4 end
              PV3 alt
                    exec ERROR;
              PV3 end
        PV2 alt
              exec ERROR;
        PV2 end
PBASE alt
        exec ERROR;
PBASE end
```

We get a superior selection, which processes V1 and contains a selection within a selection within . . . in some way resembling a Chinese box. It is a completely correct solution with a component type from the approved assortment. But doesn't it look a little too bushy? ERROR occurs in four places though it is to be executed just once.

The corresponding logical data structure diagram begins with a selection in which one part could be named "Base transaction with V1 OK" and the other part "Base transaction with V1 err". This is the only executable check at the highest level, figure 3.2.

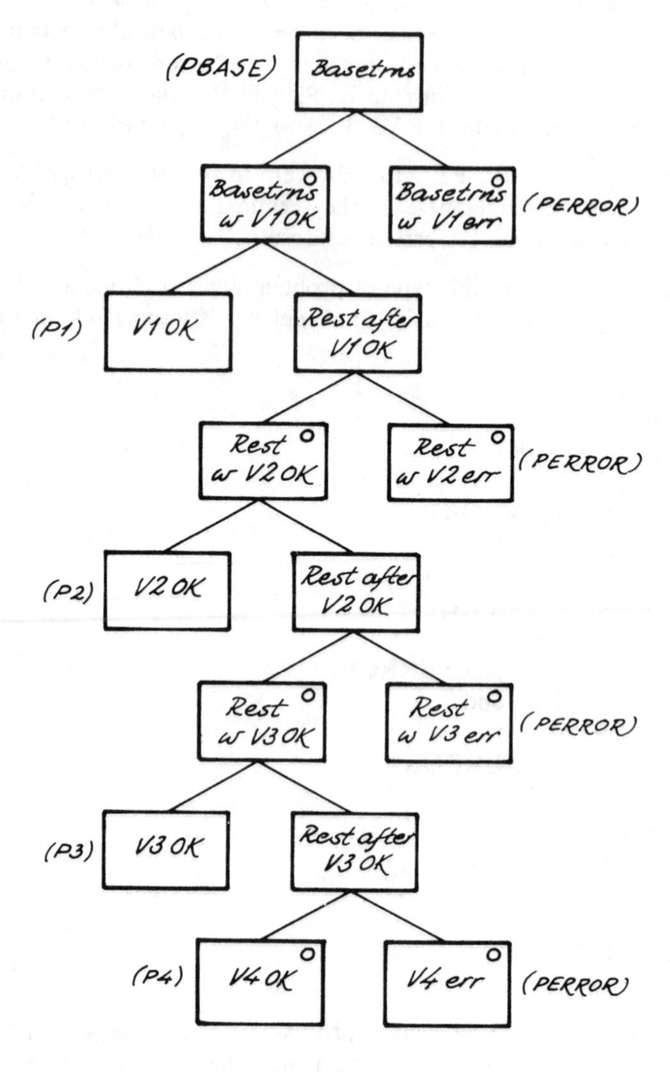

Fig 3.2

In the figure we have noted the program names within parentheses beside the appropriate boxes. There is consequently a number of places where (as said above) ERROR occurs. What makes the structure diagram entangled is that we are forced to show several error combinations:

V1 error
V1 OK, V2 error
V1 OK,V2 OK, V3 error
V1 OK, V2 OK, V3 OK, V4 error

But the problem is only to distinguish between a correct and an erroneous transaction. The logical data structure ought to look like this:

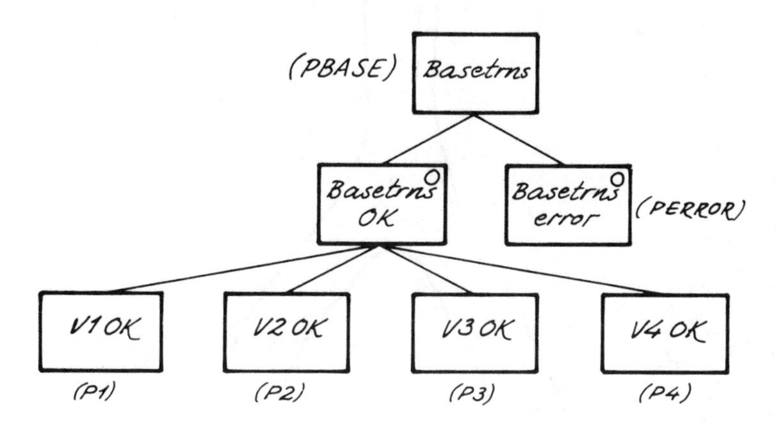

Fig 3.3

The base transaction is either correct or erroneous. If it is correct then it is a sequence of V1 OK, V2 OK, V3 OK and V4 OK. If it is erroneous then it is enough to say so.

Here, we are not interested in which of the numbers causes the transaction to be rejected.

The structure diagram in figure 3.3 is lucid and mirrors the problem. There is just one fault: we can't use it the way it is.

3.2. A Backtracking Analogy or What to Do When Uncertain

The local canoe club has organized a fête one Saturday morning in the middle of summer. Club members have to paddle upstream along the local river, figure 3.4.

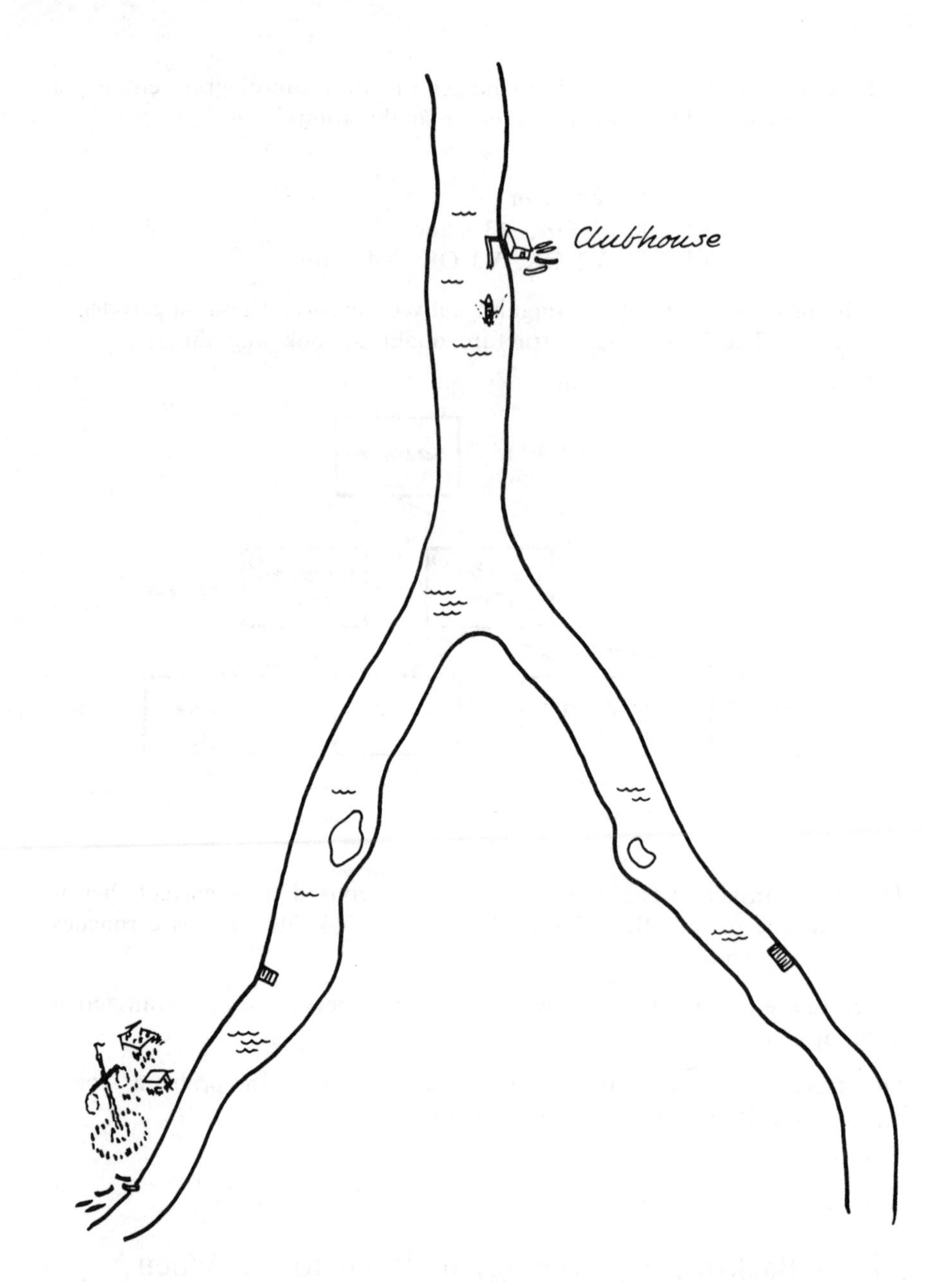

Fig 3.4

The starting point is the clubhouse. The members of the Keel family are early risers and start first. In addition to Mr. and Mrs. Keel, the family includes Careen (6 years old) and Keelson (4 years old). Careen has recently learnt to read (this is of some importance to the story) something Keelson has not yet done. Before starting off, they are given two pieces of paper by an official of the club — one is a description of the route they are to take further upstream and the other, a list of things to be done on the trip. Careen is given the piece of paper with the route description on it.

The Keels set off up river in their canoe. Keelson, sitting behind his big sister, is none too pleased. She is allowed to do things which Keelson is not allowed to do — like taking care of an important document. Slowly and exercising the utmost care Keelson moves his hand towards the scrap of paper Careen is holding tightly in her fist. Suddenly, he grabs at the piece of paper. But unfortunately for Keelson Careen is holding the paper so tightly that all he manages to do is tear off a small piece of it. Pandemonium! Mr. Keel, sitting behind his son, takes a firm grip on Keelson and tries to retrieve the piece of paper. Keelson, realizing that it can only be a matter of time before he will be forced to give up his hard won trophy, takes the only course available to him. He puts the scrap of paper in his mouth and eats it. Not a complete victory by any means but not bad in the circumstances.

Once peace has been restored, the Keel family continue their journey until they arrive at a fork in the river. It is now up to Careen to read the route description, figure 3.5.

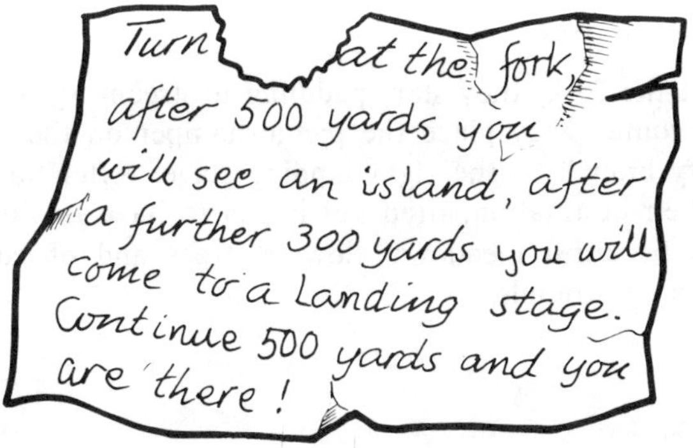

Turn at the fork,
after 500 yards you
will see an island, after
a further 300 yards you will
come to a landing stage.
Continue 500 yards and you
are there!

Fig 3.5

Unfortunately, the piece of paper swallowed by Keelson contained the not unimportant information "left" or "right". Mr. Keel who has studied statistics and the theory of probabilities is not dismayed: "We have a 50 % chance of choosing the right way so let's take the left branch of the river." (And of course left could be right.)

The Keels continue paddling up the left branch of the river in an optimistic mood. After covering an estimated 500 yards, they reach a small island. According to their list of things to do, they are supposed to place a picnic hamper on the island for use on the return journey. This Mr. Keel does. They must also catch a fish weighing at least one pound. Here, Keelson gets lucky and manages to catch a bream that meets the requirements, something which consoles him considerably.

They continue their trip and, after having paddled an additional 300 yards, they arrive at a landing stage. They are now almost convinced that they have chosen the right route. Mrs Keel, in accordance with their instructions, attaches a small leafy branch to the landing stage and off they go again. They paddle and paddle and paddle. Still no sight of their final destination. After having covered a good 500 yards, Mr. Keel is forced to admit that there was also a 50 % risk of their making the wrong decision back at the fork.

There is only one thing to do: return to the fork in the river. But what about all the things they have done according to their list of instructions? Well, the leafy branch at the landing stage can be left where it is. Having attached to the landing stage can be considered as a neutral side effect. There is no reason to throw Keelson's fish back into the river. Having caught the fish can be regarded as a favourable side effect. What about the picnic hamper? Putting it on the wrong island must be considered as an intolerable side effect. The hamper must be retrieved. This Mr. Keel does on their way down river.

Once back at the fork, they start paddling upstream again, only this time on the right route. They place the picnic hamper on the right island and attach a leafy branch to the right landing stage. After another 500 yards they reach their destination, tired but happy to have finally arrived at the fête with its beautiful meadows, flowers, trees and of course ice-cream stalls and merry-go-rounds.

3.3. The Backtracking Technique

What kind of connection has backtracking with the analogy above? We are going to discuss that soon. Let's return to the problem of the base transaction with four numbers. At the end of section 3.1 we wished that we could use the structure in figure 3.3. It has a fork: either a correct base transaction or an erroneous one, like the river with the two branches. But how can anyone seriously suggest we draw a structure diagram like that? We need some help, let's engage a good demon, figure 3.6.

Fig 3.6

"But this is ridiculous!" you probably exclaim. "I have spent years studying numerical analysis, logical algebra, information analysis, program languages etc. to be able to work as a professional programmer, and now I'm asked to believe in fairy-tales!" Don't worry! One of the greatest scientists ever, Maxwell, engaged a good demon to help him get started on proving a complicated mathematical premise. If Maxwell could use a demon, so can we.

Our good demon is clairvoyant, able to look into the future. As soon as we ask him if this is a correct base transaction he answers truthfully. If the answer is "yes" we can confidently draw a selection part where V1, V2, V3 and V4 are correct in the specified order and consequently a program structure with a sequence of P1, P2, P3 and P4. If the answer is "no" we draw a selection part with an erroneous base transaction which gives rise to the program component ERROR. Thanks to the good demon we are able to draw an uncomplicated structure.

In the first backtracking step, consequently, we draw data structures and program structure assisted by the good demon. We make an operations list, allocate the operations and write a schematic logic. The schematic logic of the program processing the base transaction looks like this (cf. fig 3.3):

```
PBASE sel (base transaction OK)
        PBASE-OK seq
                exec P1;
                exec P2;
                exec P3;
                exec P4;
        PBASE-OK end
PBASE alt
        exec ERROR:
PBASE end
```

As soon as we have written the last *end* the good demon disappears like Cinderella's coach at midnight. Now we have to do without the good demon. Then we do like the Keel family: look for landmarks and check them against the route description. We go on untiringly in the chosen direction as long as we find the right landmarks. But as soon as the real world doesn't correspond to the route description we are forced to admit that we have chosen the wrong way, return to the fork and go along the other way. This is accomplished by manipulating the schematic logic. Replace *select* by *posit* and *alt* by *admit*. Insert *quit* in all places where landmarks can be checked. Then we get a schematic logic like this:

```
PBASE posit (base transaction OK)
      PBASE-OK seq
PBASE quit (V1 not OK)
            exec P1;
PBASE quit (V2 not OK)
            exec P2;
PBASE quit (V3 not OK)
            exec P3;
PBASE quit (V4 not OK)
            exec P4;
      PBASE-OK end
PBASE admit (base transaction not OK)
      exec ERROR;
PBASE end
```

A *quit* is nothing mysterious, it is a conditional "go to", but a strictly controlled one.

The posit part processing can give rise to side effects which can be

- favourable
- neutral
- intolerable

Favourable side effects require no action. If we undo them we are then forced to repeat in the admit part the processing which gave rise to those favourable side effects. Neutral side effects can be taken care of or not. Intolerable side effects *have to be considered.* In the base transaction example, P1 can imply that a record is written into a data base. If *quit* is executed later and this implies that the record already written was erroneous, well, then we have to undo the write operation. So instead of writing the record in the original place of the program we store the record in the primary storage and don't write it into the database until all *quits* are passed, i.e. all *quits* that can disqualify the record.

When you apply backtracking you have to work in three *completely separate steps.*

1. Engage the good demon (trust him, he is a professional seer) and design the program using a selection where the clairvoyance of the good demon replaces our inability to evaluate the selection condition. That is, draw data structures and the basic program structure, make an operations list and allocate the operations, write a schematic logic. Then the good demon disappears. — The program doesn't work.
2. Replace *select* by *posit, alt* by *admit.* Check the landmarks against the route description and insert *quit.* Still, the program doesn't work. (*Ignore side effects for the time being.* If you start worrying about both *quit* and side effects you run the risk of getting yourself entangled and rearranging operations so the correct structure will be destroyed and the program will be unreliable.)
3. Now you can take care of the intolerable side effects and check that all *quits* are executable. Finally, the program works.

When solving a problem by using the backtracking technique, you get the chance to design a simple and uncomplicated program based upon data structures which reflect the problem. There is a much smaller risk of getting entangled in long trains of thought difficult to reproduce.

Only one *posit* part and one *admit* part are allowed. This means that you sometimes have to apply backtracking at more than one level. This causes a complicated problem to be divided into simpler problem parts.

Note that only the schematic logic is to be manipulated The preceding design documentation should be left as it is. It mirrors the basic problem solution.

How to code *posit, admit* and *quit* is shown below.

Cobol:

```
A posit correct       A-POS.
                          - - -
A quit (cond-1)           IF cond-1 GO TO A-ADMIT.
     ———                  - - -
A quit (cond-2)           IF cond-2 GO TO A-ADMIT.
     ———                  - - -
                          GO TO A-END.
A admit (error)       A-ADMIT.
     ———                  - - -
A end                 A-END.
```

Fortran:

```
A posit correct          0143
      ———                      - - -
A quit (cond-1)                IF (cond-1) GO TO 0144
      ———                      - - -
A quit (cond-2)                IF (cond-2) GO TO 0144
      ———                      - - -
                               GO TO 0199
A admit                  0144  CONTINUE
      ———                      - - -
A end                    0199
```

Algol:

```
A posit correct          Aposit:
      ———                      ———
A quit (cond-1)                if cond-1 then go to Aadmit;
      ———                      ———
A quit (cond-2)                if cond-2 then go to Aadmit;
      ———                      ———
                               go to Aend;
A admit                  Aadmit:
      ———                      ———
A end                    Aend:
```

Note that *quit* is defined by the *posit* name and implies a jump from the *posit* part *to that corresponding admit* part. Furthermore *quit* has to be coded "in line", ie. it has to appear in the *posit* part text and not be "hidden" in a PERFORM paragraph, a subroutine or procedure.

Exercise 3.1

Code the schematic logic of PBASE on page 000 if the following conditions apply to correct numbers in the base transaction:

$V1 \leq K$
$V2 > X+V1$
$V3 \geq Y$
$V4 < X+Y$

Exercise 3.2

A correct transaction file consists of groups of three transactions each. The transactions within any one group have the same group number. All transactions are of type A. However, a transaction file can be erroneous because of mistakes during the data collection or the punching. There may be groups consisting of more or less than three transactions. There may also be transactions of other types than A.

Apply backtracking in designing a program which reads the transaction file and writes an output file containing only correct transaction groups. Furthermore, an error list is to be printed containing error lines with the group numbers of the erroneous transaction groups. The error list shall have a heading. You need not take paging into consideration.

If you consider a code desk test more convincing than a schematic logic desk test you can code the final shematic logic of exercise 3.2 in Cobol, Fortran, Algol, PL/I, Simula or whatever. To make things simpler (if you don't code in Cobol) you can presume in applicable cases that the opening and closing of files is executed automatically at the first read and at the program termination respectively. You can also presume read and write record-wise to be executed by subroutines. ("Read trans file" in the schematic logic is Cobol influenced and implies reading one *record* from the transaction file).

Exercise 3.3

A competition with a large number of questions and corresponding choice of answers is organised with the aid of optically-readable forms. The optical reader produces a sequential file with the competition entries in it. Every answer is stored as a record (type 1), and every entry has fifty answers on it. One record (type 0) containing the competitor's name and address preceeds the records for each entry. The correct answers are stored on a direct-access file, used as a reference file, where the key is formed by the question number and the correct choice of answer.

A program has to read the file of competition entries, check the answers against the reference file and print out the names and addresses of the first 20 (maximum) correct entries on a winners' list, and then end execution.

Design a program, including the schematic logic.

3.4. More Notes on Backtracking

The Correct Part or the Error Part first?

In many problems, the location of the CORRECT part first or last can be a decision of some importance. In the base transaction example the same error handling program would be executed as soon as there was *some* error in the transaction. We were not asked to indicate specifically which errors had been found. Here is another problem where all specific errors are to be reported:

Exercise 3.4

A transaction which can be input via a terminal consists of 10 fields. 10 small subroutines (P1—P10) are to be executed to make decisions "correct/error" possible. If all the fields are correct the program P0 is to be executed. If any field or fields are erroneous this shall be reported to the terminal operator. The error message is to be an analysis line with an E below each erroneous field and an error specification line per erroneous field, figure 3.7.

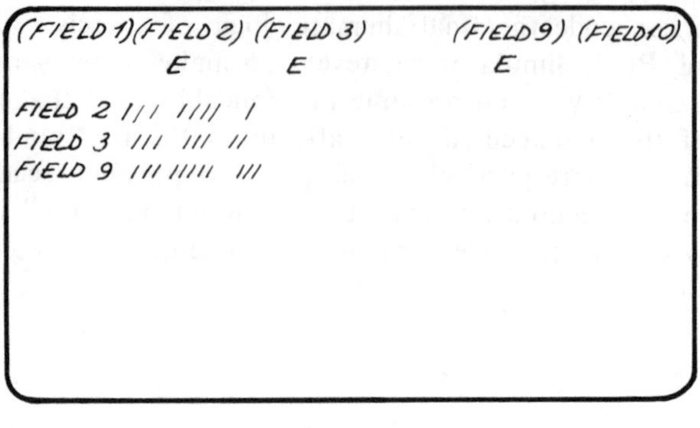

```
(FIELD 1)(FIELD 2) (FIELD 3)          (FIELD 9) (FIELD 10)
             E          E                 E

FIELD 2 /// //// /
FIELD 3 /// /// //
FIELD 9 /// ///// ///
```

Fig 3.7

(If you place the CORRECT part first this will contain 10 *quits,* i.e. 10 IF statements. Exactly the same IF statements have to occur in the ERROR part. It is simpler to place the ERROR part first. Try!)

The exercise above dealt with a number of fields in the analysis line. These fields are usable in the *quit* conditions. The fields resemble somewhat switches. They have however the positive property of being parts of the output data and exist consequently in the real world of the user. Besides they don't give rise to "wild" GO TO's but are used in the *quit* statement which has a well defined standard function. Of course you find similar problems where an error switch table can be necessary and where the connection with external data is indirect. But otherwise it is better to avoid switches.

In other cases, the basic rules for choice of posit and admit parts are these:

Alternative #1. Presume, *posit,* that branch which has a specific structure (eg. a special sequence), and confirm, *admit,* the branch which has a general structure (eg. an iteration).

Alternative #2. Presume that the element being sought is *not* there, and confirm that it exists (eg. table searching).

Alternative #3. (Last resort). If it's difficult to position the quit statements, swop the branches and try again!

Multiple Read Ahead

The exercise 3.2 dealt with analysis of a transaction file with record groups containing three transactions each. If any group did not meet the specific conditions (three transactions per group, no more no less, all of type A) one error line per group was to be printed. Return to this exercise in order to remind yourself of the problem specification. You see, we are going to complicate the problem a little. — Here is the complication: the contents of each transaction record belonging to an erroneous group are to be printed after the error line containing the group number. The consequence of this complication is that we have to look back at a number of records. The input equipment ought to be "backspaceable". If the equipment lacks this feature we can compensate by means of multiple read ahead. So we declare buffer areas, in this specific case 3+1 areas, figure 3.8.

B1	EF1	RECORD n
B2	EF2	RECORD n+1
B3	EF3	RECORD n+2
B4	EF4	RECORD n+3

Fig 3.8

An end of file flag is attached to each buffer area. (These flags are of a different kind than an ordinary switch. They could just as well be stored in the secondary storage together with the transactions. If we were to use switches *one* would be enough.) To handle these buffers you can either always read into the lowest one and successively move the records upwards or manipulate pointers and cyclicly read into the buffer areas. Applying the first principle described above you write a paragraph (subroutine, procedure) like this Cobol example:

```
MREAD.      MOVE B2 TO B1.
            MOVE B3 TO B2.
            MOVE B4 TO B3
            READ INPUT-FILE INTO B4 AT END MOVE 1 TO EF4.
```

At the beginning of the program the multiple read ahead is accomplished by four MREAD statements. Then all buffers will contain records, provided the file contains at least four records. B1 will contain the first record. If the file happens to be empty, EF1 will have the value = 1. Compare the schematic logic below with the one in the solution to exercise 3.2.

```
P seq
    Open files;
    do MREAD;
    do MREAD;
    do MREAD;
    do MREAD;
    Write header;
    PBODY iter until EF1 = 1
        PGRP seq
            Save groupno;
            PGRPBDY posit correct group
                quit PGRPBDY if transtype in B1 ≠ A;
                quit PGRPBDY if EF2 = 1;
                quit PGRPBDY if transtype in B2 ≠ A;
                quit PGRPBDY if new groupno in B2;
                quit PGRPBDY if EF3 = 1;
                quit PGRPBDY if transtype in B3 ≠ A;
                quit PGRPBDY if new groupno in B3;
                quit PGRPBDY if the same groupno in
                                B4 and EF4 = 0;

                Write B1 into output file;
                Write B2 into output file;
                Write B3 into output file;
                do MREAD;
                do MREAD;
                do MREAD;
            PGRPBDY admit (erroneous group)
                Write error line;
                PERRBDY iter until EF1 = 1 or new groupno in B1
                    Print B1;
                    do MREAD;
                PERRBDY end
            PGRPBDY end
        PGRP end
    PBODY end
    Close files;
P end
```

Three records are consumed, three new ones have to be read.

The error line is to be printed first in each group.

QUIT in Iteration

The backtracking technique gives you a fair chance to design simple and straightforward programs though facing a dilemma: you need a selection with a condition which can't be evaluated until the first selection part is partly or completely executed. A similar dilemma can arise concerning an iteration: the terminating condition can't be evaluated until a part of the iteration is executed. We can use **quit** in this case too. Then a schematic logic can look like this:

```
PA iter
    do B1;
    quit PA if cond-1;
    do B2;
    quit PA if cond-2;
    do B3;
PA end
```

It is not common that an iteration has to be interrupted somewhere in the middle but if it does happen side effects can appear. These have to be treated in the same way as in ordinary backtracking.

quit in an iteration is coded like this:

```
P iter                 Cobol:  P-ITER.
                                        - - -
     ———
     quit P if cond-1;                  IF cond-1   GO TO P-END.
     ———                                - - -
     quit P if cond-2;                  IF cond-2   GO TO P-END.
                                        - - -
P end                                   GO TO P-ITER.
                               P-END.

                      Fortran: 0102     CONTINUE
                                        - - -
                                        IF (cond-1) GO TO 0199
                                        - - -
                                        IF (cond-2) GO TO 0199
                                        - - -
                                        GO TO 0102
                               0199     CONTINUE

                        Algol: P-iter:
                                        — — —
                                        if cond-1 then go to P-end;
                                        — — —
                                        if cond-2 then go to P-end;
                                        — — —
                                        go to P-iter;
                               P-end:
```

Example: A conversation on a visual display terminal begins by sending a customer number. If the customer number exists in the customer file (which is a direct-access one), you will get a discount code in respons. If the customer number is not in the file, the response is CUSTNO. 99999 DOES NOT EXIST. You cannot continue with the conversation before an existing customer number is sent. (There is of course the option of breaking off contact, but we'll leave that aside for this example).

The input and output data streams can always be treated as sequential files. We can then draw the structures for the beginning of the conversation described as shown in Figure 3.9.

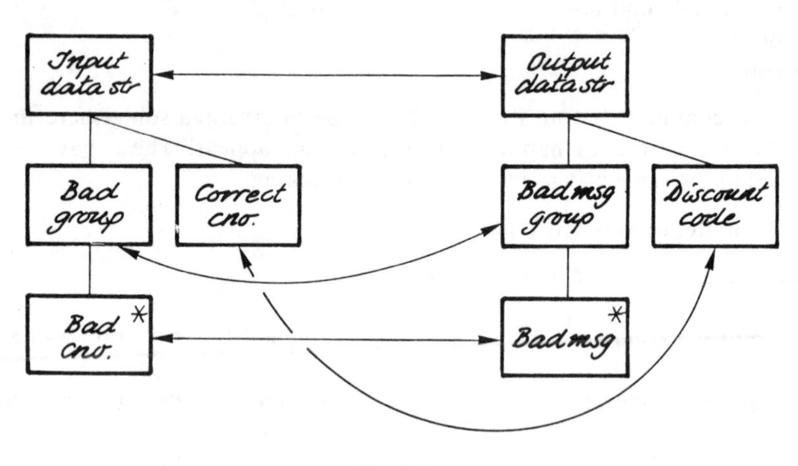

Fig 3.9

The program structure is dependent on the conversational data stream structure – the customer file does not add to the program structure, because direct access can be made as often as required, and in random order.

Operations list:

1. Read Custno.-in
2. Read Cust file with key=custno.-in
3. Write discount code
4. Write CUSTNO. 99999 DOES NOT EXIST

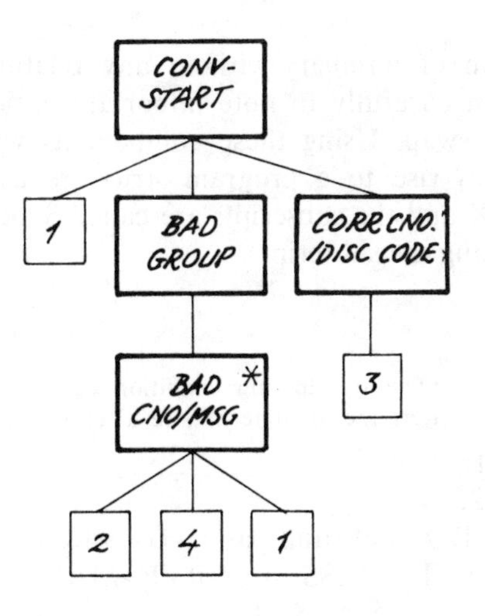

Structure text after backtracking, step 3:

```
CONV-START seq
    Read custno.-in;
    BAD-GROUP itr
        BAD-CNO/MESSAGE seq
            Read cust file with key=custno.-in;
    BAD-GROUP quit (found)
            Write CUSTNO. 99999 DOES NOT EXIST;
            Read custno.-in;
        BAD-CNO/MESSAGE end
    BAD GROUP end
    Write discount code;
CONV-START end
```

Another example: an array of numbers is to be sorted in increasing order by the bubble sort method (compare neighbours and swap).

The simplest version of bubble sort looks through the whole array repeatedly while comparing pairs of numbers. If a number has a lower subscript and higher value than its neighbour (*i.e. the one with the higher subscript*) then they have to be swapped. When a pass is executed without any swap, the array is completely sorted. This final pass is called "null pass".

In this case we can really talk about logical data structure. The physical data structure doesn't give rise to any constraints. There is only an array which is an iteration of numbers without any relations. So we read the problem specification carefully to note important entities. We note array, pass, null pass, and swap. Using these components we can create a data structure which gives rise to a program structure as in figure 3.9. The numbers are called X and the subscripts are called S and T where $T = S + 1$. A PASS starts initiating the subscripts.

Schematic logic step 1:

```
PSORT itr                  (The terminating condition can't be evaluated here as the
      PASS seq             iteration shall terminate after execution of a null pass.)
           S := 1;
           T := 2;
           PASS-BDY sel (null pass)  (The selection condition can't be eva-
                NULL-PASS itr until (T>MAXSUBSCR)  luated here.
                      S := S+1;                     Backtracking
                      T := T+1;                     is necessary.)
                NULL-PASS end        (You're right, NULL-PASS can't work
           PASS-BDY alt              of course, but we are dealing right now
                NOT-NULL-PASS seq    with step 1 of backtracking design.)
                      PFIRST itr until (X(S)>X(T))
                            S := S+1;
                            T := T+1;
                      PFIRST end
                      swap;
                      S := S+1;
                      T := T+1;
                      PLAST itr until (T>MAXSUBSCR)
                            PPAIR sel (X(S)>X(T))
                                  swap;
                                  S := S+1;
                                  T := T+1;
                            PPAIR alt
                                  S := S+1;
                                  T := T+1;
                            PPAIR end
                      PLAST end
                NOT-NULL-PASS end
           PASS-BDY end
      PASS end
PSORT end
```

Step 2:

Now we have to modify the schematic logic. The selection PASS-BDY is to be converted into a *posit – admit* construction. The PASS-BDY *quit* is to be inserted at appropriate places in the *posit* part and PSORT *quit* is to be placed somewhere in order to interrupt the superior iteration PSORT.

```
PSORT itr
        PASS seq
             S := 1;
             T := 2;
             PASS-BDY posit (null pass)
                  NULL-PASS itr until (T>MAXSUBSCR)
             PASS-BDY quit (X(S)>X(T))  (We have to
                         S := S+1;      abandon PASS-BDY posit here.)
                         R := T+1;
                  NULL-PASS end
                                        (This statement will be executed only if a
PSORT quit                              null pass is encountered. Then the iteration
             PASS-BDY admit             PSORT is to be interrupted.)
                  NOT-NULL-PASS seq
                         PFIRST itr until (X(S)>X(T))
                         S := S+1;
                         T := T+1;
                         PFIRST end
                         swap;
                         S := S+1;
                         T := T+1;
                         PLAST itr until (T>MAXSUBSCR)
                               PPAIR sel (X(S)>X(T))
                                    swap;
                                    S := S+1;
                                    T := T+1;
                               PPAIR alt
                                    S := S+1;
                                    T := T+1;
                               PPAIR end
                         PLAST end
                  NOT-NULL-PASS end
             PASS-BDY end
        PASS end
PSORT end
```

Step 3:

Let's now examine side effects. What is executed before the first *quit* statement (PASS-BDY *quit* (X(S)>X(T))? At least S and T are initiated by 1 and 2 respectively. S and T could also have been incremented one or more times. Since we abandon the *posit* part when X(S)>X(T) we will skip the iteration PFIRST and arrive at "swap" after PFIRST *end.* We will correctly start rearranging numbers at the first unsorted place in the array. The subscripts are incremented to point at that place which undoubtedly is a favourable side effect and the component PFIRST can consequently be omitted.

The next question is what side effect does PSORT *quit* give rise to? We interrupt the iteration when a null pass is executed. What's happened is only the incrementing of the subscripts. This is totally harmless so no modifications are needed.

Finally we ask ourselves if the statement PASS-BDY quit X(S)>X(T) is executable. The answer is "yes".

The program we have designed above is not optimized. The three statements after PFIRST *end* (swap; S := S+1; T := T+1;) can be omitted as we will arrive at the first of the selection parts in PPAIR *select* anyway. This part contains the same set of statements.

You have surely discovered at least one further possibility of optimizing. But remember: the more you optimize, the less understandable your program will be! Let's conclude the discussion of bubble sort by studying the effects of the *quit* statements. Look at the relevant code:

```
PSORT-ITER.       — — —
                  — — —
PASS-BDY-POSIT. — — —
NULL-PASS-ITER.
        IF T>MAXSUBSCR GO TO NULL-PASS-END.
        IF X(S)>X(T) GO TO PASS-BDY-ADMIT.
        — — —
NULL-PASS-END.
        GO TO PSORT-END.        (GO TO PASS-BDY-END. is omitted for
PASS-BDY-ADMIT.                  obvious reasons.)
        — — —
        — — —
PASS-BDY-END.
PASS-END.
PSORT-END.
```

Valid Data — Error Data

Backtracking deals very often with error handling. Note that error data structures have to be considered as carefully as correct data structures. From the program point of view there is no fundamental difference in writing a record in a file of correct data or in writing a record in a print file with the header "Error Data". Both classes of data are to be processed correctly in accordance with the program specification. Correct data and error data belong therefore to the class of *valid data.* What then are invalid data? They are data not considered at all in the program specification. If a program is presented with invalid data then the result has to be unspecified. A numeric field can for instance have a check digit. If the check procedure discovers that the input digits are erroneous then the procedure executes those statements foreseen in the program design. If non-numeric data is input into the same field and this is not anticipated in the program specification then the program behaviour is unspecified. It is exposed to invalid data.

It is important to understand the difference between valid and invalid data. A program has to be based upon data structures including *all* valid data, consequently both correct and error data. It is wrong to base the program structure upon correct data only. If you hope to be able to supplement the program, for instance during the coding, so that error data are processed then you lead yourself astray. The result will probably be a "switch-sorry-go-round" in a brushy structure.

Normalization

Böhm and Jacopini worked out, as earlier mentioned, the theories of program structuring. Thanks to these theories a firm base of program design exists. However it was also proved that each *flowchart* could be "normalized" so that the same processing could be carried out by the standard component types. This can give rise to the misunderstanding that the difference between a flowchart and a program of standard components is just formal and that flowchart-thinking would do as well. *But this is not what program design deals with!* It's true that we use standard component types — but it is of paramount importance that the components and their relationships be based upon the real world represented by data.

Besides, normalization is accomplished by adding switches.

4 The Chapter that Contains so Many Different Things that One Doesn't Know What to Call It

4.1. More on Program Inversion

Serial Inversion

The philosophy when you face a structure clash is simple: solve the problem by using two programs and one intermediate file. The intermediate file shall contain a component which is common to the clashing structures. But what if there is no common component? Then more intermediate files and programs can be used as in figure 4.1.

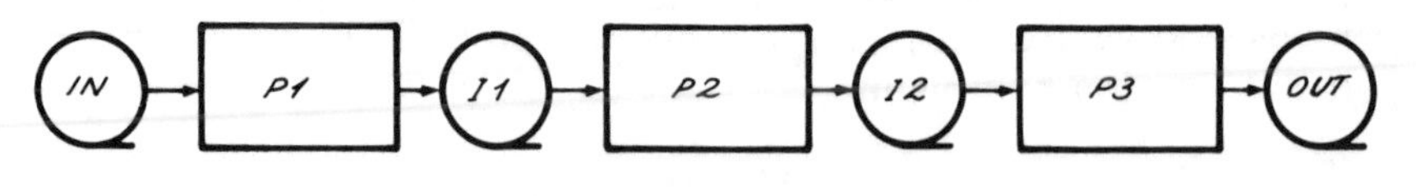

Fig 4.1

Program inversion can be applied in different ways. Here is one:

- P1 as a main program calling the subroutine P2W.
- P2 inverted with respect to I1 becoming P2W which at the same time is a main program calling the subroutine P3W.
- P3 inverted with respect to I2.

Serial inversion can of course be applied in all systems where physical intermediate files are to be eliminated.

Parallel Inversion and the Status Vector (Multithreading)

Interleaving clash is a special case of ordering clash and can be solved by sorting in a batch processing system, but not efficiently in a real time system. Furthermore, the nature of an interleaving clash is not the same as that of an

2.1) are ordered *with respect to that item*. The relevant solution is to separate the records into item groups. This philosophy is realized by so called multithreading or parallel inversion. The best way to describe parallel inversion is to use an example. Here we go:

An automatic mine transport system is controlled by a computer installation and some system data are recorded. The start and stop times of each transport are stored on a log tape, together with other data. The transports are numbered chronologically. A part of the log file is shown in figure 4.2.

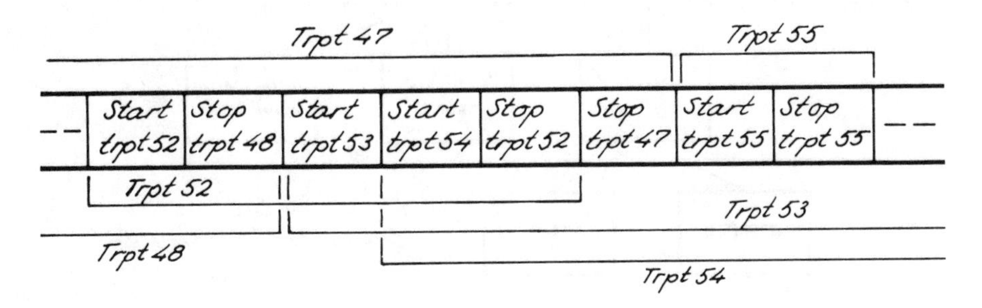

Fig 4.2

We want a report stating the number of transports and the average transport time. The data structures are shown in figure 4.3.

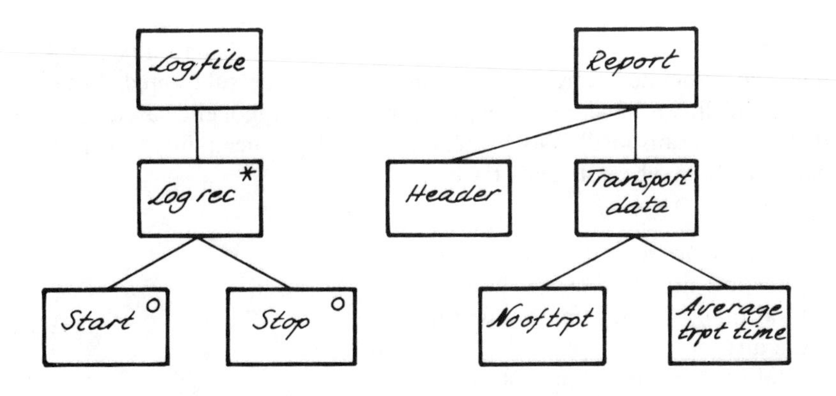

Fig 4.3

Too easy? Well, let's do it, using the structure shown in figure 4.4.

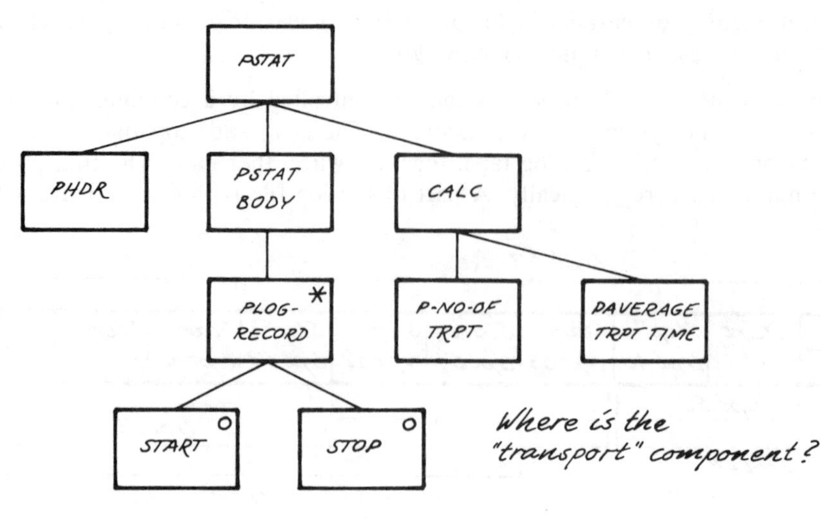

Fig 4.4

In this solution we first process the log file and then produce the statistics. If we try to allocate the operation "add 1 to number of transports" we get into trouble. This operation has to be executed once every time a transport is processed. But there is no component called PROCESS TRANSPORT to which this operation can be allocated. And to calculate the transport time, the associated start and stop times have to be subtracted. What went wrong? Well, we have neglected an important component based upon the real world: "Transport". No problem? You don't need the transport component? Well, maybe not. Let's try it.

```
– – –
PLOGREC sel (start record)
        transport no := transport no+1;
        total time := total time−start time;
PLOGREC alt
        total time := total time+stop time;
PLOGREC end
```

Yes, it is an elegant solution and it works certainly — but is it an easy-to-modify solution? How do we modify the program if, for instance, the statistics are to be supplemented by the longest and shortest transport times? There is only one thing to do and that is rewrite the program. If a PROCESS TRANSPORT component existed then we could easily supplement the program.

How should we design a program or a system of programs which contains, somewhere, the component PROCESS TRANSPORT? Well, we use many programs and small intermediate files, one for each transport. Each intermediate file contains one start record and one stop record, figure 4.5.

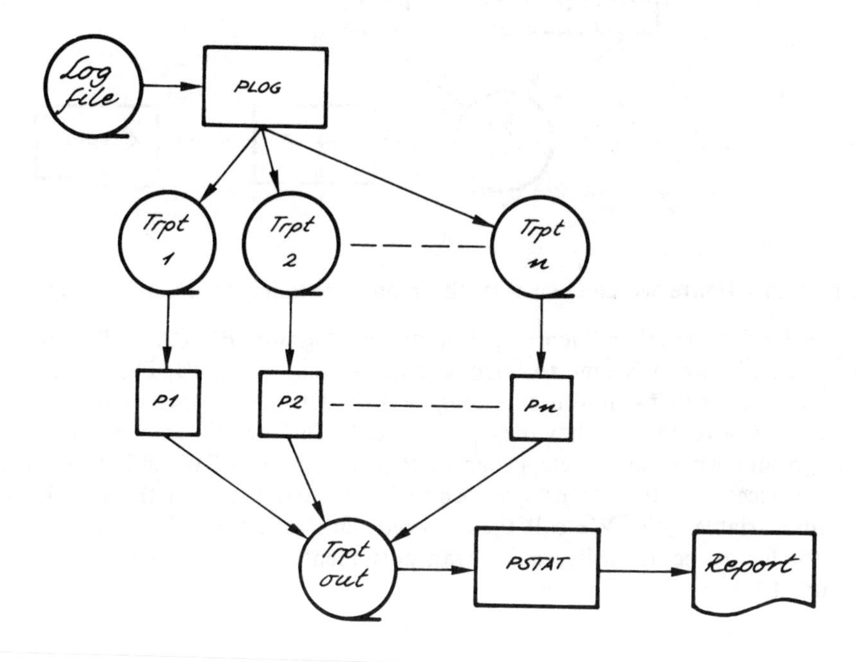

Fig 4.5

PLOG reads the log file and writes start and stop records into the files Trpt 1, Trpt 2, ... Trpt n respectively. The intermediate files are read by one program each, P1, P2, ... Pn respectively.

These programs calculate the transport times and write them in an output file "Trpt out" common to all programs. PSTAT counts the number of transports, calculates the average time and prints the report.

Now we are going to invert. P1, P2, ... Pn are to be inverted with respect to the corresponding intermediate files, figure 4.6.

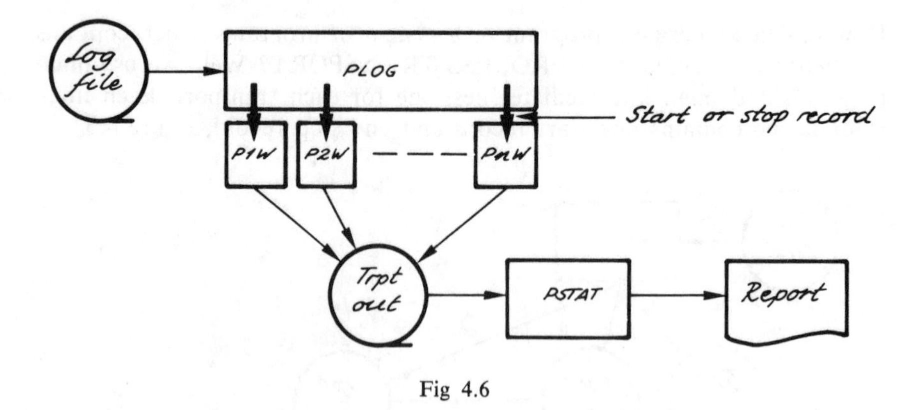

Fig 4.6

From this figure we can see why the name "parallel inversion" is applied.

Here we face another dilemma: how many programs P1, P2,... Pn are to be written? Now it's time to introduce the status vector. P1, P2,... Pn are as identical as twins (if you can imagine an indefinite number of twins...). The only difference is that they process data for specific transports. Let's design and write one single program P, invert it into PW and store in a direct access file the "transport specific" data together with the respective status variable QSn. We call these stored data status vectors. Each status vector has to be accessible using transport identification number as a key, figure 4.7.

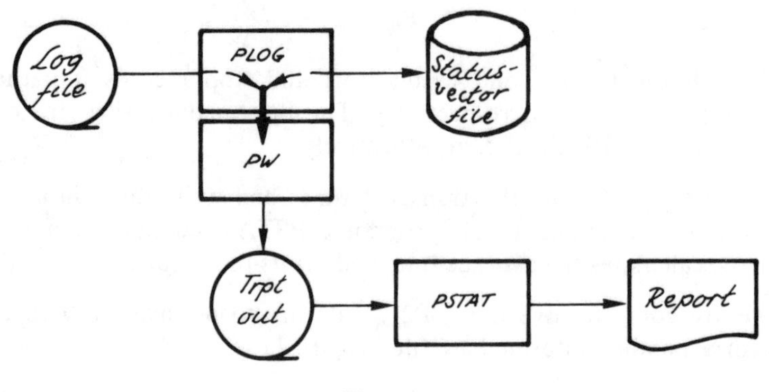

Fig 4.7

With the key as a parameter, status vector handling shall allow: read (with the result "found" or "not found"), addition of a new status vector, update and delete, i.e. the common direct access file operations.

If PLOG reads the status vector file before calling PW then PLOG can present to PW both start and stop records and the status vector. In addition we shall use a communication area. The principle of parallel inversion when the status vector is introduced can be described by the PLOG schematic logic with comments:

```
PLOG seq
        EF-LOG := 0;
        Open log file;
        Read log file;
        PLOG-BDY itr until (EF-LOG=1)
                Read status vector (transport id no);
                PSTATV 1 sel not found                            (Comment 1)
                        Create status vector;
                        Add status vector (transport id no);
                        Open call PW (record, status vector, commarea);
                PSTATV 1 alt
                PSTATV 1 end
                P call PW (record, status vector, commarea);      (Comment 2)
                PSTATV 2 sel (EOF-TRPT)                           (Comment 3)
                        Close call PW (record, status vector, commarea);
                        Delete status vector (transport id no);
                PSTATV 2 alt
                        Update status vector (transport id no);
                PSTATV 2 end
                Read log file;
        PLOG-BDY end
        Close log file;
PLOG end
```

Comment 1:
If PLOG doesn't find any status vector with the current transport ID No. then a status vector has to be created and stored in the status vector file. PW is then called with OPEN in the communication area.

Comment 2:
"P call" implies a call for PW where the communication area contains PROCESS.

Comment 3:
When PW has found and processed a stop record, it puts EOF-TRPT into the communication area. A transport (intermediate) file is the sum of all (here two in total) records which PLOG has presented. PLOG makes a close call for PW and deletes the current status vector. (Yes, it may seem a bit fussy and can of course be "optimized". But an "unoptimized" program is easier to modify.)

Since inversion is accomplished by modifying the code we describe PW by commenting the PW code:

```
— — —
PROCEDURE DIVISION USING RECORD, STATUS-VECTOR,
                               COMMAREA.
PW-SLCT.
      IF COMMAREA NOT = "OPEN" GO TO PW-SLCT-END.
      MOVE 1 TO QS.                              (Comment 4)
      EXIT PROGRAM.
PW-SLCT-END.
TRPT-SEQ.
      GO TO Q1, Q2, Q3 DEPENDING ON QS.  (Comment 5)
Q1.   MOVE START-TIME TO ST-TIME.
      MOVE 2 TO QS.
      EXIT PROGRAM.
Q2.   SUBTRACT ST-TIME FROM STOP-TIME GIVING
      TRPT-TIME.
      MOVE "EOF-TRPT" TO COMMAREA.
      MOVE 3 TO QS.
      EXIT PROGRAM.
Q3.   WRITE TRPT-TIME.
      EXIT PROGRAM.
TRPT-SEQ-END.
```

Comment 4:
PW must put 1 into QS the first time per transport, i.e. when PLOG calls PW with OPEN in COMMAREA.

Comment 5:
Before inversion the program contained three READ statements (according to the READ AHEAD rule, a rule without exceptions). Consequently we will have three paragraph names in the GO TO . . . DEPENDING statement.

PSTAT is suitably inverted with respect to the TRPT-OUT file. This makes PW a main program from the PSTATW point of view.

The communication area has to be supplemented by OPEN — CLOSE TRPT-OUT with regard to PSTATW. PLOG reports when the log file EOF appears and PW hands it over to PSTATW. This is not shown in the PW code.

The programs discussed above are not "optimized". A modification demand, for instance, to process queue standstill per transport is simple to meet by adding a level in PW below TRPT-SEQ. PW can also be modified to process incomplete data from PLOG, i.e. if start or stop time is missing.

4.2. What's so Special About Technical Programming?

Sometimes people state that JSP is not applicable in "technical programming". But the expression "technical programming" is rather undefined. What we need is a more tangible problem classification.

Is it "technical programming" if you have small input-output data sets but extensive processing? Developing modern military aircraft implies a lot of test flights. From each test flight of say half an hour hundreds of thousands of data values are recorded, data originating from different subsystem measurements. These are evaluated in computers producing a lot of tables and diagrams. The processing can be more or less complicated, in many cases simple. Has this anything to do with "technical programming" or not?

A warehouse firm has a central haulage, many regional stores and still more local stores. Some distribution lines are handled by the firm's own lorries. How much is the solvency of the firm affected (*one* output datum) if the official discount rate is raised by 1 % (*one i*nput datum)? Has this anything to do with "technical programming" or not?

Can the two examples above have something in common? In the aircraft case, external data structures reflect the subsystems. In the haulage firm case, external data have no structure. To get an answer to the question about the haulage firm's solvency we must have data on the firm. These data are used internally in the program and shall be given a structure which is a model of the firm.

Both cases have the following in common: the problem solution structure has to be a *model of the real world*. They differ in one respect: the model structure in the aircraft case is found in external data, the model structure in the distribution firm case is found in internal data.

Process control is a problem area where data often arrive at random. But in this case too the programs can (and should) be structured as a model — a model which corresponds to the control system. A big refinery company in the USA has successfully applied JSP in this way.

4.3. When the Talking Has to Stop . . .

This book deals mainly with the theory of JSP. Its objective is, of course, to inspire and persuade you to use JSP in practice. And to enable you to design correct and easy-to-modify programs with confidence.

What difficulties does a programmer experience when he/she starts applying JSP? As we pointed out at the beginning of the book, it is sometimes difficult to analyze and create logical data structures. That phase demands most of the programmer's creative ability. The model concept can be helpful.

Sometimes programmers ask how they can know whether an operation list is complete. There is no known method guaranteeing a programmer a complete operation list. Here professional knowledge and experience are needed.

As a first "practice case" a task not too big, not too small is suitable. What is "not too big, not too small"? Well, the programmer is the right person to decide which case has the right size with respect to his/her experience. Note the possibilities to divide a program into separate structure parts and to solve the problem by team work. The common design method and easy-to- interpret notation facilitate team work considerably.

It happens now and then that a programmer experiences the first steps of JSP design as more difficult than for instance the start of flowcharting. There is an explanation and even a good reason for this. Consider a program specification. It is essentially a description of problems to be solved and some problems are not obvious. Regardless of design method, the problems have to be solved. The more rudimentary the design method, the easier it is to start programming and the greater the likelihood of unexpected problems requiring solution turning up during the testing stage. In addition there are risks that the program will still contain errors when it enters the production runs. A good design method reveals the problems at an early stage and forces us to solve them before going on. It is, by far, much cheaper to solve the problems in the design phase than during testing. Furthermore there is a good chance that the program is correct when it starts its productive life.

"JSP involves a lot of drawing and writing" is an objection raised by some programmers who have started to use JSP. In this context it is appropriate to refer to Dijkstra. He has stated that a reasonable proportion of documentation volumes of program design/program code is ten to one. Consequently Dijkstra wouldn't raise his eyebrows if a source code of ten pages is based upon design documentation of one hundred pages. He has pointed out that *it is not the design documentation that is extensive but the source code that is compressed!*

It is probably this fact, that the source code is compressed, which has established a specific view of program documentation. Besides, a program is an abstract phenomenon compared with, for instance, an electromechanical gadget. If you visit a design office and ask for another type of screw in said gadget for the next production series the design manager will probably tell you that he needs 30 design hours to achieve the modification. If you ask why, you'll find out that a lot of drawings and part lists have to be gone through, modified, checked and approved. Designers and manufacturers have learnt a long time ago that design documentation has to be complete and rigorously updated if the manufacturing process is to produce the intended products. So at the design office they have resources for documentation and modification work. One reason for this is that it is easy to demonstrate the complexity of a gadget and gain a hearing for demands for resources. It is more difficult to demonstrate the scope of a program and as a result be allotted resources corresponding to those of the design office. At programming departments, the resources for documentation work are often sadly inadequate.

The structure diagrams are more extensive than for instance BNF notation of course. But structure diagrams allow man to benefit from a human property far superior to that of machines: pattern recognition. It is always easier for us to go to an unknown destination with the help of a route drawn on a map than with the help of a route description.

Finally: don't quit JSP if your first efforts imply set-backs. Do you remember your very first programs? That's it! You didn't quit coding just because it wasn't easy! And to *design* programs is necessary too.

Thousands of programmers apply JSP. JSP is a really practical method of program design — the answer to wishes of many people to tackle problems methodically. JSP is worth the effort — and you are worthy of JSP. Good luck!

5 Answers

1.1

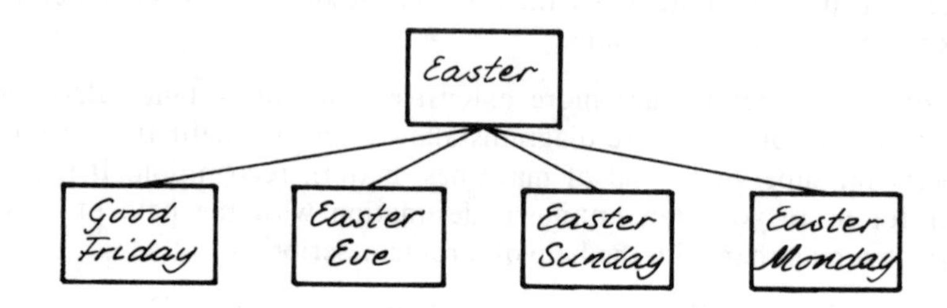

Fig 5.1

1.2

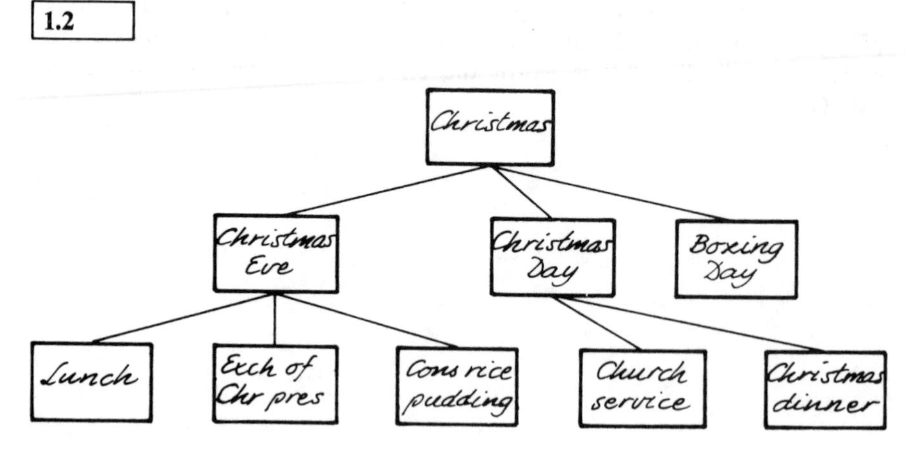

Fig 5.2

1.3

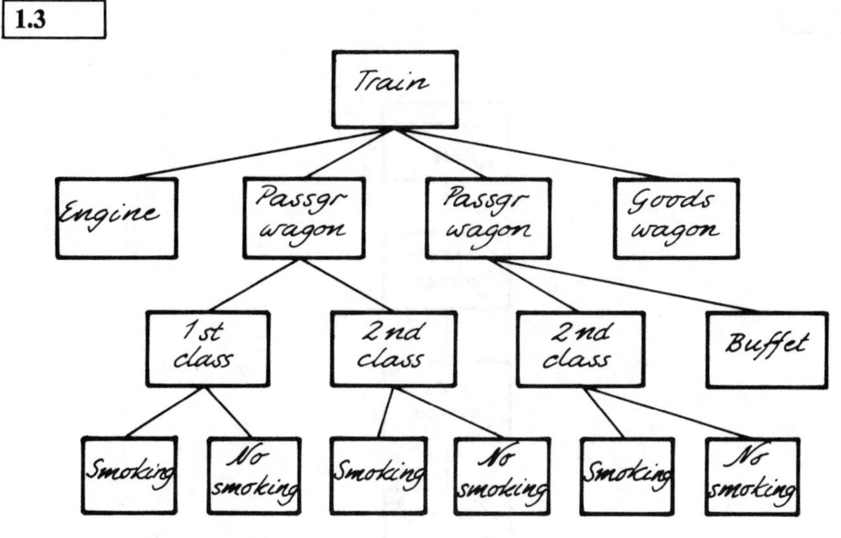

Fig 5.3

1.4

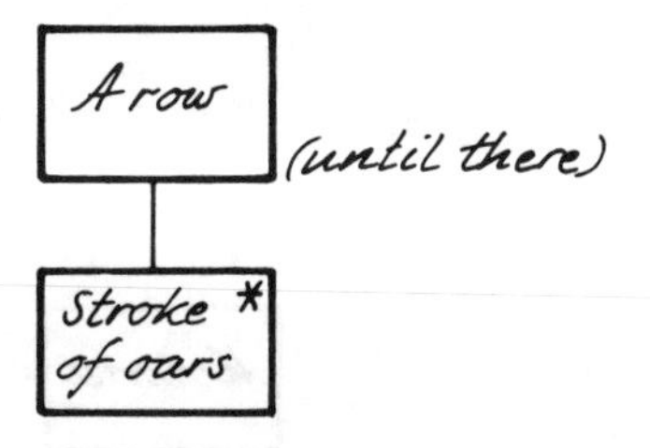

Fig 5.4

1.5

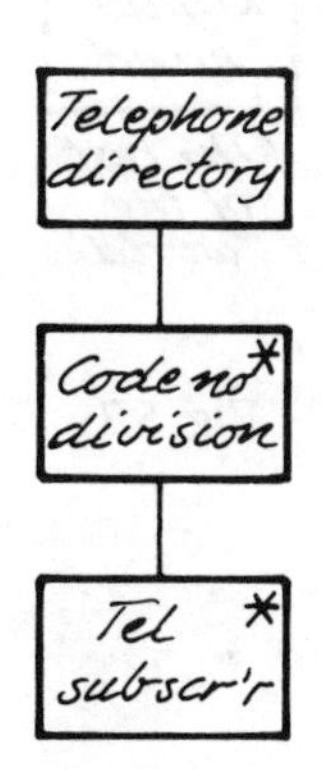

Fig 5.5

1.6

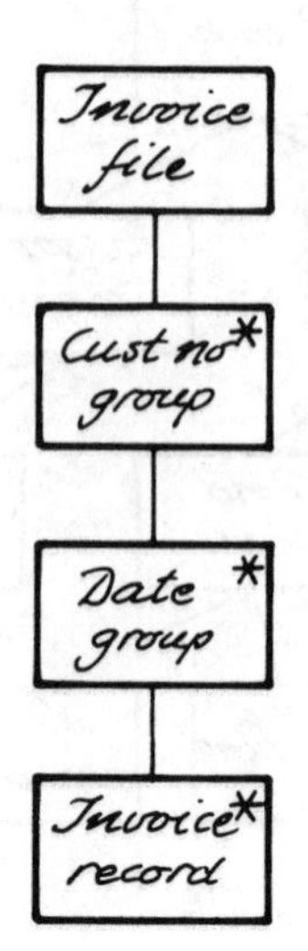

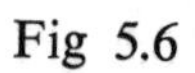

Fig 5.6

1.7

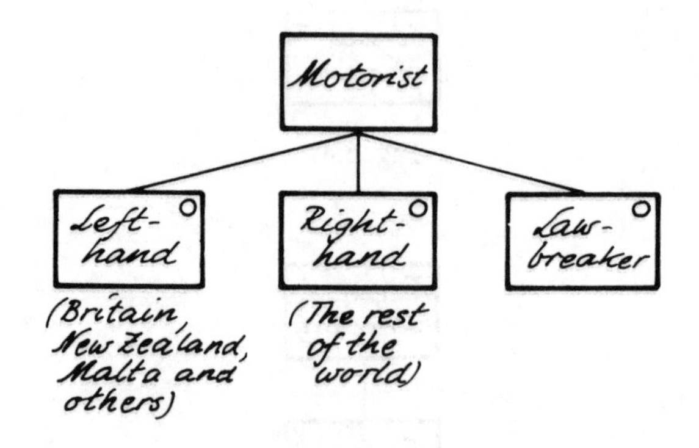

Fig 5.7

1.8

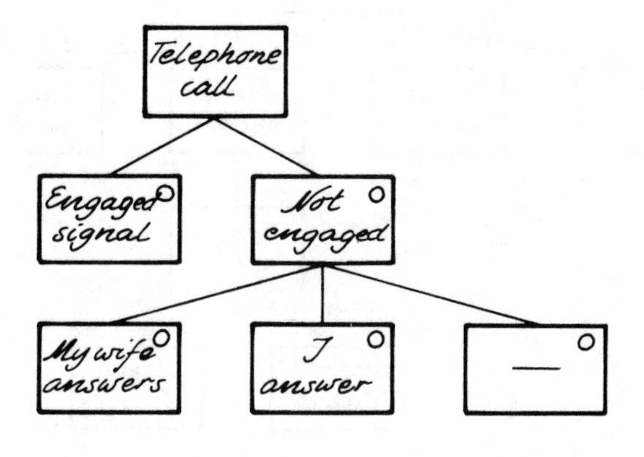

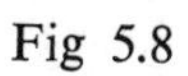
Fig 5.8

1.9

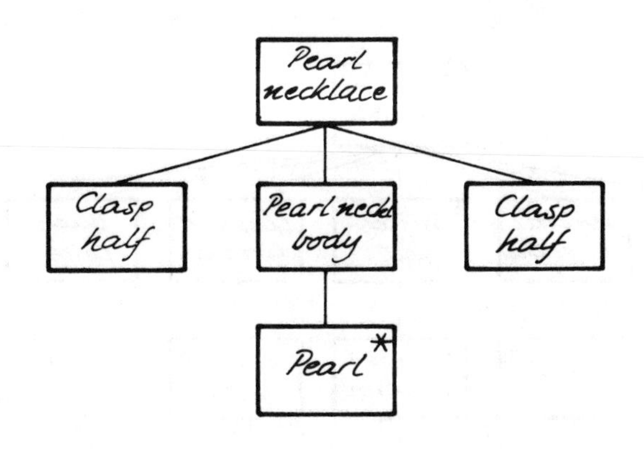

Fig 5.9

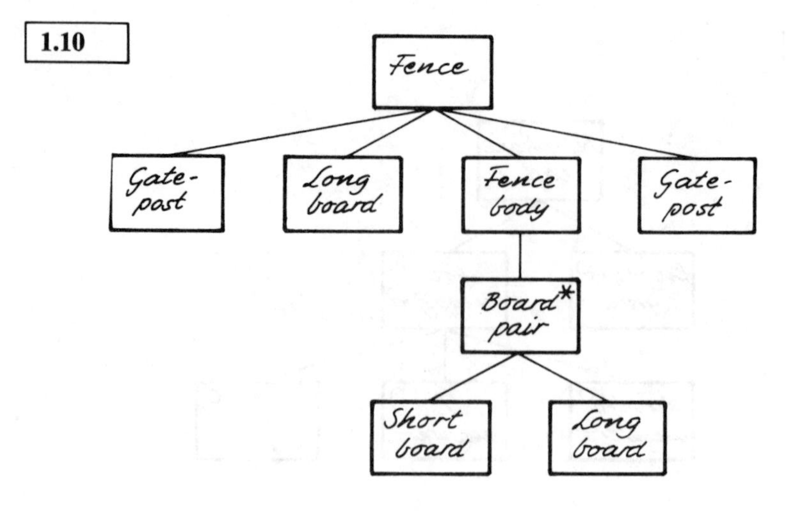

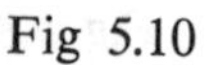
Fig 5.10

Note that the fence can't be described as a selection of a long or a short board! A selection doesn't imply any specific order of the selection parts.

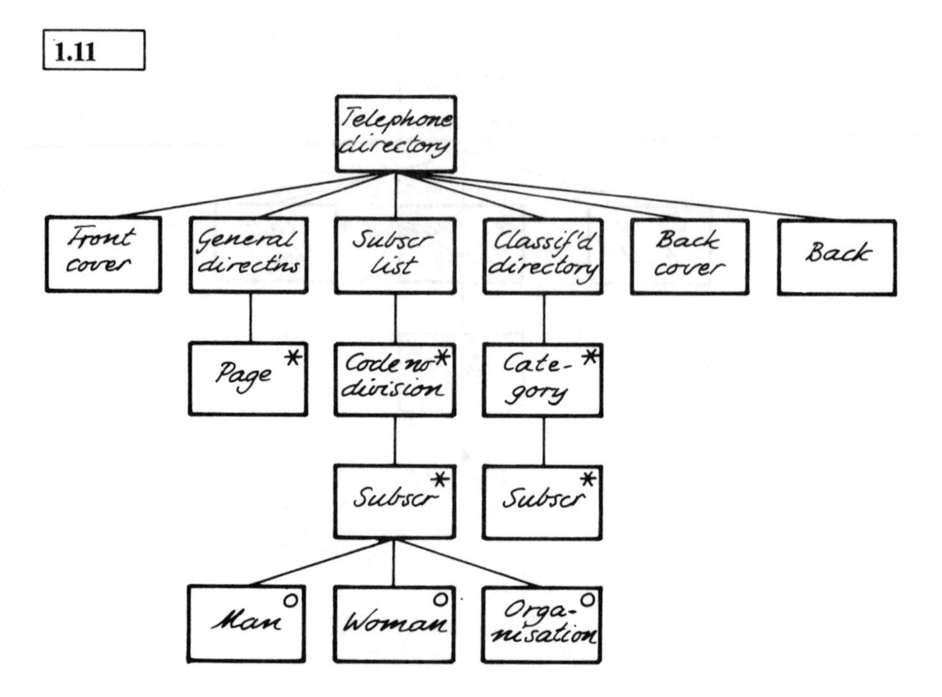

Fig 5.11

1.12

```
PR itr until (C1)
    PB sel (C2)
        exec J;
    PB alt
        K seq
            exec L;
            exec M;
        K end
    PB end
PR end
```

1.13

```
A seq
    B sel (C1)
        E sel (C3)
            exec J;
        E alt
            exec K,
        E end
    B alt
        exec F;
    B end
    C itr until (not C2)
        G seq
            exec L;
            exec M;
            exec N;
        G end
    C end
    D seq
        exec H;
        exec I;
    D end
A end
```

1.14

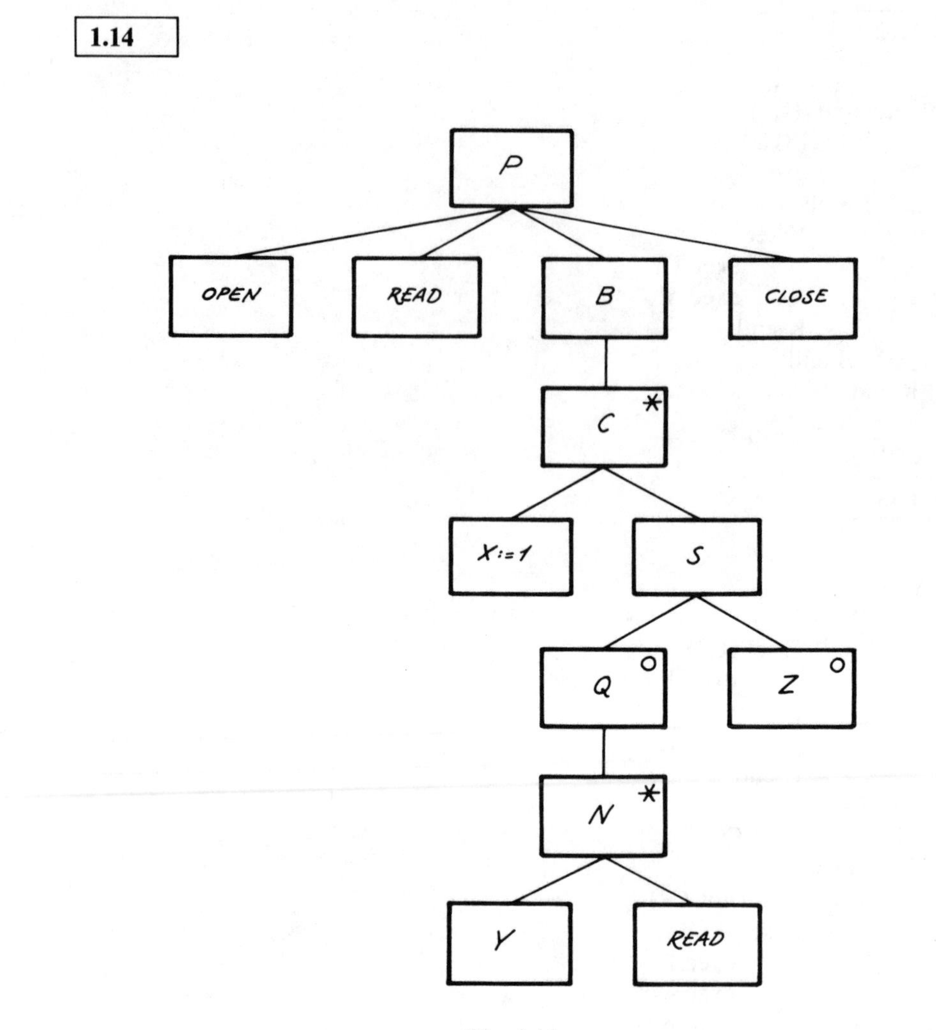

Fig 5.12

1.15

```
PSEQ.     MOVE 0 TO IE.
          MOVE 1 TO KA.
BPITER.   IF KA > 10 GO TO BPEND.
BBSEQ.    MOVE 10 TO LFLT.
BTSLCT.   IF NOT(COND=N) GO TO BTOR.

          SUBTRACT 1 FROM LFLT.
          COMPUTE MT = IE + 2 * KA.
          ADD 2 TO IE.
          GO TO BTEND.
BTOR.     ADD 1 TO IE.
BTEND.
          ADD 1 TO KA.
BBEND.
          GO TO BPITER.
BPEND.
PEND.     STOP RUN.
```

```
P seq: begin
     IE := 0;
     KA := 1;
     BPiter: if KA>10 then go to BPend;
          BBseq:    LFLT := 10;
                    BT sel: if cond ≠ N then go to BT or;
                         LFLT := LFLT — 1;
                         MT := IE + 2 * KA;
                         IE := IE + 2;
                         go to BTend;
                    BTor:
                         IE := IE + 1;
                    BTend:
                         KA := KA + 1;
                    BBend:
                    go to BPiter;
          BPend:
Pend:     end
```

```
0101  IE=0
      KA=0
0202  IF(KA.GT.10) GO TO 0299
0301  LFLT=10
0403  IF(COND.NE.N) GO TO 0404
      LFLT=LFLT-1
      MT=IE+2*KA
```

1.15 (continued)

```
      IE=IE+2
      GO TO 0499
0404  IE=IE+1
0499  CONTINUE
      KA=KA+1
0399  CONTINUE
      GO TO 0202
0299  CONTINUE
0199  STOP
      END
```

1.16

```
ASEQ.
BSLCT.   IF NOT(TYPE = T1) GO TO BOR.
ESLCT.   IF NOT(CLASS = C1) GO TO EOR.
         PERFORM J.
         GO TO EEND.
EOR.     PERFORM K.
EEND.
         GO TO BEND.
BOR.     PERFORM F.
BEND.
CITER.   IF NOT (TYPE = T3) GO TO CEND.
GITER.   IF NOT (CLASS = C3) GO TO GEND.
LSEQ.
         PERFORM M.
         PERFORM N.
LEND.
         GO TO GITER.
GEND.    PERFORM P.
         GO TO CITER.
CEND.
DSLCT.   IF NOT (CLASS = C1) GO TO DOR.
         PERFORM H.
         GO TO DEND.
DOR.                        }Empty selection part
DEND.                       }
AEND.    STOP RUN.
```

1.16 (continued)

```
Aseq:  begin
       — — —
       Bsel: if ¬(type = T1) then go to Bor;
             Esel: if ¬(class = C1) then go to Eor;
                   J (a, b, . . .);
                  [go to Eend;]
            [Eor:] K(c,d, . . .);
             Eend:
            [go to Bend;]
      [Bor:] F(e, f, . . .);
       Bend:
       Citer: if ¬(type = T3) then go to Cend;
             Giter: if ¬(class = C3) then go to Gend;
                   Lseq: M(g, h, . . .);
                         N(i, j, . . .);
                   Lend:
                  [go to Giter;]
            [Gend:]
             P(k, 1, . . .);
            [go to Citer;]
      [Cend:]
       Dsel: if ¬(class = C1) then go to Dor;
             H(m, n, . . .);
            [go to Dend;]
      [Dor:]                 }Empty selection part
       Dend:
Aend:  end
```

```
0101  CONTINUE
0203  IF(TYPE.NE.T1)GO TO 0204
0303  IF(CLASS.NE.C1)GO TO 0304
      CALL J(A, B, ...)
     [GO TO 0399]
[0304] CALL K(C, D, ...)
0399  CONTINUE
     [GO TO 0299]
[0204] CALL F(E, G, ...)
0299  CONTINUE
0402  IF(TYPE.NE.T3) GO TO 0499
0502  IF(CLASS.NE.C3) GO TO 0599
0601  CALL M(I,J, ...)
      CALL N(K,L, ...)
0699  CONTINUE
     [GO TO 0502]
[0599] CONTINUE
```

1.16 (continued)

```
      CALL P(Q, R, ...)
      GO TO 0402
0499  CONTINUE
0703  IF(CLASS.NE.C1) GO TO 0704
      CALL H(S, T, ...)
      GO TO 0799
0704  CONTINUE  }Empty selection part
0799  CONTINUE
      STOP
0199  END
```

1.17a)

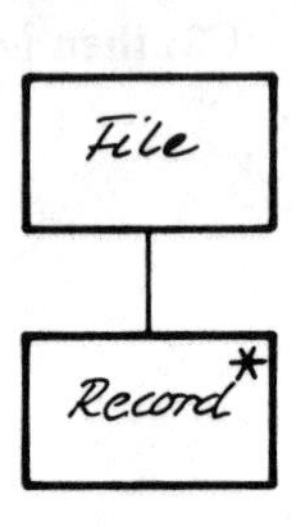

Fig 5.13

1.17b)

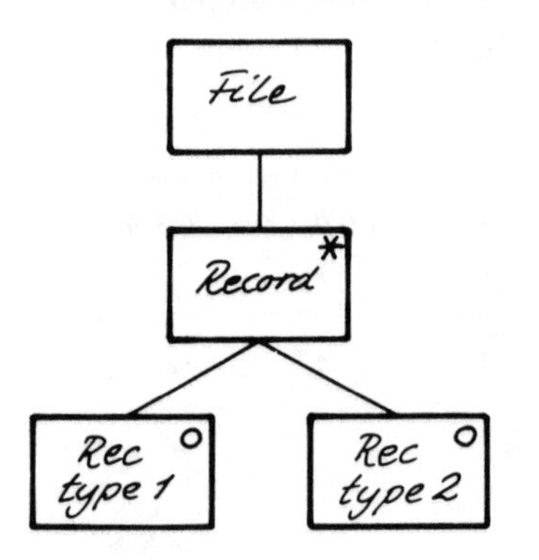

Fig 5.14

1.17c) = the structure of b).

1.18a)

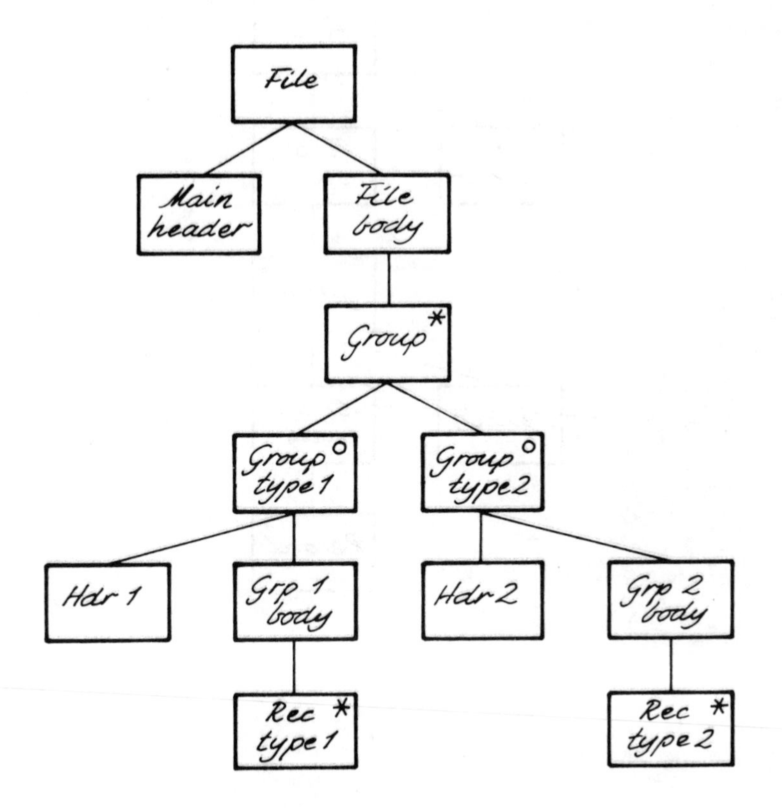
File
Main header
File body
Group *
Group type1 o
Group type2 o
Hdr 1
Grp 1 body
Hdr 2
Grp 2 body
Rec type1 *
Rec type2 *

Fig 5.15

1.18b)

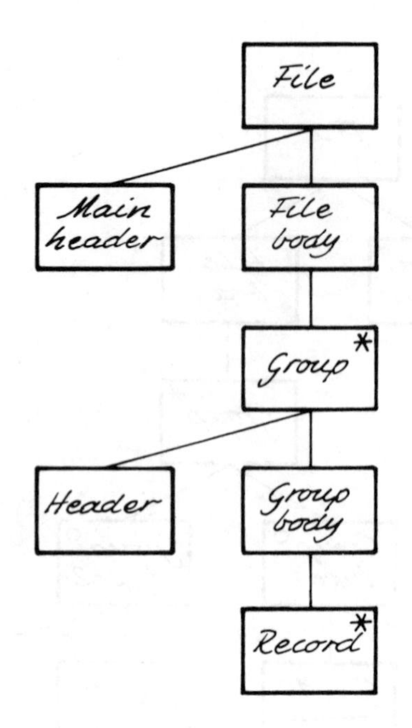

Fig 5.16

1.19

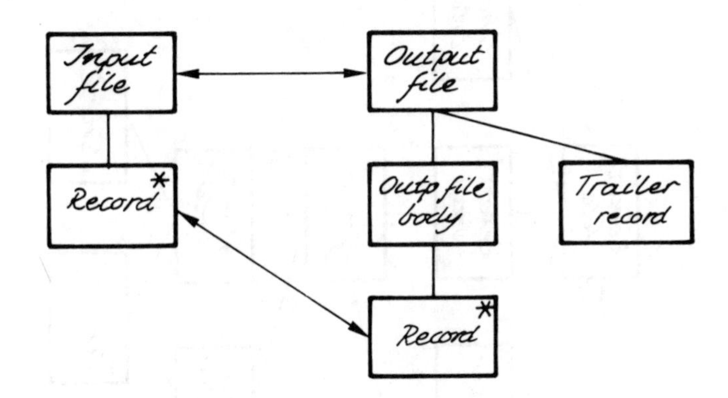

Input file
Output file
Record
Outp file body
Trailer record
Record

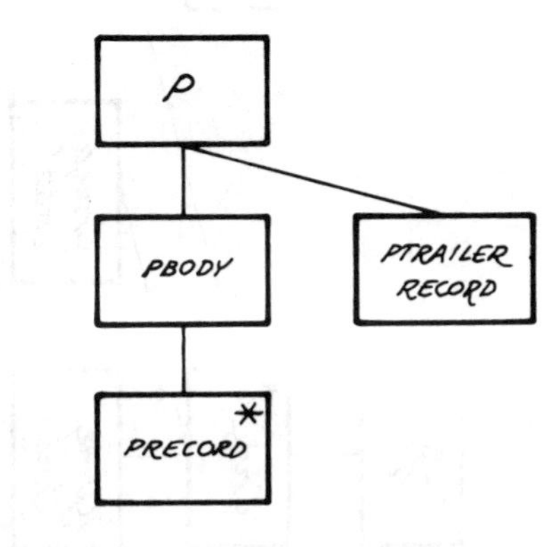

P
PBODY
PTRAILER RECORD
PRECORD

Fig 5.17

1.20

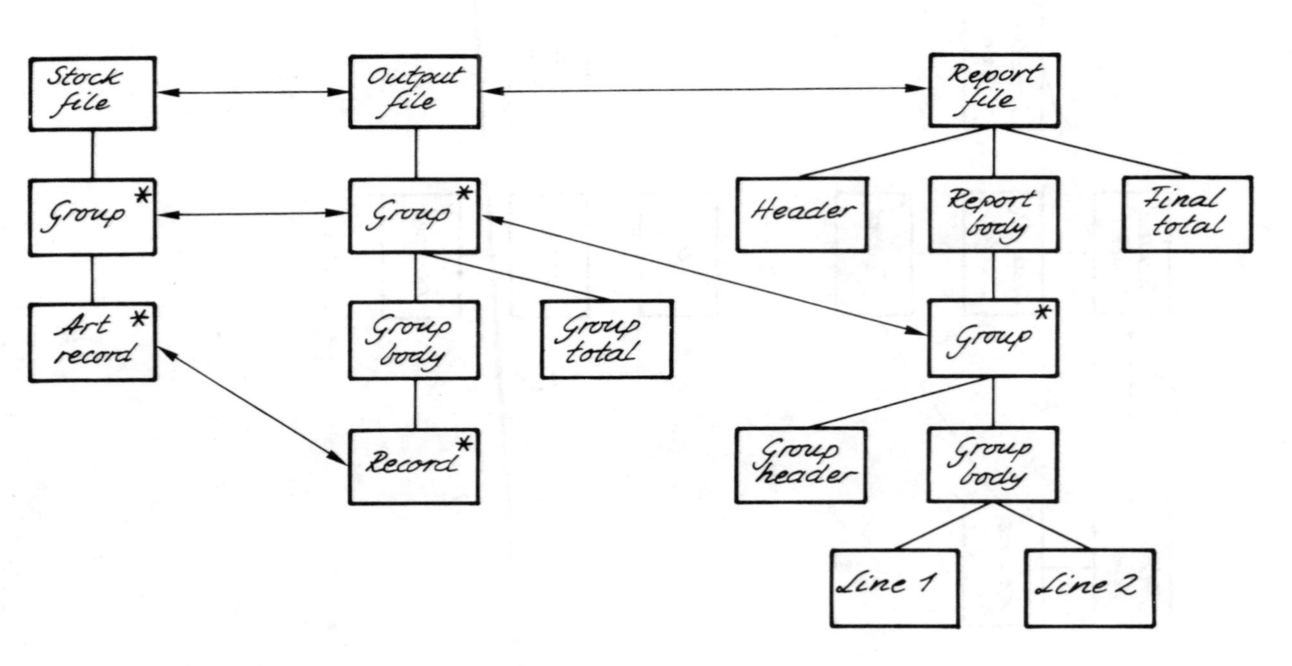

Stock file
Group *
Art record *
Output file
Group *
Group body
Record *
Group total
Report file
Header
Report body
Final total
Group *
Group header
Group body
Line 1
Line 2

Fig 5.18

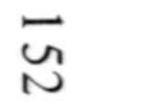

1.20 (continued)

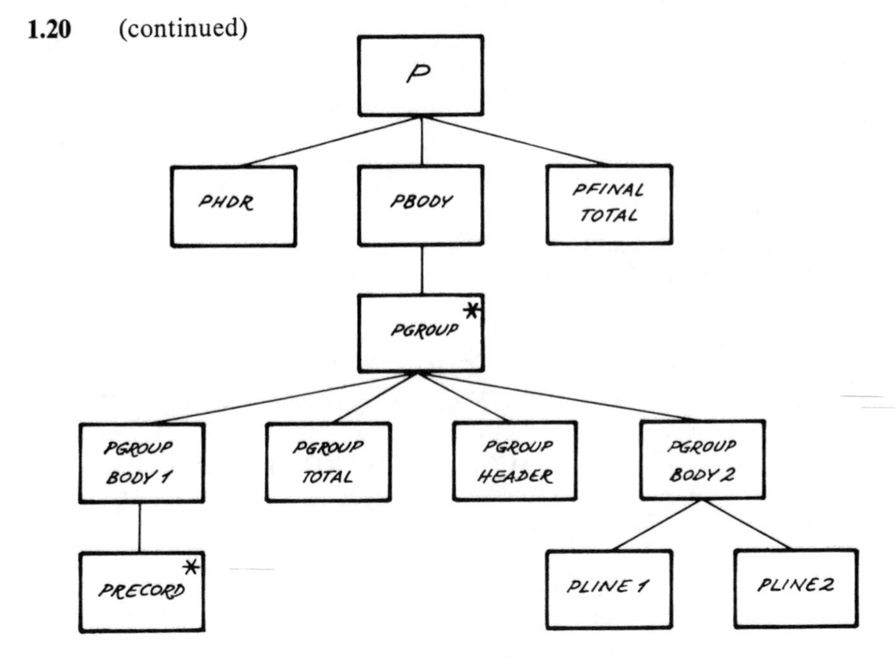

Fig 5.19

1.21

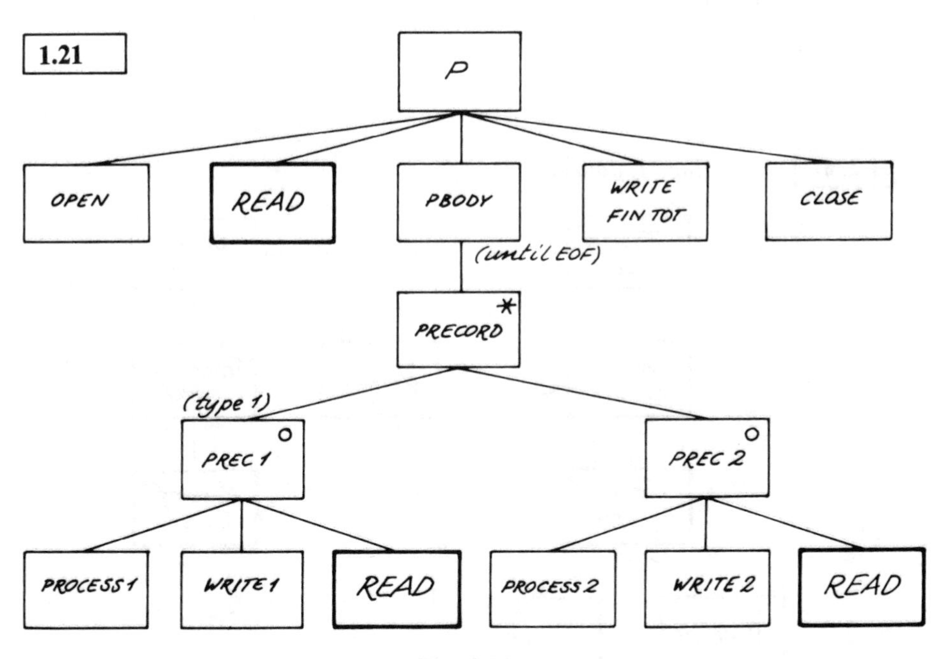

Fig 5.20

1.22

```
P seq
        Open files;
        EF := 0;
        ACCFT := 0;
        Read; Note: at end of file EF := 1
        PBODY itr until (EF=1)
                PCGRP seq
                        ACCDT := 0;
                        GRPNO := CNO,
                        PCGRPBDY itr until (GRPNO ≠ CNO or EF=1)
                                PREC seq
                                ACCDT := ACCDT+INVAMT;
                                Write output rec;
                                Read;
                                PREC end
                        PCGRPBDY end
                        ACCFT := ACCFT+ACCDT;
                        Write ACCDT;
                PCGRP end
        PBODY end
        Write ACCFT;
        Close files;
P end
```

1.23a) *Stage 1, data structures:*

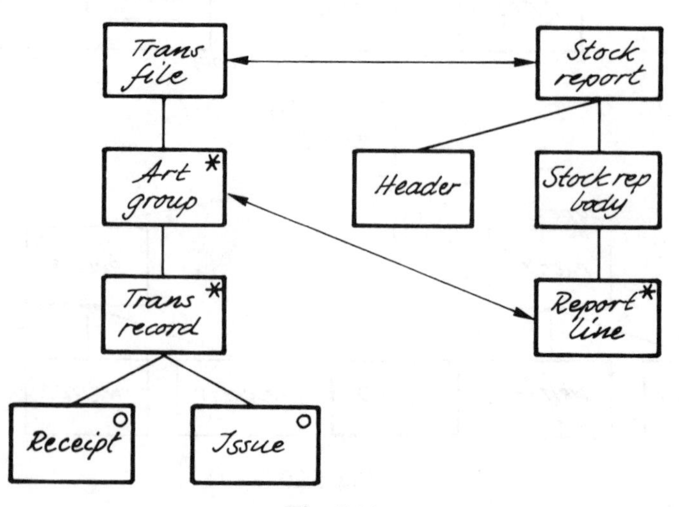

Fig 5.21

1.23a) (continued)

Stage 2, basic program structure:

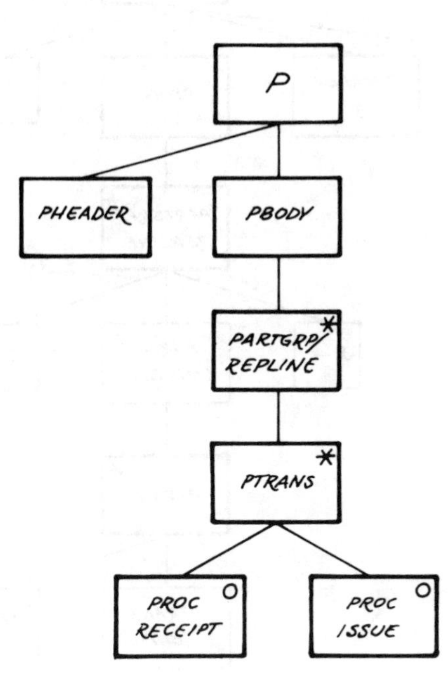

Fig 5.22

Stage 3, operations list:

1. Open files
2. EF := 0
3. GRPNO := ARTNO
4. ACC := 0
5. ACC := ACC+QUANT
6. ACC := ACC—QUANT
7. Process report line
8. Write header
9. Read
10. Close files

(Process report line = editing and printing. "Read" is presumed to access a complete transaction record.)

Stage 3 (continued), allocate the operations:

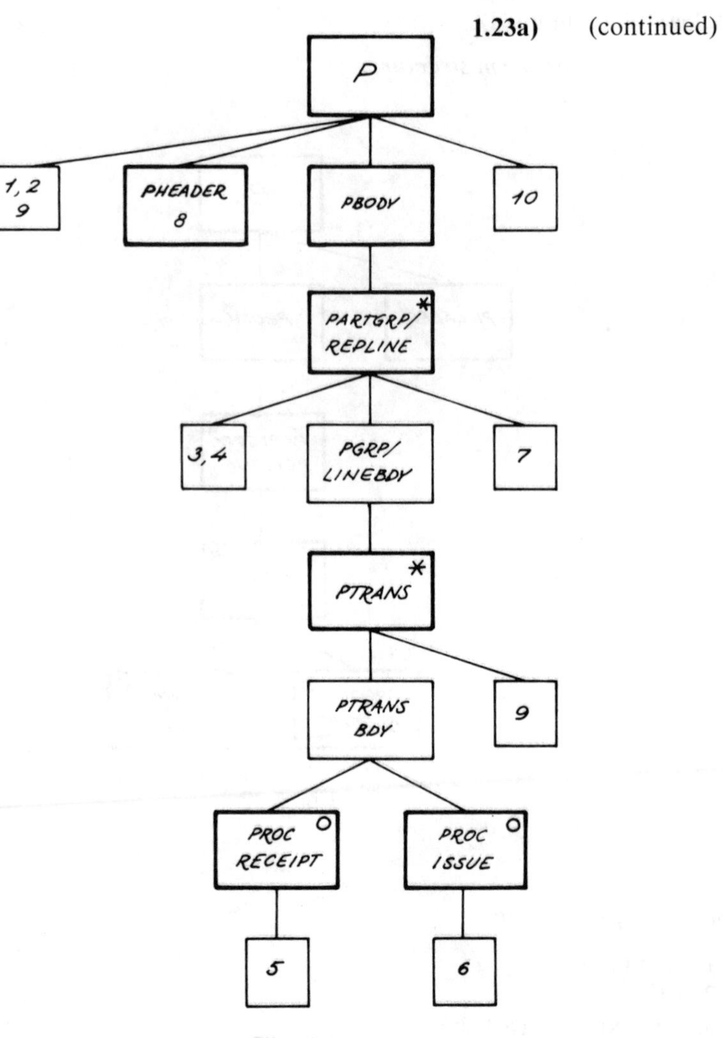

Fig 5.23

Stage 4, schematic logic:

```
P seq
      Open files;
      EF := 0;
      Read; Note: at end of file EF := 1;
      Write header;
      PBODY itr until (EF := 1)
              PARTGRP/REPLINE seq
                      ACC := 0;
                      GRPNO := ARTNO;
```

1.23a) (continued)

```
                    PGRP/LINEBDY itr until (ARTNO ≠ GRPNO
                                            or EF=1)
                         PTRANS seq
                              PTRANSBDY sel (TRANSCODE
                                    =R)
                                    ACC := ACC+QUANT;
                              PTRANSBDY alt
                                    ACC := ACC−QUANT;
                              PTRANSBDY end
                              Read;
                         PTRANS end
                    PGRP/LINEBDY end
                    Process report line;
              PARTGRP/REPLINE end
    PBODY end
    Close files;
P end
```

1.23b)

No, let us avoid switches. Why, we will discuss later on (section 1.8). We can still solve the problem easily. Which component will be executed if *no* asterisk is to be printed? Well, it is PROCISSUE. Then we can add the operation "replace asterisk by space" first under the header PROCISSUE (the second selection part PTRANSBDY *alt*). And we start PARTGRP/REPLINE by editing "put an asterisk at the end of the report line".

1.24

The answer is easiest to achieve by drawing a set diagram.

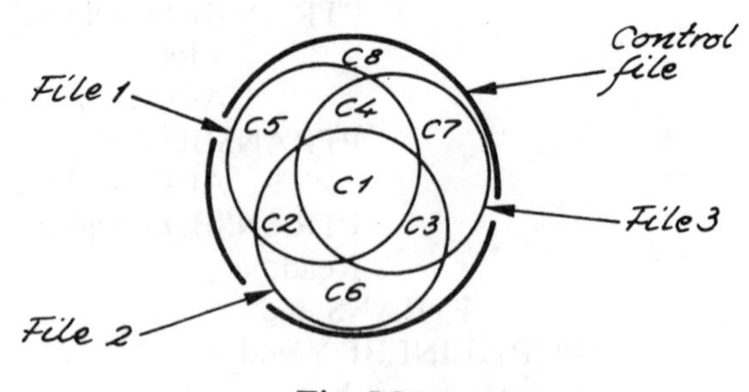

Fig 5.24

Consequently eight cases.

In general:
Maximum number of collating cases $= 2^n$ where $n =$ the number of files to be matched (the control file is excluded).

1.25

Stage 1, data structures:

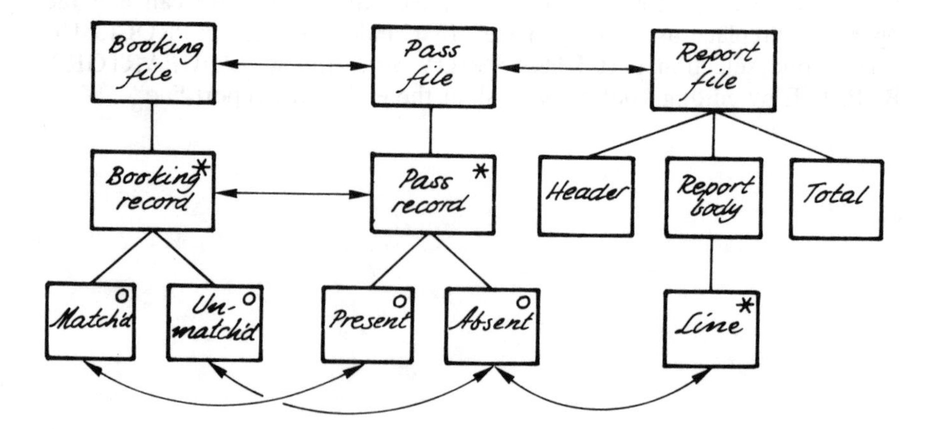

Fig 5.25

1.25 (continued)

The booking file is also a control file. "Passrec" includes both present and absent records. So there are as many "Passrec" as "Bookrec". As "Passfile" is a direct access file "Passrec" can be accessed in the same order as "Bookrec". Consequently there is a 1—1 correspondence between "Passrec" and "Bookrec". A similar 1—1 correspondence also exists between present "Passrec" and matched "Bookrec", between absent "Passrec" and unmatched "Bookrec" and between absent "Passrec" and "Line".

Stage 2, basic program structure:

The sequence "Report file" (Header — Repbdy — Sum) can be inserted at level 2 in the other structures. PBOOK/PASSREC will then get the header PBODY which is no contradiction.

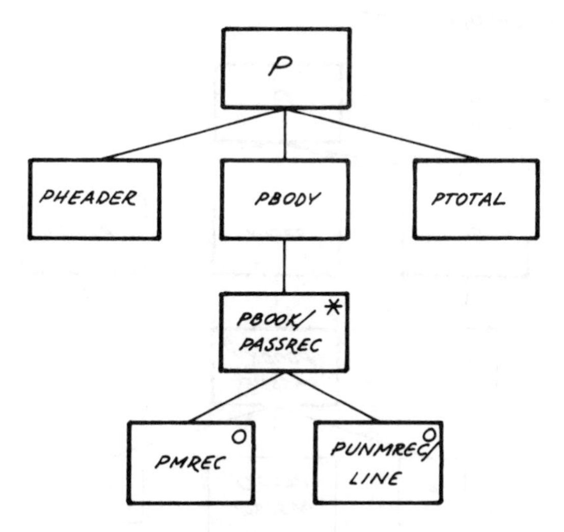

Fig 5.26

Stage 3, make an operations list . . .	*Frequency and order:*
1. Open files	Once per P, at the beginning
2. Close files	Once per P, at the end
3. Read Booking file	Once immediately after open Once immediately after a "Bookrec" is consumed
4. Read Pass file	Once immediately before the collating selection (direct acces file)
5. Write line	Once per PUNBREC/LINE
6. Write header	Once per PHDR
7. COUNTER := 0	Once per P, at the beginning
8. COUNTER := COUNTER+1	Once per PUNBREC/LINE
9. Write sum	Once per PSUM
10. EFB := 0	Once per P, at the beginning before the first read

. . . and allocate the operations:

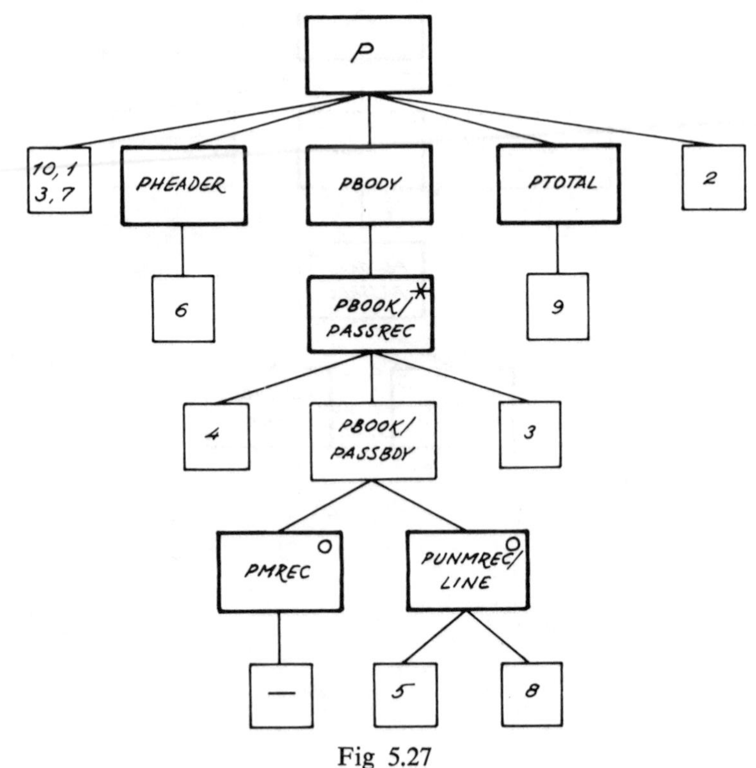

Fig 5.27

1.25 (continued)

PMBREC (Process Matched Booking Record) gets no operation. It becomes an empty selection part.

Stage 4, schematic logic:

```
P seq
    EFB := 0;
    Open files;
    Read Booking file;
    COUNTER := 0;
    Write header;
    PBODY itr until (EFB=1)
            PBOOK/PASSREC seq
                    Read Pass file (Key=ticket number in Book rec);
                    PBOOK/PASSBDY sel (FOUND)
                    PBOOK/PASSBDY alt
                            Write line;
                            COUNTER := COUNTER+1;
                    PBOOK/PASSBDY end
                    Read Booking file;
            PBOOK/PASSREC end
    PBODY end
    Write sum;
    Close files;
P end
```

1.26 *Stage 1, data structures:*

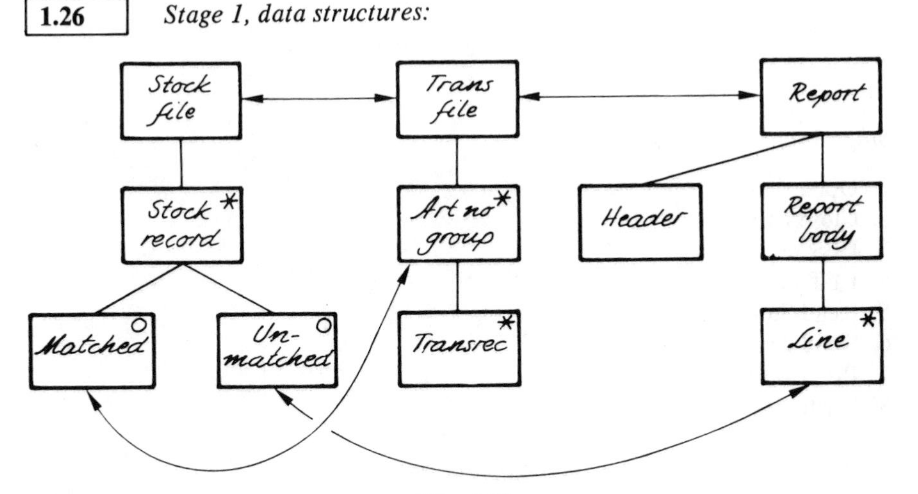

Fig 5.28

Note, here is a correspondence like that in figure 1.23! There are the same number of matched stock records as article number groups and in the same order. There is also the same number of unmatched stock records as lines and in the same order.

Stage 2, basic program structure:

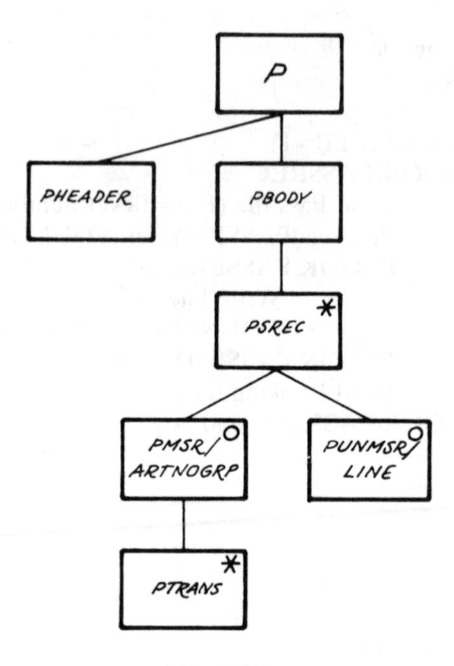

Fig 5.29

Stage 3, operations list:

1. Open files
2. Close files
3. EFS := 0
4. EFT := 0
5. Read Stock file
6. Read Transaction file
7. Process line
8. Write header

Stage 3 (continued). Allocate the operations:

1.26 (continued)

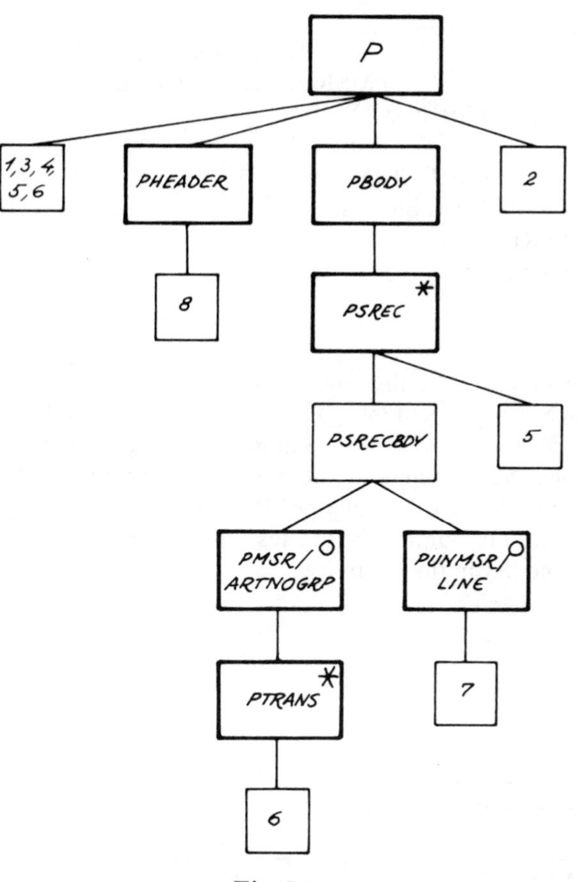

Fig 5.30

Stage 4, schematic logic:

```
P seq
        Open files;
        EFS := 0;
        EFT := 0;
        Read Stock file;
        Read Transaction file;
        Write header;
        PBODY itr until (EFS=1)
                PSREC seq
                        PSRECBDY sel (Tartno=Sartno)
                                PMSR/ARTNOGRP itr until (EFT=1 or
                                                          Tartno ≠
                                                          Sartno)
```

```
                    Read Transaction file;
                PMSR/ARTNOGRP end
            PSRECBDY alt
                Process line;
            PSRECBDY end
            Read Stock file
        PSREC end
    PBODY end
    Close files;
P end
```

It is not necessary to save the stock article number to make the condition test Tartno ≠ Sartno executable. The stock record including stock article number is accessible during the "skimming through" of an article in the transaction file. Nevertheless, a more general and thus a better solution is to save the article number once per PSREC and in the beginning and to use this saved article number in the test. Then the program will be easier (and safer) to modify in the future.

1.27

Stage 1, data structures:

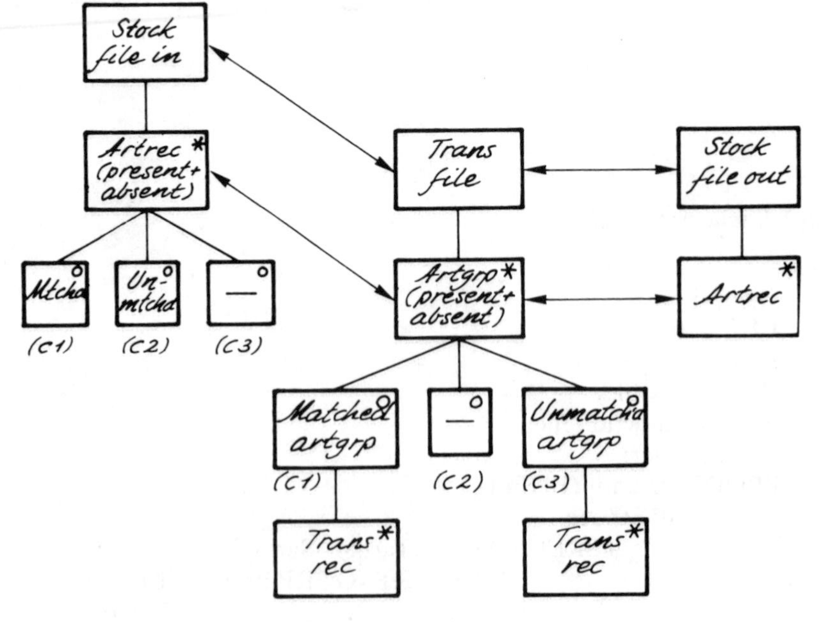

Fig 5.31a

1.27 (continued)

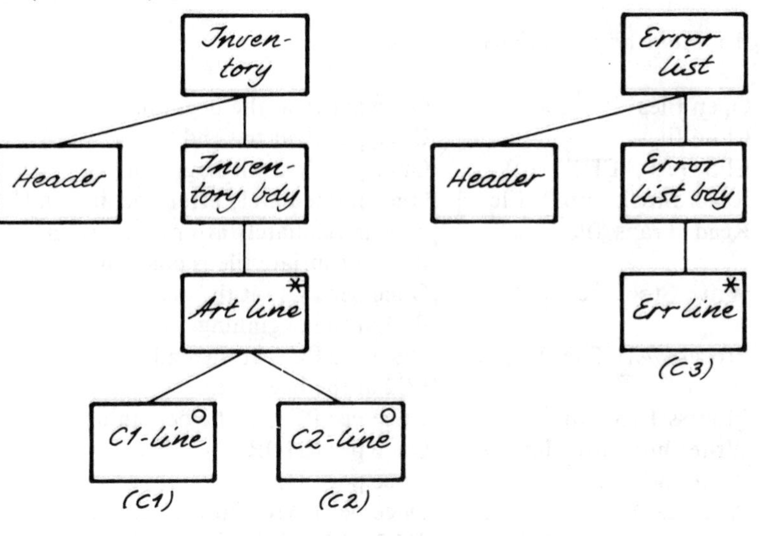

Fig 5.31b

Art line is essentially the same in C1 and C2. The selection parts are shown here only to clarify the correspondences to the other structures.

The remaining correspondences are obvious because of the names C1, C2 and C3.

Stage 2, basic program structure:

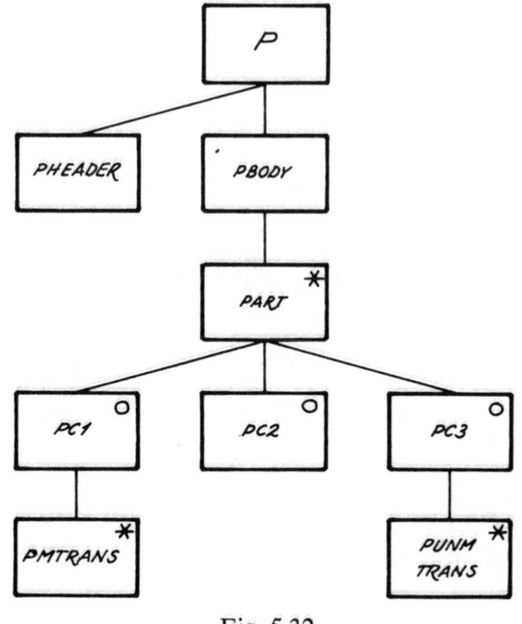

Fig 5.32

Stage 3, make an operations list . . .

Operation	When
1. Open files	Once per P, at the beginning
2. Close files	Once per P, at the end
3. EFS := 0, EFT := 0	Once per P, at the beginning
4. Read Stock input file 5. Read Trans file	Once immediately after opening and once immediately after a record in the appropriate file is consumed
6. Write Stock rec	Once per PC1, at the end, PC2 at the beginning
7. Process Art line a)	Once per PC1, at the end, PC2 at the beginning
8. Process Error line a)	Once per PC3, at the beginning
9. Write hdr Stocklist	Once per PHDR
10. Write hdr Error list	Once per PHDR
11. ACC := 0	Once per PART, at the beginning
12. ACC := ACC + QUANT	Once per PMTRANS, at the beginning
13. Update Art rec	Once per PC1, at the end
14. Artno := min (Sartno, Tartno)	Once per P, at the beginning Once per PART, at the end

a) Process line includes editing and printing.

. . . and allocate the operations:

1.27 (continued)

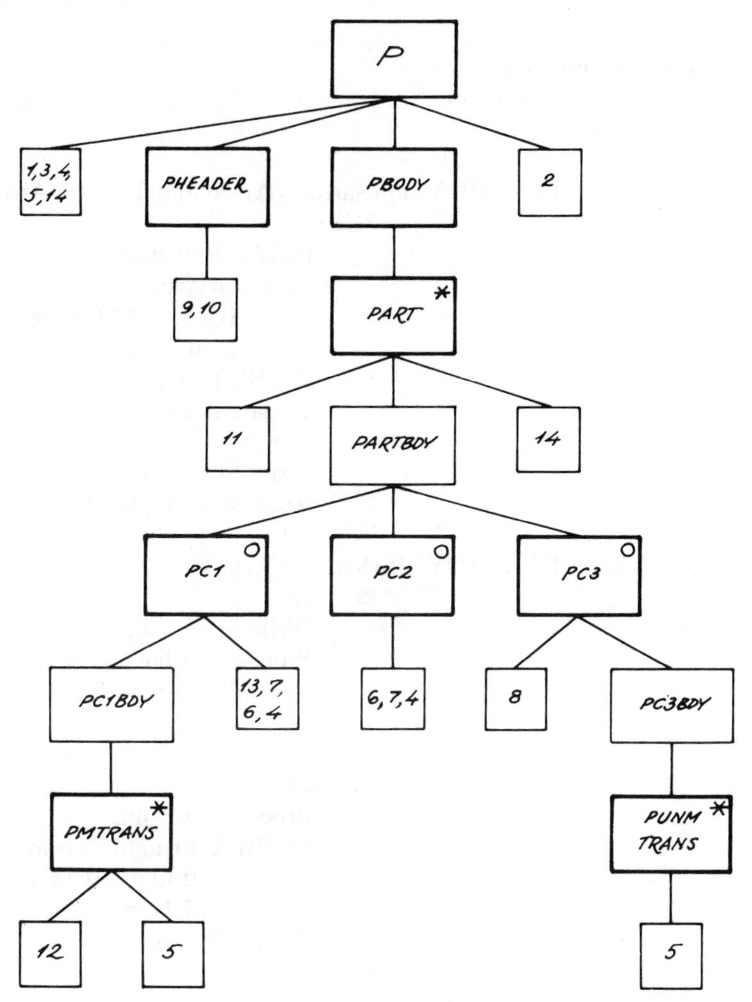

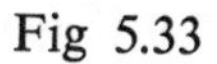
Fig 5.33

Stage 4, schematic logic:

P seq

Open files;
EFS := EFT := 0;
Read Stock input file;
Read Trans file;
Artno := min (Sartno, Tartno)
Write header Stock list;
Write header Error list;

Note: At end of file the appropriate Artno is given a preposterously high value;

```
    PBODY itr until (EFS=1 and
                 EFT=1)
         PART seq
              ACC := 0;
              PARTBDY sel (Sartno=Artno and Tartno=Artno)
                          PC1 sec
                              PC1BDY itr until (EFT=1 or
                              Tartno ≠ Artno)
                                   ACC := ACC+QUANT;
                                   Read Trans file;
                              PC1BDY end
                              Update Art rec;
                              Process Art line;
                              Write Stock rec;
                              Read Stock input file;
                          PC1 end
              PARTBDY alt (Sartno=Artno)
                          PC2 seq
                              Write Stock rec;
                              Process Art line;
                              Read Stock input file;
                          PC2 end
              PARTBDY alt
                          PC3 seq
                              Process Error line;
                              PC3BDY itr until Tartno ≠
                                   ≠ Artno or EFT=1
                                   Read Trans file;
                              PC3BDY end
                          PC3 end
              PARTBDY end
              Artno := min (Sartno, Tartno);
         PART end
    PBODY end
    Close files;
P end
```

2.1 a)

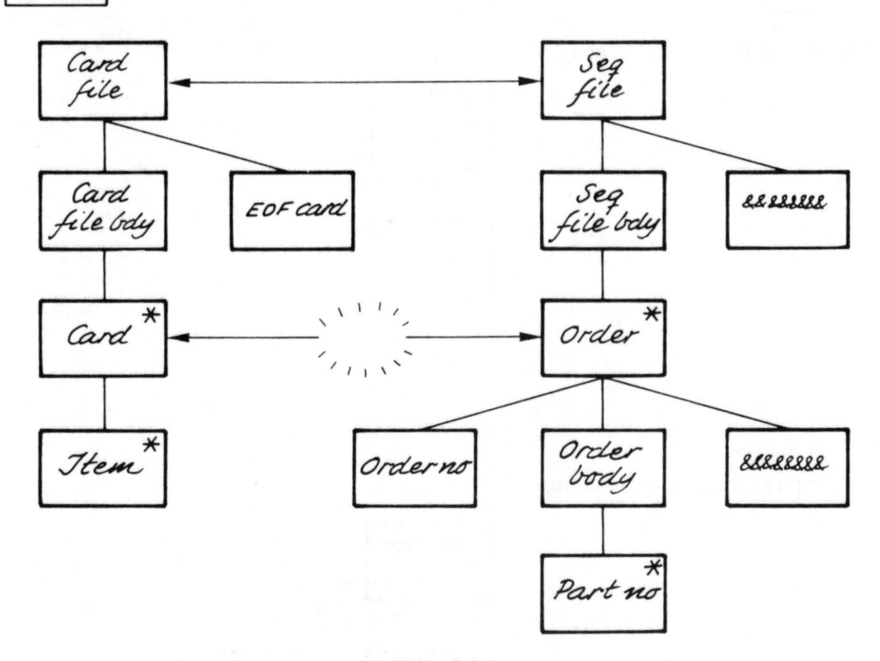

Fig 5.34

There is a structure clash between card and order because they are different entities without any relationships. Note that there is no sense in specifically showing the order number, part number and &&&&&&&& in the card file. These items have specific relationships in the sequential output file only.

As for the intermediate file, we can have a discussion like the one in the "spanned record" case. To store the whole card file as one single record would demand too big a primary storage space. Character as a record gives rise to an unacceptable number of calls for the inverted program. Consequently item remains as the common entity in both files (each card consists of an integer number of items).

2.1 b)

The intermediate file as seen by P1:

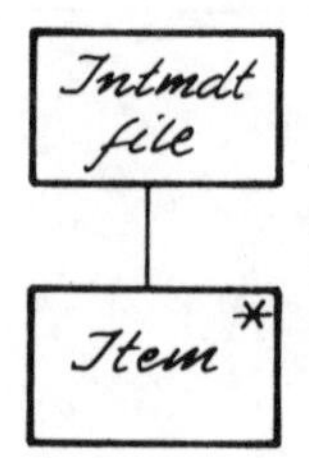

Fig 5.35

The intermediate file as seen by P2:

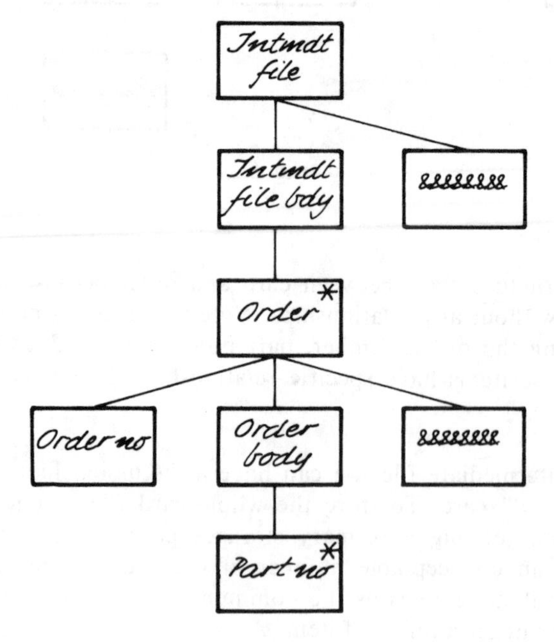

Fig 5.36

Each record in the intermediate file consists of one item only, the context "card record" having disappeared. P2 can now regard the items as "order groups" which is natural from the P2 point of view.

2.2 a)

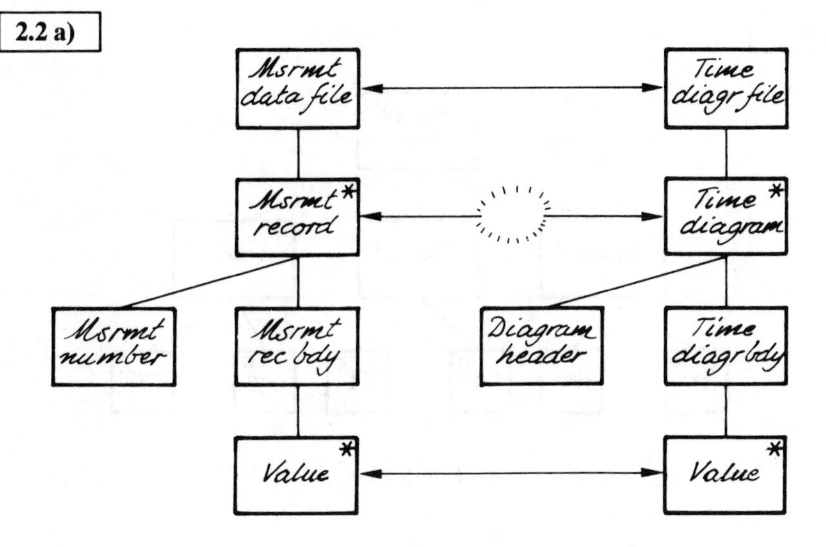

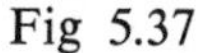

Fig 5.37

There is a structure clash between Measurement position record and Time diagram. There are no relationships between them. It is of no use that Value pairs in both files are the same in number and order. They appear in incompatible contexts.

The intermediate file records should therefore consist of Values (Measurement position number, Reading and Time respectively).

2.2 b)

The intermediate file as seen by P1:

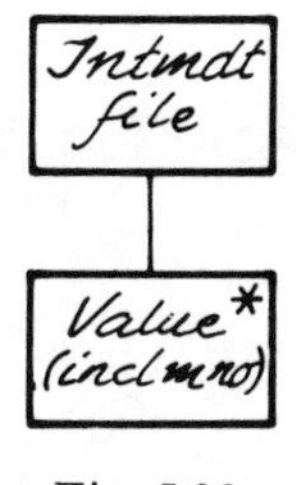

Fig 5.38

The intermediate file as seen by P2 will look like the time diagram file because Values can be arranged in the Time diagram context.

2.3

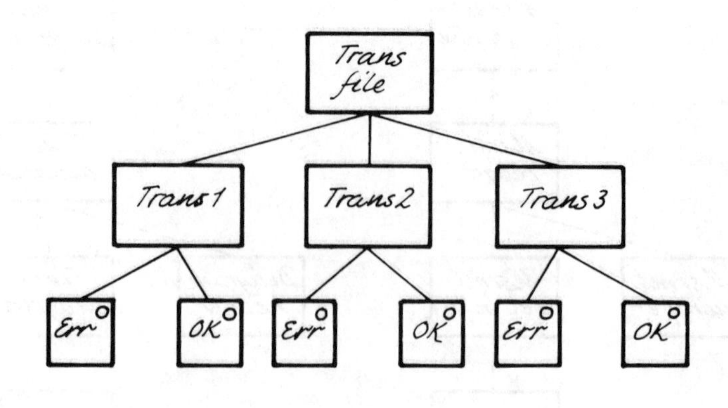

Fig 5.39

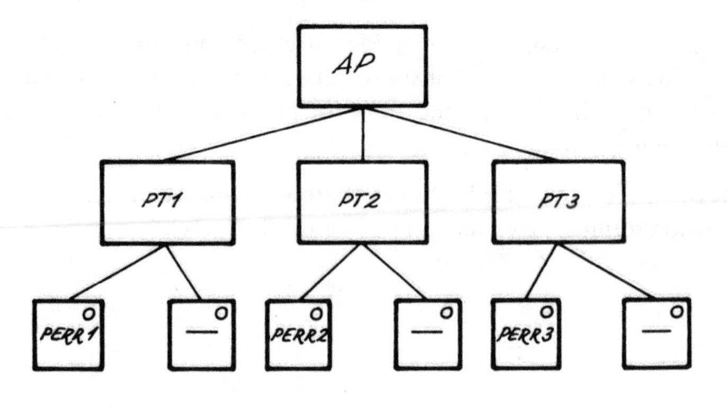

Fig 5.40

1. Open Trans file (Cobol)
2. Close Trans file (Cobol)
3. Error flag := 1
4. Move Error text 1
5. Move Error text 2
6. Move Error text 3
7. Read Trans file

2.3 (continued)

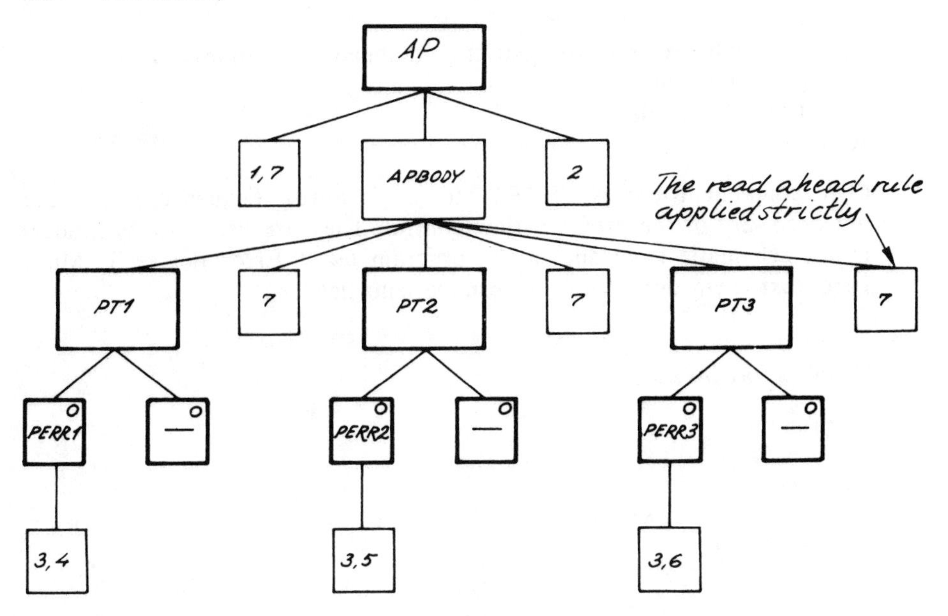

Fig 5.41

```
AP seq
    Open Trans file;
    Read Trans file;
    APBODY seq
        PT1 sel (trans type ≠ 1)
            Error flag := 1;
            Move Error text 1;
        PT1 alt
        PT1 end
        Read Trans file;
        PT2 sel (trans type ≠ 2)
            Error flag := 1;
            Move Error text 2;
        PT2 alt
        PT2 end
        Read Trans file;
        PT3 sel (trans type ≠ 3)
            Error flag := 1;
            Move Error text 3;
        PT3 alt
        PT3 end
```

```
        Read Trans file; (strict read ahead application)
    APBODY end
    Close Trans file;
AP end
```

(The component names PERR1 etc. are omitted. Sequence names are not necessary in the program flow control. They are used just as headers in the schematic logic and in the program text. "Error flag := 1; Move Error text 1; etc. don't demand a summarizing header.)

Cobol, before inversion:

```
- - -
PROCEDURE DIVISION.
AP-SEQ.       OPEN INPUT TRANS-FILE.
              READ TRANS-FILE AT END MOVE 1 TO EF-T.
APBODY-SEQ.
PT1-SLCT.     IF TRANS-TYPE = 1 GO TO PT1-OR.
              MOVE 1 TO ERROR-FLAG.
              MOVE ERROR-TEXT-1 TO ERROR-TEXT.
              GO TO PT1-END.
PT1-OR.
PT1-END.
              READ TRANS-FILE AT END MOVE 1 TO  EF-T.
PT2-SLCT.     IF TRANS-TYPE = 2 GO TO PT2-OR.
              MOVE 1 TO ERROR-FLAG.
              MOVE ERROR-TEXT-2 TO ERROR-TEXT.
              GO TO PT2-END.
PT2-OR.
PT2-END
              READ TRANS-FILE AT END MOVE 1 TO EF-T.
PT3-SLCT.     IF TRANS-TYPE = 3 GO TO PT3-OR.
              MOVE 1 TO ERROR-FLAG.
              MOVE ERROR-TEXT-3 TO ERROR-TEXT.
              GO TO PT3-END.
PT3-OR.
PT3-END.
              READ TRANS-FILE AT END MOVE 1 TO EF-T.
APBODY-END.
              CLOSE TRANS-FILE.
AP-END.
              STOP RUN.
```

2.3 (continued)

(The empty selection parts are coded. If you prefer to simplify the program slightly by eliminating the empty selection parts then you must be prepared to do a lot more thinking the day (or night) you are asked to modify the program to process correct transactions. As the code is presented above, it is *very* easy to modify according to the demand just mentioned. If your Cobol doesn't allow empty paragraphs you will have, of course, to add EXIT in the appropriate places.)

Inverted program:

```
- - -
WORKING-STORAGE SECTION.
77 QS PICTURE 9 VALUE 1.
- - -
PROCEDURE DIVISION USING ERROR-FLAG, ERROR-
TEXT, TRANS-TYPE.
AP-SEQ. GO TO Q1, Q2, Q3, Q4 DEPENDING ON QS.
Q1.                                        (← first READ)
PT1-SLCT. IF TRANS-TYPE = 1 GO TO PT1-OR.
          MOVE 1 TO ERROR-FLAG.
          MOVE ERROR-TEXT-1 TO ERROR-TEXT.
          GO TO PT1-END.
PT1-OR.
PT1-END.
          MOVE 2 TO QS.                    }
          EXIT PROGRAM.                    }(← second READ)
Q2.                                        }
PT2-SLCT. IF TRANS-TYPE = 2 GO TO PT2-OR.
          MOVE 1 TO ERROR-FLAG.
          MOVE ERROR-TEXT-2 TO ERROR-TEXT.
          GO TO PT2-END.
PT2-OR.
PT2-END.
          MOVE 3 TO QS.                    }
          EXIT PROGRAM.                    }(← third READ)
Q3.                                        }
PT3-SLCT. IF TRANS-TYPE = 3 GO TO PT3-OR.
          MOVE 1 TO ERROR-FLAG.
          MOVE ERROR-TEXT-3 TO ERROR-TEXT.
          GO TO PT3-END.
PT3-OR.
PT3-END.
```

```
              MOVE 4 TO QS.
              EXIT PROGRAM.             (← fourth READ)
Q4.
AP-END.       EXIT PROGRAM.
```

Fortran, before inversion (subroutines "read record" (READRC) and "move string" (MOVEST) are presumed):

```
- - -
0101  CALL READRC(TRANS)
0201  CONTINUE
0303  IF(TRTYP.EQ.1) GO TO 0304.
      ERRFL=1
      CALL MOVEST(ERRTX1,ERRTX).
      GO TO 0399
0304  CONTINUE
0399  CONTINUE
      CALL READRC(TRANS)
0403  IF(TRTYP.EQ.2) GO TO 0404
      ERRFL=1
      CALL MOVEST(ERRTX2,ERRTX)
      GO TO 0499
0404  CONTINUE
0499  CONTINUE
      CALL READRC(TRANS)
0503  IF(TRTYP.EQ.3) GO TO 0504
      ERRFL=1
      CALL MOVEST(ERRTX3,ERRTX)
      GO TO 0599
0504  CONTINUE
0599  CONTINUE
      CALL READRC(TRANS)
0299  CONTINUE
0199  STOP
      END
```

Inverted program:

```
- - -  (L01 is given the initial value = 1 by the main program)1)
0101   GO TO (01001, 01002, 01003, 01004), L01
01001  CONTINUE                        (← first CALL READRC)
```

1) Better to use a communication area, cf. section 4.1.

2.3 (continued)

```
0201   CONTINUE
0303   IF(TRTYP.EQ.1) GO TO 0304
       ERRFL=1
       CALL MOVEST(ERRTX1,ERRTX)
       GO TO 0399
0304   CONTINUE
0399   CONTINUE
       L01=2                  )
       RETURN                 }(← second CALL READRC)
01002  CONTINUE               )
0403   IF(TRTYP.EQ.2) GO TO 0404
       ERRFL=1
       CALL MOVEST(ERRTX2,ERRTX)
       GO TO 0499
0404   CONTINUE
0499   CONTINUE
       L01=3                  )
       RETURN                 }(← third CALL READRC)
01003  CONTINUE               )
0503   IF(TRTYP.EQ.3) GO TO 0504
       ERRFL=1
       CALL MOVEST(ERRTX3,ERRTX)
       GO TO 0599
0504   CONTINUE
0599   CONTINUE
       L01=4                  )
       RETURN                 }(← fourth CALL READRC)
01004  CONTINUE               )
0299   CONTINUE
0199   RETURN
       END
```

Algol, before inversion (procedures "read record" (readrec) and "move string" (movestring) are presumed):

```
begin integer transtype, errorflag;
    ———
    AP-seq: readrec(trans);
        APBODY-seq:
            PT1-slct: if transtype = 1 then go to PT1-or;
                errorflag := 1;
                movestring(errortext1, errortext);
                go to PT1-end;
```

```
            PT1-or:
            PT1-end;
                  readrec(trans);
            PT2-slct:
                  if transtype = 2 then go to PT2-or;
                  errorflag := 1;
                  movestring(errortext2, errortext);
                  go to PT2-end;
            PT2-or:
            PT2-end:
                  readrec(trans);
            PT3-slct:
                  if transtype = 3 then go to PT3-or;
                  errorflag := 1;
                  movestring(errortext3, errortext);
                  go to PT3-end;
            PT3-or:
            PT3-end:
      APBODY-end:
                  readrec(trans);
AP-end: end
```

Inverted program:

```
          procedure APW (transtype, errorflag, errortext, QS);

          begin (QS is given the initial value = 1 by the main program)1)

                   switch S := Q1, Q2, Q3, Q4;
(first readrec →)   AP seq: go to S[QS];
                Q1:  PT1-slct: if transtype=1 then go to PT1-or;
                               errorflag := 1;
                               movestring (errortext1, errortext);
                               go to PT1-end;
                      PT1-or:
                      PT1-end:
                               QS := 2
(second readrec →){
                               go to AP-end;
                Q2:  PT2-slct: if transtype=2 then go to PT2-or;
                               errorflag := 1;
                               movestring (errortext2, errortext);
                               go to PT2-end;
```

1) Better to use a communication area, cf. section 4.1.

2.3 (continued)

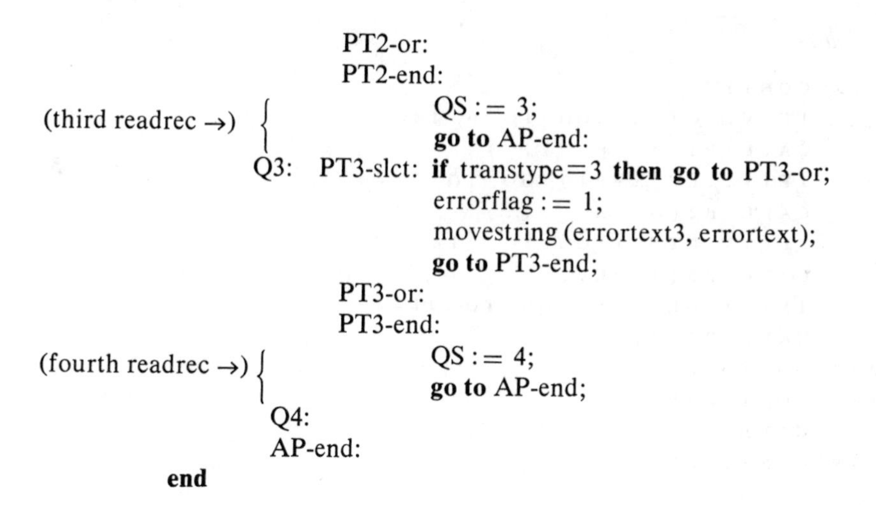

```
                              PT2-or:
                              PT2-end:
(third readrec →)  {                   QS := 3;
                                       go to AP-end:
                   Q3:  PT3-slct:      if transtype=3 then go to PT3-or;
                                       errorflag := 1;
                                       movestring (errortext3, errortext);
                                       go to PT3-end;
                              PT3-or:
                              PT3-end:
(fourth readrec →) {                   QS := 4;
                                       go to AP-end;
                     Q4:
                     AP-end:
          end
```

3.1

Cobol:

```
PBASE-POSIT.      - - -
PBASE-OK-SEQ.     IF V1 > K GO TO PBASE-ADMIT.
                  PERFORM P1.
                  IF V2 < OR = (X + V1) GO TO
                  PBASE-ADMIT.
                  PERFORM P2.
                  IF V3 < Y GO TO PBASE-ADMIT.
                  PERFORM P3.
                  IF V4 > OR = (X + Y) GO TO PBASE-
                  ADMIT.
                  PERFORM P4.
                  GO TO PBASE-END.
PBASE-OK-END.
PBASE-ADMIT.
                  PERFORM ERROR.
PBASE-END.        - - -
```

Fortran:

```
0143  CONTINUE
0201  IF(V1.GT.K) GO TO 0144
      CALL P1(A, B, ...)
      IF(V2.LE.X+V1) GO TO 0144
      CALL P2(G, H, ...)
      IF(V3.LT.Y) GO TO 0144
      CALL P3(J, K, ...)
      IF(V4.GE.X+Y) GO TO 0144
      CALL P4(P, Q, ...)
0299  GO TO 0199
0144  CONTINUE
      CALL ERROR(V, Z, ...)
0199  CONTINUE
      - - -
```

Algol:

```
PBASEposit:
        PBASEOKseq: if V1 >K then go to PBASEadmit;
                    P1 (a, b, ...);
                    if V2 ≤ (X + V1) then go to PBASEadmit;
                    P2 (g, h, ...);
                    if V3 < Y then go to PBASEadmit;
                    P3 (j, k, ...);
                    if V4 ≥ (X + Y) then go to PBASEadmit;
                    P4 (p, q, ...);
                    go to PBASEend;
        PBASEOKend:
PBASEadmit:
                    ERROR (V1, Z, ...);
PBASEend:           end
                    ———
```

3.2

Data structures:

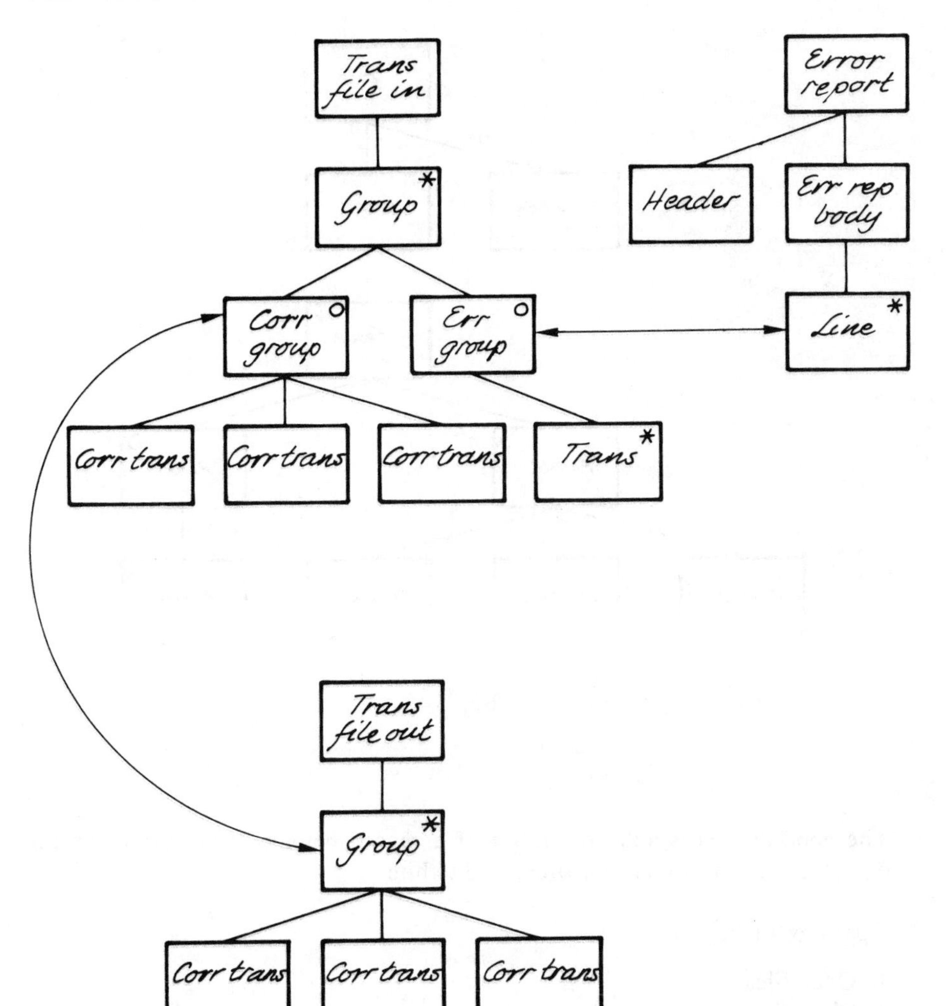

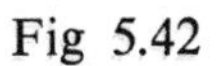
Fig 5.42

Basic program structure:

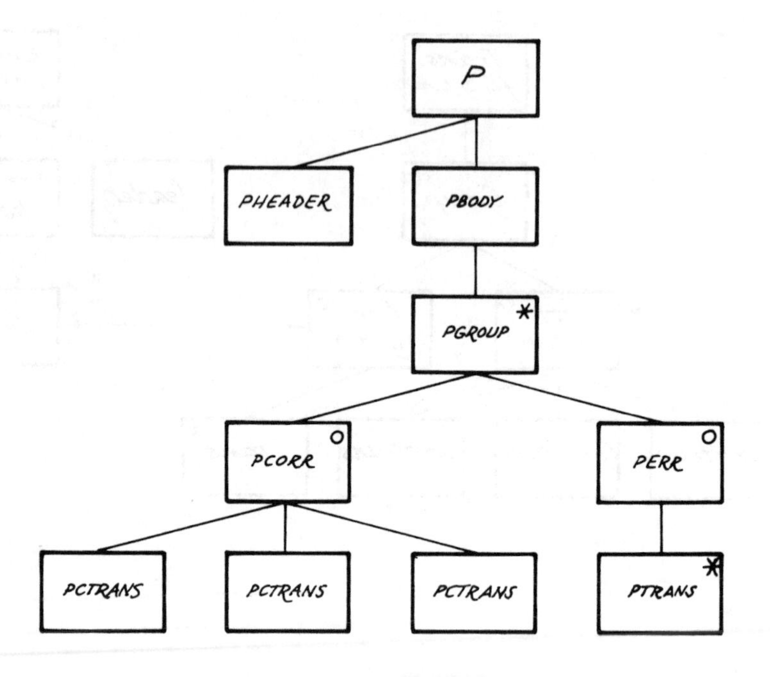

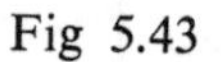
Fig 5.43

The good demon is able to tell you if a record belongs to a correct group or not, *each* time a record is presented to him.

Operations list:

1. Open files
2. Close files
3. Read trans file
4. Write trans record
5. Write error line
6. Save groupno
7. Write header

3.2 (continued)

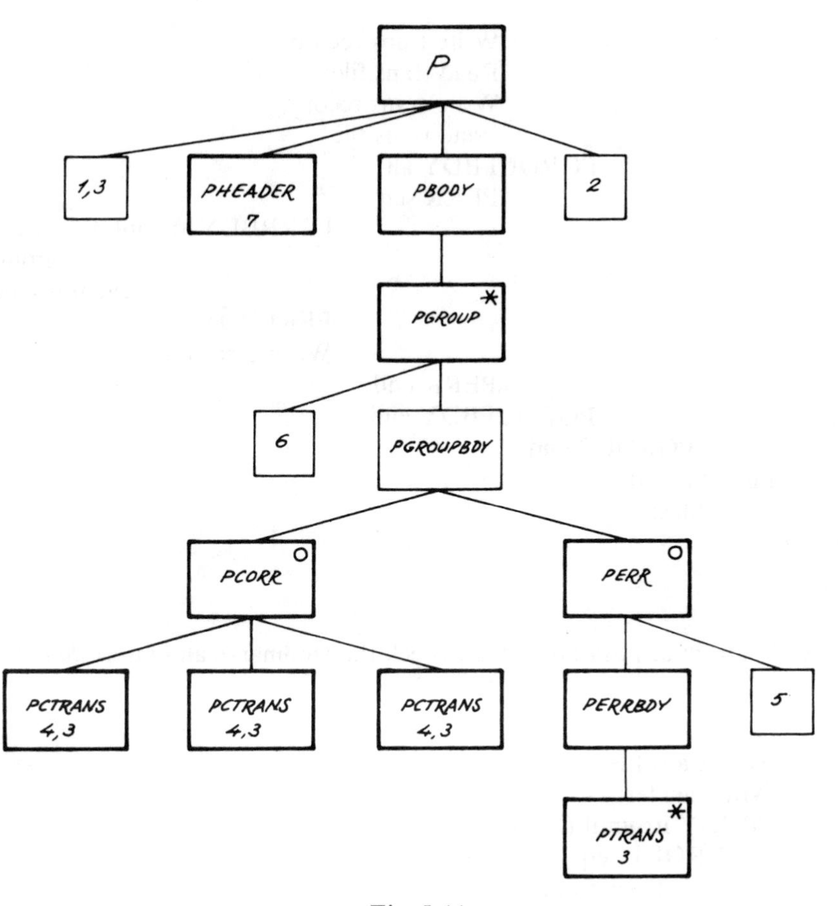

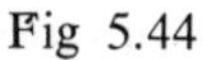

Fig 5.44

Schematic logic, step 1:

```
P seq
     Open files;
     Read trans file;
     Write header;
     PBODY iter until (EF=1)
            PGROUP seq
                    Save groupno;
                    PGROUPBDY sel (correct group)
                            Write trans record;
                            Read trans file;
```

```
                              Write trans record;
                              Read trans file;
                              Write trans record;
                              Read trans file;
                    PGROUPBDY alt
                              PERR seq
                                        PERRBDY itr until (EF=1 or
                                                          new group)
                                                  Read trans file;
                                        PERRBDY end
                                        Write error line;
                              PERR end
                    PGROUPBDY end
          PGROUP end
     PBODY end
     Close files;
P end
```

Step 2: introduce *posit* and *admit,* check the landmarks and insert *quit.*

```
P seq
     Open files;
     Read trans file;
     Write header;
     PBODY itr until (EF=1)
        PGROUP seq
                Save groupno;
(check the     } PGROUPBDY posit (correct group)
first trans)   } PGROUPBDY quit (transtype ≠ A)
                             Write trans record;
                             Read trans file;
(check the     { PGROUPBDY quit (trans type ≠ A)
second trans)  { PGROUPBDY quit (new groupno)
               { PGROUPBDY quit (EF=1)
                             Write trans record;
                             Read trans file;
(check the     { PGROUBDY quit (trans type ≠ A)
third trans)   { PGROUPBDY quit (new groupno)
               { PGROUPBDY quit (EF=1)
                             Write trans record;
                             Read trans file;
```

3.2 (continued)

```
(check the      } PGROUPBDY quit (the same groupno and
fourth trans)   } EF=0)
                      PGROUPBDY admit
                           PERR seq
                                PERRBDY itr until (EF=1 or
                                                    new groupno)
                                     Read trans file;
                                PERRBDY end
                                Write error line;
                           PERR end
                      PGROUPBDY end
                 PGROUP end
     PBODY end
     Close files;
P end
```

Step 3: take care of intolerable side effects, check that every *quit* is executable.

```
P seq
     Open files;
     Read trans file;
     Write header;
     PBODY itr until (EF=1)
               PGROUP seq
                      Save groupno;
                      PGROUPBDY posit (correct group)
"Write trans       }  PGROUPBDY quit (trans type ≠ A)
record"=           }           Save trans record in T1;
intolerable        }           Read trans file;
side effect,       }  PGROUPBDY (quit trans type ≠ A)
the transaction    }  PGROUPBDY (quit new group no)
can belong to an   }  PGROUPBDY (quit EF=1)
erroneous group    }           Save trans record in T2;
                               Read trans file;
                      PGROUPBDY (quit trans type ≠ A)
                      PGROUPBDY (quit new groupno)
                      PGROUPBDY (quit EF=1)
                               Save trans record in T3;
                               Read trans file;
                      PGROUPBDY (quit the same groupno and
                                                     EF=0)
```

3.2 (continued)

```
                        Write T1; (Here all transactions can be
                        Write T2; output. Passing the last quit
                        Write T3; means that we have found a
                                   correct group.)
                PGROUPBDY admit
                        PERR seq
                                PERRBDY itr until (EF=1 or
                                                   new groupno)
                                        Read trans file;
                                PERRBDY end
                                Write error line;
                        PERR end
                PGROUPBDY end
        PGROUP end
    PBODY end
    Close files;
P end
```

3.3

Backtracking, Step 1:

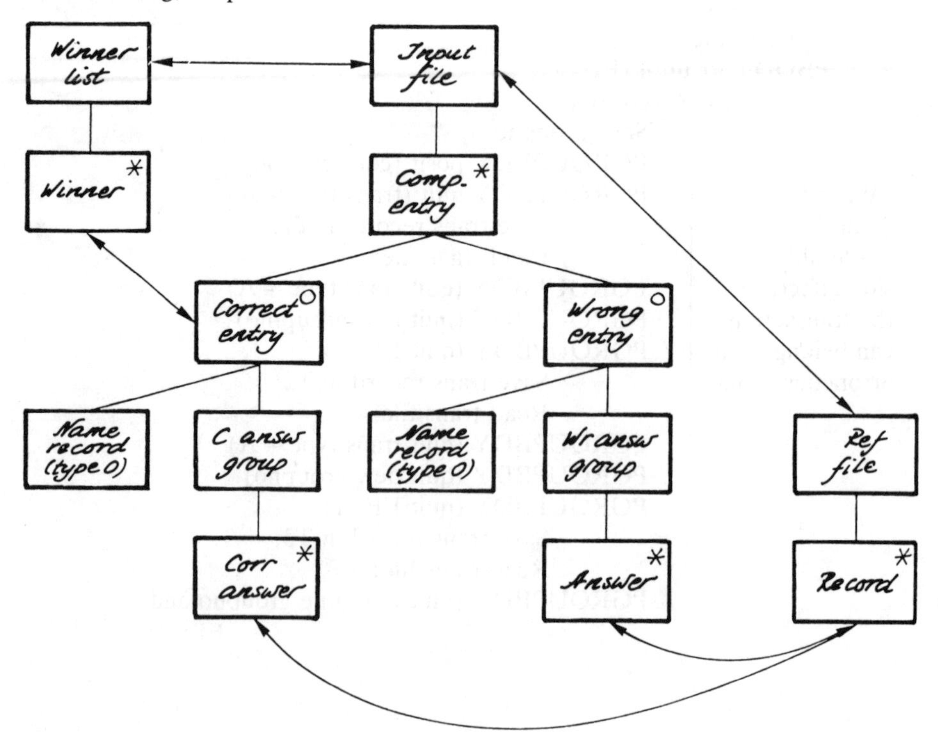

Fig 5.45

Program structure = input file structure. (There are as many "Correct entries" in the input file as "Winners" in the list of winners, and in the same order; the records in the reference file can be read as many times as the total number of answers in the input file, and in the same order).

Operations list:

1. Close files
2. Open files
3. Write winner-line
4. Zeroise winner-counter
5. Add 1 to the winner-counter
6. Read the reference file with key = answerno.+answer alternative
7. Read input file
8. EF := 0

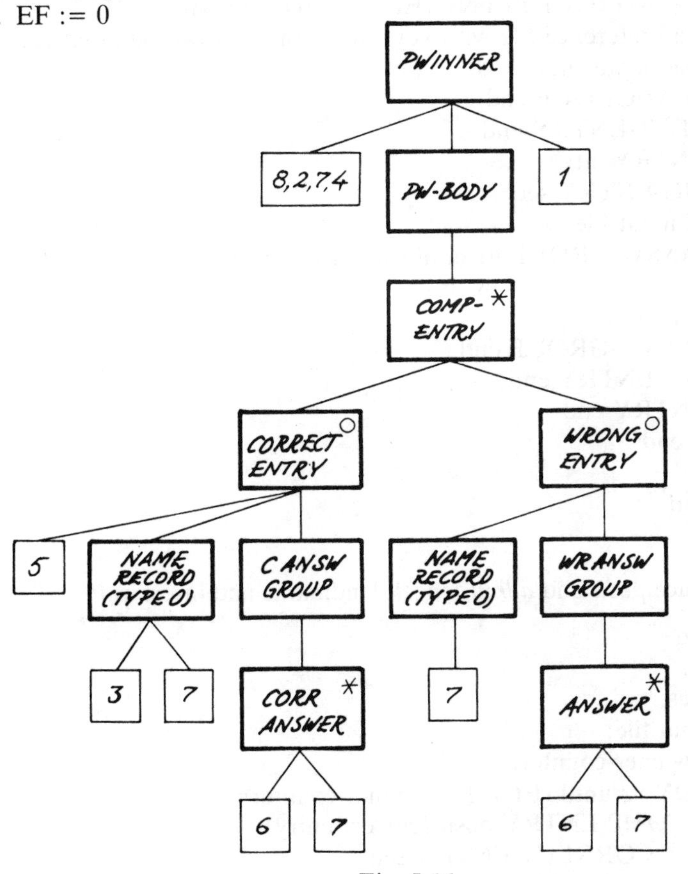

Fig 5.46

3.3 (continued)

Schematic logic:

```
PWINNER seq
  EF := 0;
  Open files;
  Read input file;
  Zeroise winner-counter;
  PW-BODY itr until (EF=1 or winner-counter=20)
    COMP-ENTRY sel (correct entry)
      CORRECT-ENTRY seq
        Add 1 to winner-counter;
        Write winner line;
        Read input file;
        CANSW-GROUP itr until (EF=1 or record=type 0)
          Read reference file with key=answerno.+answer alternative;
          Read input file;
        CANSW-GROUP end
      CORRECT-ENTRY end
    COMP-ENTRY alt
      WRONG-ENTRY seq
        Read input file;
        WRANSW-GROUP itr until (EF=1 or record=type 0)
          Read reference file with key=answerno.+answer alternative;
          Read input file;
        WRANSW-GROUP end
      WRONG-ENTRY end
    COMP-ENTRY end
  PW-BODY end
  Close files;
PWINNER end
```

Step 2: introduce *posit* and *admit,* check landmarks and insert *quit.*

```
PWINNER seq
    EF := 0;
    Open files;
    Read input file;
    Zeroise winner-counter;
    PW-BODY itr until (EF = 1 or winner-counter=20)
            COMP-ENTRY posit (correct entry)
                CORRECT-ENTRY seq
                        Add 1 to winner-counter;
```

```
                        Writer winner line;
                        Read input file;
                        CANSW-GROUP itr until (EF=1 or record=type 0)
                            Read reference file with key=answerno.
                            +answer alternative;
(First          COMP-ENTRY quit (not found))
error found)                Read input file;
                        CANSW-GROUP end
                    CORRECT-ENTRY end
                COMP-ENTRY admit
                    WRONG-ENTRY seq
                        Read input file;
                        WRANSW-GROUP iter until (EF=1 or record=
                        =type 0)
                            Read reference file with key=answerno.+
                            +answer alternative;
                            Read input file;
                        WRANSW-GROUP end
                    WRONG-ENTRY end
                COMP-ENTRY end
        PW-BODY end
        Close files;
PWINNER end
```

Step 3: take care of intolerable side-effects, and check that all *quits* are executable.

```
PWINNER seq
  EF := 0;
  Open files;
  Read input file;
  Zeroise winner-counter;
  PW-BODY itr until (EF=1 or winner-counter=20)
    COMP-ENTRY posit (correct entry)
      CORRECT-ENTRY seq
(Writing winner
line before           Store winner-line;
whole entry
analysed=             Read input file;
intolerable           CANSW-GROUP itr until (EF=1 or record=type 0)
side-effect)            Read reference file with key=answerno.+anser
                        alternative;
```

3.3 (continued)

```
    COMP-ENTRY quit (not found);
                        Read input file;
                      CANSW-GROUP end
(Operation put
forward. Earlier      Add 1 to winner-counter;
calculation ->
intolerable           Write stored winner-line; (NOW we can write)
side-effect)
      CORRECT-ENTRY end
    COMP-ENTRY admit
      WRONG-ENTRY seq
(We do not need
to start from         Read input file;
the beginning
of the entry –        WRANS-GROUP itr until (EF=1 or record=type 0)
records already
read=good
side-effect)

(This operation
can be 'optimised       [Read reference file . . .]
out' – it is enough
to find the first
error)
                        Read input file;
                      WRANS-GROUP end
      WRONG-ENTRY end
    COMP-ENTRY end
  PW-BODY end
  Close files;
PWINNER end
```

3.4

Step 1: (the good demon).

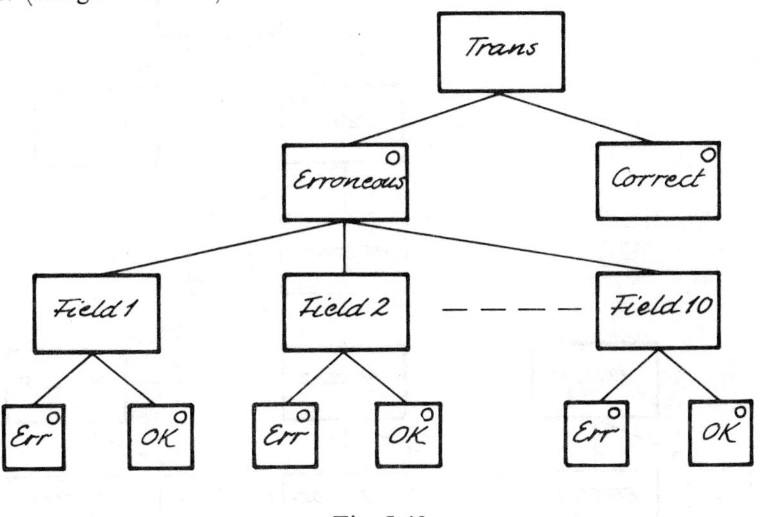

Fig 5.48

The good demon can determine whether the *transaction* is erroneous or not. We ourselves can determine which *field* or *fields* are erroneous.

The structure of the error message is the same as that of the error branch in the transaction structure so we can use the transaction structure as a basic program structure.

1. ANALYSIS-FIELD(N) := E
2. ERROR-LINE(N) := ERROR-TEXT(N)
3. Edit and send error message
4. Perform P(N)
5. Perform P0

3.4 (continued)

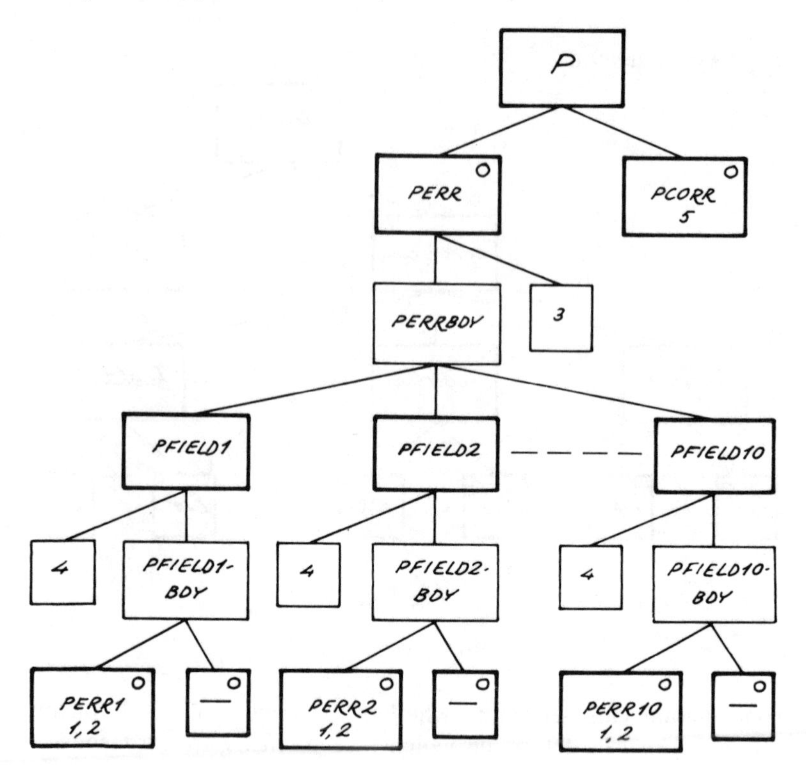

Fig 5.49

```
P sel error trans
    PERR seq
        PERRBDY seq
            PFIELD1 seq
                exec P1;
                PFIELD1-BDY sel (FIELD1 error)
                    ANALYSIS-FIELD(1) := E;
                    ERROR-LINE(1) := ERROR-TEXT(1);
                PFIELD-BDY end
            PFIELD1 end
            PFIELD2 seq
                exec P2;
                PFIELD2-BDY sel (FIELD2 error)
```

```
                ANALYSIS-FIELD(2) := E;
                ERROR-LINE(2) := ERROR-TEXT(2);
            PFIELD2-BDY end
        PFIELD2 end
        - - -
        - - -
        - - -
        PFIELD10 seq
            exec P10;
            PFIELD10-BDY sel (FIELD10 error)
                ANALYSIS-FIELD(10) := E;
                ERROR-LINE(10) := ERROR-
                TEXT(10);
            PFIELD10-BDY end
        PFIELD10 end
    PERRBDY end
    Edit and send error message;
  PERR end
P alt
  exec P0;
P end
```

Step 2: (posit – admit, quit).

Replace P *select* by *posit* and P *alt* by P *admit.*

Where can we insert *quit?* It is possible only after all field analyses have been done, that is after PERRBDY *end.* Here we insert: P *quit* ANALYSIS-FIELD(1) to and including ANALYSIS-FIELD(10)=SPACE. If at least one F occurs the *quit* will not be executed, the error message will be edited and sent and the *admit* part will be skipped.

Step 3: (side effects, *quit* executable).

If the *quit* is executed, only P1 to and including P10 are executed. These procedures have to be executed anyway to enable testing of the fields. This is a favourable side effect. The only *quit* is executable.

Appendix 1

Coding rules

The purpose of the rules are

- to make it easier to trace components from the design documents to the code text
- to get a block structure with a nest free code, *making subroutines reentrant* when program inversion is used.

The coding rules are not specifically stated to create an easy-to-read code. *You need not read the code to understand the program,* since you have better look at the data structures, program structure, operations-list, program structure with allocated operations and schematic logic, in other words: the design documents. As a JSP-programmer *you need the code only to get the computer system to do what you have designed in detail.*

COBOL

Sequence:

```
A seq                                A-SEQ.
  ---                                  ---
  ---                                  ---
A end                                A-END.
```

Iteration:

```
B itr until (C1)                B-ITR. IF C1 GO TO B-END.
  ---                             ---
  ---                             ---
                                  GO TO B-ITR.
B end                           B-END.
```

Selection:

```
C sel (C1)                      C-SEL. IF NOT C1 GO TO C-ALT1.
  ---                             ---
                                  GO TO C-END.
C alt (C2)                      C-ALT1.  IF NOT C2 GO TO C-ALT2.
  ---                             ---
                                  GO TO C-END.
C alt (else)                    C-ALT2.
  ---                             ---
C end                           C-END.
```

Backtracking in selection:

```
D posit                         D-POSIT
  ---                             ---
  ---                             ---
D quit (C1)                     IF C1 GO TO D-ADMIT.
  ---                             ---
                                  GO TO D-END.
D admit                         D-ADMIT.
  ---                             ---
D end                           D-END.
```

Backtracking in iteration:

```
E itr                           E-ITR.
  ---                             ---
  ---                             ---
E quit (C1)                       IF C1 GO TO E-END.
  ---                             ---
                                  GO TO E-ITR.
E end                           E-END.
```

Program inversion, F calls G:

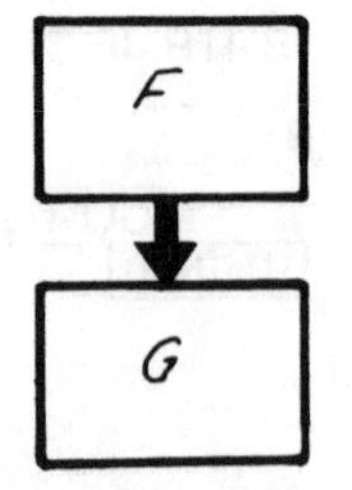

Fig A.1.1

(Below, the schematic logic is modified to accomodate program inversion. The coding technique is of course the same as in chapter 2.)

```
F seq                                  F-SEQ.
  ---                                    ---
  Call G (Message);                      CALL 'G' USING MESSAGE.
  ---                                    ---
  FA itr until (C1)                    FA-ITR. IF C1 GO TO FA-END.
    ---                                  ---
    Call G (Message);                  CALL G' USING MESSAGE.
    ---                                  ---
                                         GO TO FA-ITR.
  FA end                               FA-END.
F end                                  F-END.

G seq                                  G-SEQ.      (QS = 1 initially)
(Open intermediate file and the            GO TO Q1, Q2, Q3, Q4
first read are omitted.)                     DEPENDING ON QS.
  ---                                  Q1. ---

                                           MOVE 2 TO QS.
  Wait for the next message;               GO TO QX.
    ---                                Q2. ---

                                           MOVE 3 TO QS.
  Wait for the next message;               GO TO QX.
    ---                                Q3. ---

  GA itr until (V2)                    GA-ITR.
                                         IF C2 GO TO GA-END.
    ---                                  ---

                                           MOVE 4 TO QS.
  Wait for the next message;               GO TO QX.
                                       Q4. GO TO GA-ITR.
  GA end                               GA-END.

                                       QX. EXIT PROGRAM.

G end                                  G-END.
```

Alternative:

```
F seq                              F-SEQ SECTION.
  ---                                ---
  Call G(Message);                   PERFORM G-SEQ.
  ---                                ---
  FA itr until (C1)                FA-ITR. IF C1 GO TO FA-END.
    ---                              ---
    Call G(Message);                 PERFORM G-SEQ.
    ---                              ---
                                     GO TO FA-ITR.
  FA end                           FA-END.
F end                              F-END. EXIT.

G seq                              G-SEQ SECTION. (QS = 1 initially)
                                      GO TO Q1, Q2, Q3, Q4
                                        DEPENDING ON QS
  ---                              Q1. ---
                                        MOVE 2 TO QS.
  Wait for the next message;            GO TO QX.
  ---                              Q2. ---
                                        MOVE 3 TO QS.
  Wait for the next message;            GO TO QX.
  ---                              Q3. ---
                                   GA-ITR.
  GA itr until (C2)                     IF C2 GO TO GA-END.
    ---                                 ---
                                        MOVE 4 TO QS.
  Wait for the next message;            GO TO QX.
                                   Q4. GO TO GA-ITR.
  GA end                           GA-END.
                                   QX. EXIT.
G end                              G-END.
```

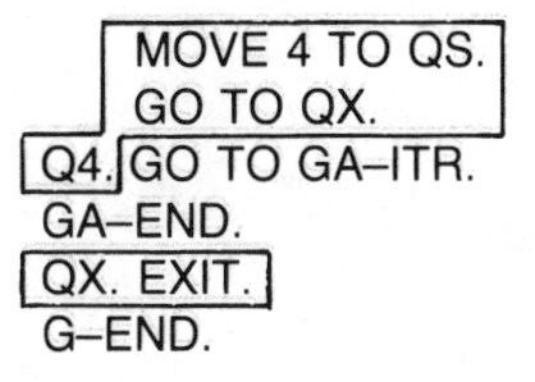

If G calls F, each "Write message" must be replaced by "Wait for the next call", which will be coded

```
        MOVE n TO QS.
        GO TO QX.
  Qn.
```

Ada

Please, read the text within the frame at page 194 before you read the code.

The block structure of Ada does not prevent program inversion if you use tasking.

Sequence:

```
A seq                                   --A SEQ
  ---                                     ---
  ---                                     ---
A end                                   --A END
```

Iteration:

```
B itr until (C1)                        --B ITR
                                          while not C1
                                          loop
  ---                                     ---
  ---                                     ---
                                          end loop;
B end                                   --B END
```

Selection:

```
C sel (C1)                              --C SEL
                                          if C1 then
  ---                                     ---
C alt (C2)                              --C ALT1
                                          elsif C2 then
  ---                                     ---
C alt (else)                            --C ALT 2
                                          else
  ---                                     ---
                                          end if;
C end                                   --C END
```

Backtracking in selection:

```
D posit
  ---
  ---
D quit (C1)

  ---

D admit
  ---
D end
```

```
-- D POSIT
  ---
  ---
-- D QUIT
  if C1 then goto D_ADMIT
  end if;
  ---
  goto D_END
<<D ADMIT>>
  ---
<<D END>>
```

Backtracking in iteration:

```
E itr

  ---
  ---
E quit (C1)

,   ---

E end
```

```
-- E ITR
  loop
  ---
  ---
  if C1 then exit
  end if;
  ---
  end loop;
-- E END
```

Program inversion, F calls G:

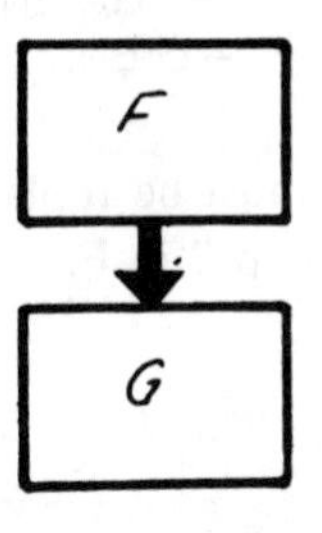

Fig A 1.2

(Below, the schematic logic is modified to accomodate program inversion.)

```
F seq
  ---
  Call G (Message);
  ---
  FA itr until (C1)
```

```
-- F SEQ
---
  FORWARD_DS (DS_MESSAGE)
  ---
  -- FA ITR
    while not C1
    loop
```

```
    ---                                    ---
    Call G (Message);;                     FORWARD_DS (DS_MESSAGE)
    ---                                    ---
                                           end loop;
  FA end                                 -- FA END
F end                                  -- F END
```

(G: a "task" with entry FORWARD_DS (DS: in DS_MESSAGE))

```
G seq                                  -- G SEQ
(Open intermediate file and the
first read are omitted.)
  ---                                    ---
  Wait for the next message;             accept FORWARD_DS (DS_MES-
                                         SAGE);
  ---                                    ---
                                       end FORWARD_DS;
  Wait for the next message;             accept FORWARD_DS (DS_MES-
                                         SAGE);
  ---                                    ---
                                       end FORWARD_DS;
  GA itr until (C2)                      -- GA ITR
                                           while not C2
                                           loop
    ---                                    ---
    Wait for the next message;             accept FORWARD_DS (DS_MES-
                                           SAGE);
                                         ---
                                       end FORWARD_DS;
  GA end                                 -- GA END
G end                                  -- G END
```

If G calls F, each "Write message" must be replaced by "Wait for the next call", which will be coded as an "accept" in F.

PASCAL

> Please, read the text within the frame at page 194 before you read the code.

Sequence:

```
A seq                                  (*A SEQ*)
  ---                                    ---
  ---                                    ---
A end                                  (*AEND*)
```

Iteration:

	nn = consecutive component number
B itr until (C1)	nn02: (*B ITR*)
	if C1 then goto nn99;
– – –	– – –
– – –	– – –
	goto nn02;
B end	nn99: (*B END*)

Selection:

C sel (C1)	nn03: (*C SEL*)
	if not C1 then goto nn04;
– – –	– – –
	goto nn99;
C alt (C2)	nn04: (*C ALT1*)
	if not C2 then goto nn05;
– – –	– – –
	goto nn99;
C alt (else)	nn05: (*C ALT2*)
– – –	– – –
C end	nn99: (*C END*)

Backtracking in selection:

D posit	nn44: (*D POSIT*)
– – –	– – –
– – –	– – –
D quit (C1)	if C1 then goto nn45;
– – –	– – –
	goto nn99;
D admit	nn45: (*D ADMIT*)
– – –	– – –
D end	nn99: (*D END*)

Backtracking in iteration:

E itr	nn02: (*E ITR*)
– – –	– – –
– – –	– – –
E quit (C1)	if C1 then goto nn99;
– – –	– – –
	goto nn02;
E end	nn99: (*E END*)

Program inversion, F calls G:

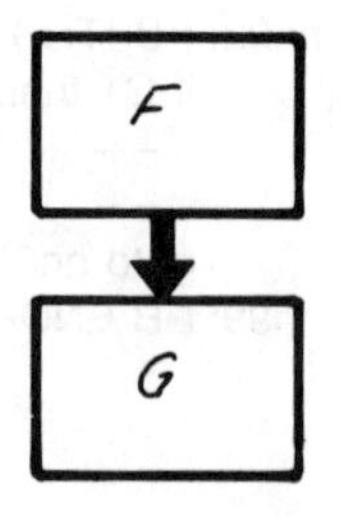

Fig A 1.3

(Below, the schematic logic is modified to accomodate program inversion. The coding technique is of course the same as in chapter 2.)

```
F seq                                   (*F SEQ*)
  ---                                   begin ---
                                           OPKOD := 'OPEN';
  Call G(Message);                         G(message);
  ---                                      ---
  F itr until (C1)                      nn02: (*FA ITR*)
                                              if C1 then goto nn99;
    ---                                         ---
                                                OPKOD := 'READ';
    Call G(Message);                            G(message);
    ---                                         ---
                                                go to nn02;
  FA end                                nn99: (*FA END*)
F end                                   end
                                        (*F END*)

G seq                                   (*G SEQ*)
(Open intermediate file and the         begin
the first read are omitted.)                  if OPKOD = 'OPEN' then QS := 1;
                                              case QS of
                                              1: goto 9901;
                                              2: goto 9902;
                                              3: goto 9903;
                                              4: goto 9904;
                                              end
                                        9901:
  ---                                         ---
                                              QS := 2;
  Wait for the next message;                  goto 9999;
  ---                                   9902: ---
                                              QS := 3;
  Wait for the next message;                  goto 9999;
  ---                                   9903: ---
  GA itr until (C2)                     nn02: (*GA ITR*)
                                                if C2 then goto nn99;
```

```
---                                  ---
                                     QS := 4;
  Wait for the next message;         goto 9999;
                                9904: goto nn02;
 GA end                         nn99:(*G END*)

G end                           9999: ((*G END*)
```

If G calls F, each "Write message" must be replaced by "Wait for the next call", which will be coded

```
        QS := nn;
        goto 9999;
99nn:
```

Appendix 2

Tools

There is a variety of program packages with code generators to facilitate implementation of JSP-programs:

- JSP-COBOL, accepts operations list and a shorthand schematic logic, has a very useful text macro function, facilitates portability from one environment to another, inverts programs automatically if you want to eliminate intermediate files, generates documents, among others, process structures on line printer, is implemented on a wide variety of computers.

- JSP-MACRO, a JSP-adapted COBOL and FORTRAN macro processor, is used e.g. to implement I/O-modules making the application programs independent of input and output media (such as files and terminals) and physical data storage.

- JSP-TOOL, is a computer aided program design software. You draw the program structure on a display unit, input the operations list, a condition list and any quit list, allocate operations etc and JSP-TOOL takes care of coding and documentation. At present (1985) there are code generators for COBOL, JSP-COBOL, Pascal and C. Documents, such as structures and schematic logic are output on line printer, where the structures are drawn in graphic mode. JSP-TOOL is implemented on IBM PC and compatible computers.

- PDF, Program Deisgn Facility, works in a similar way as JSP-TOOL. It has code generators for COBOL, FORTRAN, PL/1, Pascal, Ada and Coral 66 and is implemented on DEC/VAX and IBM PC.

- JSP 800 is similar to JSP-TOOL, has a BASIC code generator and is implemented on ABC 800 and Facit DTC.

Appendix 3

Reading list

1. M. A. Jackson: System Development, Prentice-Hall 1983.
2. John Cameron: JSP & JSD: The Jackson Approach to Software Development, IEEE Computer Society, IEEE Catalog number EHO206–3.
3. M.A. Jackson: Principles of Program Design, Academic Press 1975.
4. Bo Sandén: System Programming in JSP, Chartwell-Bratt Ltd 1985.